Staging History

Staging History

Brecht's Social Concepts of Ideology

Astrid Oesmann

State University of New York Press

Published by
State University of New York Press, Albany

© 2005 State University of New York

For information, address State University of New York Press,
90 State Street, Suite 700, Albany, NY 12207

Production by Michael Haggett
Marketing by Michael Campochiaro

Library of Congress Cataloging-in-Publication Data

Oesmann, Astrid, 1961–
    Staging history : Brecht's social concepts of ideology / Astrid Oesmann.
        p. cm.
    Includes bibliographical references and index.
    ISBN 0-7914-6385-0 (alk. paper) — ISBN 0-7914-6386-9 (pbk. : alk. paper)
    1. Brecht, Bertolt, 1898–1956—Political and social views. 2. Brecht, Bertolt, 1898–
1956—Criticism and interpretation. I. Title.
PT2603.R397Z79442 2005
832'.912—dc22

                                                                    2004007224

10 9 8 7 6 5 4 3 2 1

Contents

Foreword

All translations of quotations from the works of Bertolt Brecht were prepared specifically for this book in order to facilitate the English speaker's reading of the analyses based on the original German passages. However, for the convenience of readers who desire access to more complete English translations of the works discussed, the translated titles of these works follow, wherever possible, those listed in:

Brecht, Bertolt. *Collected Plays.* 8 vols. Edited by John Willett and Ralph Manheim. London: Methuen, 1970–1987.

Brecht, Bertolt. *Poems, 1913–1956.* Edited by John Willett and Ralph Manheim. London: Methuen, 1976.

Brecht, Bertolt. *Brecht on Theatre: The Development of an Aesthetic.* 2d ed. Edited and translated by John Willett. New York: Hill and Wang, 1978.

Brecht, Bertolt. *The Good Person of Szechwan, Mother Courage and Her Children, Fear and Misery of the Third Reich.* Translated by John Willett. New York: Arcade, 1993.

Brecht, Bertolt. *The Measures Taken and Other Lehrstücke.* Edited by John Willett and Ralph Manheim. New York: Arcade, 2001.

Brecht, Bertolt. *Stories of Mr. Keuner.* Translated by Martin Chalmers. San Francisco: City Lights Books, 2001.

CHRIS LONG

Acknowledgments

I would like to thank the National Endowment for the Humanities and the College of Liberal Arts at The University of Iowa who supported this project through a fellowship and a grant respectively. I also want to thank the professional staff of the Brecht-Archive in Berlin for the patient assistance during the time I spent working there.

Parts of this book were originally published elsewhere. The first part of chapter 2 appeared in *The German Quarterly* 70.2 (Spring 1997), and the second part of the same chapter appeared in *The Brecht Yearbook* 26 (Fall 2001). I thank the editors of those journals for permission to use that material here.

This book is the result of a long and complex process of thinking about Brecht and his works. From this perspective I thank my parents for keeping an old recording of *The Threepenny Opera* and my brother Rainer for playing it because this introduced me to Brecht when I was a child. I also want to thank my high school teachers for withholding Brecht's works from us and thus for not spoiling for us the pleasures of his texts. More recently, Andreas Huyssen, my dissertation advisor at Columbia University, fostered a productive dialogue and provided insightful observations about my research and writing. Joachim Lucchesi, Jan Knopf, Siegfried Mews, and Marc Silberman have also stimulated my work through their discussions and comments on multiple talks, papers, and chapters. I would especially like to thank Jan Knopf and Marc Silberman for their thorough readings and valuable critiques of my various writings on Brecht. I am also grateful to Chris Long for her exemplary work editing the final version of my manuscript and translating into English the Brecht material quoted in this book as well as to James Peltz and Michael Haggett at SUNY Press for their dedication to this project. Finally, *Staging History* would not have been realized without James Sidbury, himself a historian, who in countless discussions about Brecht and perusals of chapter drafts made the transition from German thought to English syntax not only possible, but enjoyable. To him I dedicate this book.

Introduction

Some years ago there was a conference in Berlin on *Die Maßnahme (The Measures Taken)*, one of Brecht's most infamous plays. It is a short play, about twenty pages, but the conference lasted four full days. Literary critics were well represented at the podium and in the audience, but, interestingly enough, a small majority of the presenters came from other academic disciplines ranging from anthropology to sociology to philosophy. Everyone struggled with the play's brutality—it presents a young communist activist being killed by his comrades for the sake of the revolution—but everyone also agreed that Brecht's theatre continues to have much to say about Marxism and that it addresses questions about past (and present) communist systems and thought in important ways. This book uses the tools of literary criticism to unravel the complexities of Brecht's theories of history and revolution, revealing in the process why such diverse thinkers continue to find the supposedly propagandistic playwright's thought so relevant more than a decade after the fall of communism in Eastern Europe.

Conventional periodizations of Brecht's career have hindered a proper appreciation of the development of his thought. His career is generally divided into an early period (1919–1927) during which he produced anarchistic and undertheorized plays, a middle period (1927–1932) during which he read Marx and wrote the "crudely propagandistic" teaching plays, and a mature phase (1933–1956) during which he developed his new and impressive theory of "epic theatre" and wrote his most famous plays (e.g., *Mother Courage* and *The Good Person of Szechwan*), which have earned him his place in the canon. *Staging History* demonstrates that Brecht's writings during Germany's Weimar Republic should be seen as a coherent whole. Prior to the triumph of National Socialism, Brecht's experiments with theatre and politics created a genuinely theatrical concept of historical materialism. This assertion does not deny the importance

experiments

1

of Brecht's readings of Marx, but it insists that he had already begun to present historical materialism on stage before he embraced Marxism in 1927. Recognizing the continuity between the "early" plays and the "teaching" plays reveals the underappreciated theoretical sophistication of his Weimar-era theatre and sheds new light on the break that the Nazi triumph in Germany produced in his work. This book shows how Brecht's supposedly inferior early work enriches our understanding of his entire career as a playwright.

I pursue this argument through five chapters, the first of which positions Brecht's work in literary theory. In chapter 1, "Brecht and Theory," I trace Brecht's awkward position among the major leftist theorists in twentieth-century Germany, mainly between members of the Frankfurt School on one side and the Soviet-oriented leftism of Georg Lukács on the other. I focus less on a comparison of theorists' contemporary political commitments—something that has been done sufficiently in the past and which can divert attention from the importance of their theories in today's world—than on Brecht's development of the concepts of mass culture, mimesis, and natural history, each of which continues to be important throughout the following chapters. Brecht's famous differences with major leftist critics in Germany were based less on ideological disagreement than on his refusal to take either ideology or history for granted; rather than treating them as static givens, he sought to release them into disturbing theatrical investigations. These investigations interrogate Marxist ideology, but they also seek to unravel Nietzsche's concepts of morality and history, Benjamin's concepts of mimesis and mass culture, and Adorno's concept of natural history. Critics have long acknowledged the ways that Brecht intersects with Benjamin and Nietzsche, but his thought is still perceived as irreconcilable with that of Adorno. This chapter shows that their concepts of natural history are, in fact, comparable in their respective diagnoses of the pathologies of twentieth-century European history. After establishing the context in which Brecht wrote, in terms of his place both in the history of ideology and in literary theory, I turn to close readings of his early writing for and about the stage.

Chapter 2, "Prehistories," shows that even at the very beginning of his career, Brecht, like Benjamin and Adorno, sought radically new ways to present history without falling into the trap of coherent historical narrative. *Trommeln in der Nacht (Drums in the Night)* and *Im Dickicht der Städte (In the Jungle of Cities)*, two of Brecht's first plays, share a commitment to the theatrical destruction of traditional notions of history and subjectivity. *Trommeln (Drums)* is set during the revolutionary upheavals that occurred in Berlin in 1919, but it is scarcely a traditional narrative of rebellion. It focuses on the return of Kragler, a soldier in World War I, from a POW camp in Africa. Kragler reemerges as a survivor, and the key to his ability to survive is his ability to adapt to new surroundings—he has become a "Negro" during his time in Africa. Kragler's gift for mimesis, rather than the rebellion in the city, is presented as the key to subaltern survival. Brecht continues to experiment with the traditional theatrical element of mimesis in *Im Dickicht (In the Jungle)*, in which two Chicago men carry on a protracted and seemingly pointless feud, transforming both socially and racially in the process of imitating one another. Both plays use the traditional theatrical trope of mimesis to present natural history, with all its incoherence and contingency, as an alternative to traditional history's grand narratives. Brecht appropriates Aristotelian mimesis to present experiments on nonlinear historical understandings.

After exploring the complexities of historical narrative and change in *Trommeln (Drums)* and *Im Dickicht (In the Jungle)*, Brecht began to interrogate the ways in which people could perceive and respond progressively to social reality. In chapter 3, "Man Between Material and Social Order," I trace Brecht's development of a concept of theatre as a "counterpublic sphere," a space in which participants (those acting and those watching) can learn to observe and understand the power relations that shape their lives and, by understanding them, learn how to act in appropriately subversive ways. In *Der Dreigroschenprozeß (The Threepenny Trial)* and *Die Straßenszene (The Street Scene)*, Brecht begins to explore how one could present reliable evidence about systematic injustices that are endemic to bourgeois society but are rendered undetectable because they are culturally accepted. In *Mann ist Mann (Man Equals Man)*, an important transitional play, Brecht returns to the theme of transformation through mimesis in order to present a man's successful adaptation to bourgeois social relations in one version of the text and to fascism in the other. That Brecht conceived of the two texts as different versions of the same play, rather than as one play about bourgeois society and another about fascism, underscores that his primary interest in this text lay less in questions of state politics and political ideology than in the role of mimetic transformation in human survival.

Chapter 3 culminates in a close reading of *Furcht und Elend des Dritten Reiches (Fear and Misery of the Third Reich)*, a play that has received much less critical attention than it merits. Here Brecht dramatizes the difficulties that individuals face in comprehending and formulating effective resistance to the effects of fascist politics and terror. Effective strategies can only be developed by those who are able to stage, observe, and respond to fascist situations within an acknowledged "counterpublic sphere." Theatre, both the conventional theatre involving actors and an audience and the theatre of everyday life informed by the techniques taught in Brecht's theatre, offers a forum in which people can learn to resist fascism in their daily lives.

Chapter 4, "Revolution: Change and Persistence," turns to Brecht's most experimental texts—the teaching plays—in which he moves from his earlier attempts to interrogate the nature of historical representation to an even more elaborate effort to explore revolutionary change on the stage. The teaching plays are brutal, and it is unsurprising, given the bloody history of twentieth-century revolution, that much critical attention has focused on this brutality. Without denying the plays' cruelty, I return to Benjamin's insight that the cultural situation in Germany following World War I was determined by poverty and the barbarism that grew out of poverty. The economic poverty of postwar Germany is obvious, but even more important, Benjamin insisted, was the cultural poverty created by the loss of an entire generation to World War I and the resulting deficit in collective social experience. Brecht's teaching plays stage the inherent brutality of people seeking to understand profound change in the absence of the experience that ordinarily guides such understanding.

The teaching plays pursue this end through radical simplification. The stage is an empty space, and the distinction between actors and spectators is largely erased. Each play's plot (or "fable" in Brechtian terminology) presents a small group of people playing out a revolutionary maxim and facing the life and death choices produced by following the logic of that maxim. Characters are cut off from the personal and communal histories that create individual personality and normally inform important choices. Brecht's use of the mask in *Die Maßnahme (The Measures Taken)*, and of the concept of masking in the other teaching plays, anticipates and enriches anthropologist Michael Taussig's famous conceptualization of "the face" by using the face both as a cultural disguise and as a tool for political education rather than as a marker of identity. It is from this scenario of depersonalization and ahistoricity that the teaching plays explore the human brutality produced by abstract social thought and the change it fosters.

Finally, chapter 5, "Brecht's Archaeology of Knowledge," uses a number of theatrical fragments (only recently made generally available) in order to synthesize the concerns of Brecht's pre-exile theatre. Of central importance to my argument is the enormous *Fatzer* fragment, a project Brecht began writing in 1926 and returned to intermittently until he abandoned it altogether in 1930 in anticipation of fascism's victory in Germany. The fragment spans much of Brecht's early career and touches on all of his theatrical concerns during that period. *Fatzer* follows four men who desert from combat and hide out in an industrial town. While in hiding they prepare to undertake a revolution through which they hope to end the war. Ultimately, they fail because they lack the patience necessary to wait for the right moment and to adapt to their conditions until that moment arrives.

Brecht uses this simple scenario to question some of the most fundamental notions of history and change. He complicates the notion of revolution by insisting that the Renaissance view of social revolution as the natural and perpetual alteration in the position of peoples and nations, which was based on the Copernican model of orbiting celestial bodies, remains a part of the "modern" sense of revolution as a complete overturning of the given social order. This fundamentally subverts standard Marxist revolutionary ideology because it rejects the belief in progress that lies at the heart of Marxist (and liberal) conceptions of history. Brecht does not turn away from revolution or Marxism as a result of this antiprogressive vision. He does, however, formulate a rather fatalistic concept of a communist society as a society in which poverty rather than plenty is equally distributed and individual intellectual progress is impossible. He brings these dark insights together in the *Geschichten vom Herrn Keuner (Stories of Mr. Keuner)* and the *Buch der Wendungen (Book of Changes)*, which he wrote while going into exile. His turn toward the aphorism as a literary form probably reflects, at least in part, his loss of access to theatres in which he could stage his experiments.

Staging History demonstrates the continuing relevance of Brecht's work in the postcommunist world. The epic plays of his late career, with their grand ideological ideas, are now firmly and deservedly entrenched in the canon. This reading of his early work as a profound response to a brutalized society that had, in the face of military and economic disaster, lost faith that it could predict the direction of history helps explain the current cross-disciplinary interest in his early plays. To a world in which "capitalism" and "the market" seem to stand as largely unquestioned social and cultural forces, Brecht's early work offers a concept of the theatre as a "counterpublic sphere," as a space in which people can play out and analyze the hidden brutality of accepted social relations. That he does all of this in the beautiful language that has made him one of Germany's greatest twentieth-century poets, and that he accomplishes it through experiments in dramatic form that continue to transform German theatre underscores Brecht's centrality to twentieth-century Western culture.

.

1

Brecht and Theory

»Ich denke oft an ein Tribunal, vor dem ich vernommen werden würde. ›Wie ist das? Ist es Ihnen eigentlich ernst?‹ Ich müßte dann anerkennen: ganz ernst ist es mir nicht. Ich denke ja auch zu viel an Artistisches, an das, was dem Theater zugute kommt, als daß es mir ganz ernst sein könnte. Aber wenn ich diese wichtige Frage verneint habe, so werde ich eine noch wichtigere Behauptung anschließen: daß mein Verhalten nämlich *erlaubt* ist.«

["I often think of a tribunal before which I am being questioned. 'What was that? Do you really mean that seriously?' I would then have to admit: Not quite seriously. After all I think too much about artistic matters, about what would go well on the stage, to be quite serious; but when I have answered this important question in the negative, I will add a still more important affirmation: that my conduct is *legitimate*."]

—Walter Benjamin, *Versuche über Brecht (Reflections)*

This 1934 remark, in which Brecht describes his attitude toward theatre and politics to Walter Benjamin, reveals how and why Brecht felt close to Benjamin as a critic. Among the German-speaking theorists, Benjamin was personally and theoretically the closest to Brecht. They had been friends since 1929, and Benjamin witnessed Brecht's most innovative work periods, ranging from his early plays to the teaching plays and Brecht's encounter with Marxism. Here, Brecht reveals to Benjamin his awareness of an issue that has continually occupied Brechtian criticism to the present: Brecht's hypocrisy regarding political principles and personal

morals. Most recently, it has been John Fuegi who voiced his disappointment with Brecht the exploitative socialist.[1] On the opposite side is
Fredric Jameson, who celebrates Brecht as a poet reminiscent of the young
Goethe.[2] Jameson discerns a transfer from intellectual into collective
activity that I will locate in the space between the critical and the hypocritical. It is the Brecht between Marx and Nietzsche, between theatre and
theory, between principle and betrayal whose work remains so intriguing
in a postcommunist world.

The Brechtian split between the critical and the hypocritical also
polarized the reception of Brecht's work by his contemporaries. While
Benjamin used this split to read Brecht's work in its relationship to the
brutality of German culture, other critical theorists, namely Theodor W.
Adorno and Georg Lukács, considered Brecht's attitude inexcusable.
Adorno and Lukács, themselves two polarizing figures in the German culture wars, were united only in their rejection of Brecht—of his ideological commitment (Adorno) and of his flippancy (Lukács). Nevertheless, a
comparative reading of all four authors shows that, despite their differences, they share an initial critique of bourgeois culture: it suffers from
"wrong projection" or, as Adorno calls it, "gesellschaftlicher
Verblendungszusammenhang" (social context of blindness). Through a
reading of their understandings of natural history and mimesis, a surprisingly broad kinship between Brecht and Adorno reveals itself in their
shared opposition to "wrong projection." This kinship may help explain
why Benjamin could feel close to both of them.

This kinship would have surprised Brecht and Adorno themselves
because the original conflict between them was real, and they nurtured
it. For Adorno, Brecht was the ideological artist who pursued political
change through a commitment to popular culture that disqualified him
from producing "autonomous art"—the art of true recognition.[3] For
Brecht, Adorno was one of the so-called "Murxisten" of the Frankfurt
Tui, who were engaged in narcissistic intellectual reflection unrelated
to the social change they claimed to seek.[4] These accusations may (or
may not) have had substance when they were made, but the course of
German history since that time has turned them into interesting historical artifacts rather than significant ideological differences. German
history after 1945 ironically reversed these positions by granting
Brecht the "durchschlagende Wirkungslosigkeit eines Klassikers"
(thoroughgoing ineffectiveness of a classic author) (Max Frisch), while
members of the Frankfurt School found themselves equated with the
"Rote Armee Fraktion" (Red Army Faction) (a CDU politician), the

terrorist organization that was supported by the German Democratic Republic, Brecht's final home.

This renders especially ironic Adorno's rejection of Brecht for his political commitment to Marxism. As Adorno puts it, "Sein didaktischer Gestus jedoch ist intolerant gegen die Mehrdeutigkeit, an der Denken sich entzündet: er ist autoritär" (His didactic style *[gestus]*, however, is intolerant of the ambiguity in which thought originates: It is authoritarian).[5] He attacks Brecht for his "pedagogical" approach to theatre, for his outspoken Marxism, and for his commitment to social change—three elements that disqualify Brecht's theatre as autonomous art.[6] In autonomous art, reality can be mediated only indirectly because it is "in sich vielfältig zur Realität vermittelt" (mediated with reality in many ways).[7] Adorno's criticism of Brecht's "commitment" was a response to Brecht's attack on autonomous art, which "wiederhole einfach, was eine Sache ohnehin sei" (simply reiterates what something is).[8] In preferring Beckett for the way his negativity goes to the core of art and life, Adorno portrays Brecht's work as enmeshed in superficial communication. In Adorno's aesthetics, what necessitates "zu jener Änderung der Verhaltensweise, welche die engagierten Werke bloß verlangen" (the change in attitude that committed works only demand) rests upon the acceptance of the incomprehensible.[9] This renders unacceptable Brecht's concept of a pedagogical theatre because the performative acts of explaining and demanding disqualify the plays by requiring only that the audience comprehend the idea being communicated. Adorno uses the term *unterjochen* (to subjugate) to point to the repression of historical guilt in Brecht's work, something that Beckett's plays unfold. Once disqualified as inartistic, Brecht's work has nothing to offer "was nicht unabhängig von seinen Stücken, und bündiger in der Theorie, erkannt worden oder den auf ihn geeichten Zuschauern vertraut gewesen wäre" (that could not have been understood apart from his didactic plays, indeed, that could not have been understood more concisely through theory, or that was not already well known to his audience).[10] For Adorno, *Lehre* (teaching) falls short in comparison with theory because it entails a commitment to obeying the rules of communication—meaning domination—and is thus unavoidably propagandistic. Committed art responds directly to reality, and through this positive commitment, it takes part in the dynamics of domination, thus losing its autonomy.

In reducing Brecht's theatre to a representation of ideology, Adorno not only ignores the form and structure of Brecht's texts, he also overlooks the fact that a dramatic text must eventually meet performance in unpredictable ways. Brecht, who always writes with the theatre in mind, is always aware of the stage's subversive force and of the idiosyncratic nature of education and entertainment; indeed, he makes it the motivating force of his plays. Through idiosyncrasy and plagiarism, Brecht demonstrates that humane ideals are intertwined with egoistic and evil motivations. His theatre thus unveils the dynamic to which Adorno accused him of succumbing.

The aesthetic principle through which Brecht achieves this effect is, surprisingly enough, mimesis. Brecht reappropriates mimesis (which is considered a traditional Aristotelian dramatic principle) as an innovative approach to history. Imitation, then, is not employed as a principle of representation, but as a social and physical exchange that produces history as genealogy. At this point, Brecht's theatrical practice intersects with Adorno's aesthetics and Benjamin's concept of history because all three use mimesis as a key concept. For Adorno, mimesis is the way the subject encounters the object; for Benjamin, mimesis combines historical experience and revolutionary activity. In Brecht's early plays and poetry, mimesis comes alive as the primary force of seduction in the midst of politics. When Heiner Müller insists that "was mich an Brecht interessiert ist das Böse" (what interests me about Brecht is the evil),[11] he points to what has kept Brechtian theatre alive up to the present: the tension between principle and its violations. This constitutes the most challenging aspect of Brecht's work today, and it is the aspect that, from the perspective of the early twenty-first century, is in surprising harmony with Adorno's aesthetic theory.

REALISM AND REVERSED PERCEPTION

> . . . under the rule, discover the abuse; under the maxim, discover the concatenation; under Nature, discover History.
> —Roland Barthes, "Brecht and Discourse"

The bitterly opposed factions within German critical theory that rallied during the first half of the twentieth century around one or another of the major Weimar cultural Marxists—Brecht, Benjamin, Adorno, and Lukács—began their critique of capitalism with the same insight: they all insisted upon the illusory nature of unmediated experience in a capitalist society. Adorno's critique of modern subjectivity finds different echoes in both Benjamin and Brecht and even, to some extent, in Lukács.

Adorno's reflections on "gesellschaftlicher Verblendungszusammenhang" (social context of blindness) through which the subject constitutes its own identity, extend to the illusory projections through which we experience the object world and apply meaning to history. This critique of enlightened subjectivity is also present in Benjamin's critique of historicism, in Lukács's critique of the "unmittelbares Erlebnis" (immediate experience), and in Brecht's theatrical techniques that seek above all to defy the processes of identification upon which bourgeois drama is founded. Beginning, as they began, with a common critique of subjectivity, we can trace their different departures into Lukács's advocacy of realism, Adorno's commitment to the avant-garde, Benjamin's understanding of mimesis, and Brecht's use of natural history. In this way we can recapture some of the fundamental insights that they shared without glossing over their differences.

These departures occur most prominently in the *Realismusdebatte* (realism debate), which began as an argument over Expressionism's impact on fascism but grew into a broader debate on realism in the wake of Lukács's "Es geht um den Realismus" (Realism in the Balance).[12] This essay opened a discussion not only on realism as an art form, but also on the relationship between art and political resistance. The debate began between Brecht and Lukács in 1937, and it was later joined by Adorno when he critiqued Lukács's defense of socialist realism. When Lukács declares realist art, especially the realist novel, to be the aesthetic norm and avant-garde art to be decadent, he places the climax of German literary history in the nineteenth century. In contrast, both Adorno and Brecht opt for historical rather than timeless aesthetic norms and see realism as appropriate for the nineteenth century in the same way that the avant-garde is the proper aesthetic norm for the twentieth century. Neither accepts Lukács's claim that the realist novel, which offers a utopian *Vorbild* (model) for a communist society that has not yet been realized, reached its climax in the past. Nor do they accept that Lukács creates a "realistic" form of idealism which Adorno calls "Realismus aus Realitätsverlust" (realism on the basis of a loss of reality).[13]

Because the poles of the realism debate are realism versus Expressionism in art and socialism versus fascism in politics, the argument between Brecht and Lukács, and later Adorno and Lukács, was mainly about perception. All three agree that the perception of capitalism and the nature of perception in a capitalist society are fundamentally distorted, and each follows Marx in this diagnosis. Lukács writes:

Und jeder Marxist weiß, daß die grundlegenden ökonomischen Kategorien des Kapitalismus sich in den Köpfen der Menschen *unmittelbar
stets verkehrt widerspiegeln.* Das heißt in unserem Fall so viel, daß die in
der Unmittelbarkeit des kapitalistischen Lebens befangenen Menschen
zur Zeit des sogenannten normalen Funktionierens des Kapitalismus
(Etappe der verselbständigten Momente) eine Einheit erleben und
denken, zur Zeit der Krise (Herstellung der Einheit der verselbständigten Momente) jedoch die Zerissenheit als Erlebnis ansehen.

[Every Marxist knows that the basic economic categories of capitalism
are always reflected in the minds of men, directly, but always back to
front. Applied to our present argument this means that in periods when
capitalism functions in a so-called normal manner, and its various
processes appear autonomous, people living within capitalist society
think and experience it as unitary, whereas in periods of crisis, when the
autonomous elements are drawn together into unity, they experience it
as disintegration.][14]

Brecht and Adorno concur with Lukács's suspicion that unmediated
Erlebnis (experience) is the reversed perception of capitalism's economic
categories. According to Lukács, conventional perception registers unity
where economic elements disperse and crisis where these elements unite.
Adorno and Brecht privilege crisis as a signifier for the systematic workings of politics, economics, and culture. What Lukács calls unmediated
experience in the reversed perception of capitalism is, for Adorno, part of
the "gesellschaftlicher Verblendungszusammenhang" (social context of
blindness), and both are comparable to Brecht's complex notion of bourgeois identification, which he seeks to destroy in his epic theatre. The different theorists do, however, attack the problem in different ways. Adorno
inserts "vielfältige Vermittlungen" (multiple mediations) between subject
and object; Brecht seeks to present the conventional as strange (estrangement); Lukács argues for a "vermittelte Unmittelbarkeit" (mediated
immediacy) that consists of revealing both the hidden connections of
society and the abstractions required to perceive them.[15] This, as Terry
Eagleton points out, "reproduces some of the key structures of bourgeois
political power."[16]

The key structures of bourgeois power lie, to a great extent, in the
connection that historian Reinhard Koselleck, though far-removed from
the social and political intentions of early twentieth-century Marxism,
sees between the temporality of the Enlightenment and the formation of
the modern subject in the eighteenth-century project of the philosophy of
history. Koselleck shows how the project of the Enlightenment depends

on a time structure determined by the privileging of *Erwartung* (expectation) over *Erfahrung* (experience). *Erfahrung* (experience) exists as recollections of the past, *Erwartung* (expectation) as projections into the future. In the process of modernity, according to Koselleck, experience and expectation lose their balance, and expectation becomes the motivating force for human action as well as the primary shaper of memory and experience. Expectation, which Koselleck defines as the future's present, casts history as the future's past.[17]

By privileging expectation over experience, subject formation encompasses the Enlightenment's enormous educational project, and the subject constitutes itself through the "Opfer des Augenblicks an die Zukunft" (sacrifice of the present moment to the future).[18] The subjectivist orientation to the future injects an ethical component called *Fortschritt* (progress) into human behavior through time. History can, as Koselleck points out, "als ein Prozeß andauernder und zunehmender Vervollkommnung begriffen werden, der, trotz aller Rückfälle und Umwege, schließlich von den Menschen selber zu planen und zu vollstrecken sei" (be regarded as a long-term process of growing fulfillment which, despite setbacks and deviations, was ultimately planned and carried out by men themselves).[19] The modern subject, then, determines her or his destination, and it is communism as destination that Lukács identifies as the way out of reversed perception.

While Lukács and Koselleck locate the process of subject formation through expectation in the eighteenth century, Adorno and Horkheimer locate the same dynamic in prehistoric times. Lukács locates reversed perception only in the macroeconomic structures of capitalism and not, like Brecht and Adorno, in the unconscious structures of subjectivity as well. Lukács constantly searches for representations of *Bewußtsein* (consciousness) for the real societal counterforces that are finally transformable into political action. Realism, then, depends on "gedankliche Erhebung" (higher intellectual vantage point) over the chaos of reality, and achieving this is, in Lukács's argument, the task of the writer.[20] Chaos becomes order as part of a historical teleology, and realism, as the right consciousness, anticipates and helps shape this emerging order.

For Adorno, the subject is both timeless and historical. It is timeless because, as he and Horkheimer argue in *Dialektik der Aufklärung (Dialectic of Enlightenment)*, the modern subject is both creator and product of the Enlightenment's philosophy of history, a genealogy that secures a subject's understanding of itself and the world. This is, however, a flawed genealogy because Enlightenment thought has failed to become the liberating and humanizing force that it proclaimed itself to be. Instead, it has become another tool for acquiring power and domination because "instrumental reason," the key to "enlightened" thought, blocks critical reflection. Instrumental reason plays the same role in Enlightenment thought that myth played in pre-Enlightenment thought, thus constituting what the authors call the *Urgeschichte* (metahistory) of the subject and illustrating the way that the Enlightenment made instrumental reason the driving force in human history. From this perspective, Horkheimer and Adorno equate myth with Enlightenment in their book's famous central thesis, arguing that the Enlightenment and myth are mutually constitutive through instrumental reason with the dominating subject as reason's timeless agent.[21]

Nonetheless, they show that the subject is historical because it cannot control the history that it generates. For Adorno and Horkheimer, this process represents the genealogy of the bourgeois individual in which the Enlightenment "Zusammenhang, Sinn, Leben ganz in die Subjektivität zurück[nimmt], die sich in solcher Zurücknahme eigentlich erst konstituiert" (relocates context, meaning, and life entirely within a subjectivity which is actually constituted only by this relocation).[22] Through internalization and identification, the subject attempts to form a coherent self for whom life and meaning merge as elements of identity:

> Das Subjekt schafft die Welt außer ihm noch einmal aus den Spuren, die sie in seinen Sinnen zurückläßt: die Einheit des Dinges in seinen mannigfaltigen Eigenschaften und Zuständen; und es konstituiert damit rückwirkend das Ich, indem es nicht bloß den äußeren sondern auch den von diesen allmählich sich sondernden inneren Eindrücken synthetische Einheit zu verleihen lernt. Das identische Ich ist das späteste konstante Projektionsprodukt.

> [From the traces the thing leaves behind in its senses the subject recreates the world outside it: the unity of the thing in its manifold properties and states; and in so doing, in learning how to impart a synthetic unity not only to the outward impressions but to the inward ones which gradually separate themselves from them, it retroactively constitutes the self. The identical ego is the most recent constant product of projection.][23]

Projection and internalization create the self and its understanding of all aspects of the outside or material world. The subject forms a coherent image of the world by processing and ordering unending sensory traces of perception, building unity from the chaotic welter of physical reality. The subject engages in this continuous process of synthesis, internalizing out-

side impressions in order to build the self retrospectively. Subject formation enters the temporal realm when the subject learns to establish what
Adorno calls "synthetische Einheit" (synthetic unity) as identity. Subjectivity is built by the self in the process of categorizing the object world, a
process through which the object world is subsumed into the newly constructed subjectivity. The self imprisons itself in a "gesellschaftlicher
Verblendungszusammenhang" (social context of blindness); this constitutes Enlightenment thought's repetitive turn into delusion. The Enlightenment as the builder of modern subjectivity, then, constitutes a history
of reversed perception in which the object becomes the subject, history
becomes nature, the past becomes the future, and, finally, Enlightenment
falls back into myth.[24]

According to Adorno and Horkheimer, Enlightenment thought contains a temporal structure that is organized around the "already" of myth
as a prehistorical force and the "falling behind" of the Enlightenment as
a historical failure. As Fredric Jameson shows, this time structure assumes
an "always-already" that locates prehistory in any present moment of the
modern world.[25] "Always-already" accounts for the timelessness of
Enlightenment. *Dialektik der Aufklärung (Dialectic of Enlightenment)*,
then, claims that myth motivates the history of the Enlightenment, a history that appears in microcosm in the formation of the modern subject,
which propels Enlightenment thought. Adorno considers the Enlightenment to be the history of self-formation by the modern subject—in his
sense of metahistory *(Urgeschichte)*—because the Enlightenment provides
the rational confirmation of the mythical formation of the self. As a teleological construction, history provides meaning by revealing the path to
enlightened subjectivity, and the subject's history is its identity. The
Enlightenment's history is thus the *Urgeschichte* (metahistory) of the subject; history internalized constitutes the subject.

Reversed perception affects macrohistory (the history of events) and
microhistory (the genealogy of the subject) equally, and herein lies the
agreement between Adorno and Brecht, both of whom have abandoned
the revolutionary optimism that drives Lukács's aesthetics. Adorno is
more critical than Brecht of the ahistoricity of Lukács's notion of consciousness. While historical conditions change, the individual, according
to Lukács, remains constant, and it is the task of the realist writer to
identify what remains constant through historical change. The split
between Lukács on the one side and Adorno and Brecht on the other is
organized along the lines of aesthetics and history and of production and
perception. According to Lukács, realism is the conscious representation

of reality and individuality. In contrast, Adorno and Brecht see a fundamental difference between intention and effect, an approach that makes
criticism an essential element of modern art. For Adorno, art is created
consciously as well as unconsciously, and the contradictions of the production process are inherent in the artwork, whether intended or not.

Reality is thus always the producer of art through countless mediations, and the task of the critic is to trace and decipher these mediations.
According to Adorno, when the autonomous artwork becomes a "Schauplatz erscheinender Objektivitäten" (arena in which objective entities
manifest themselves),[26] the occurrence of these objectivities is an unpredictable result of the gulf separating production and perception. "Die
Lage wird dadurch so kompliziert, daß weniger denn je eine einfache
›Widergabe der Realität‹ etwas über die Realität aussagt. . . . Die
eigentliche Realität ist in die Funktionale gerutscht. Die Verdinglichung
der menschlichen Beziehungen, also etwa die Fabrik, gibt die letzteren
nicht mehr heraus" ("The situation becomes so complicated because a
simple 'reproduction of reality' says less than ever about reality. . . . True
reality has slipped over into functional reality. The reification of human
relations, that is, the factory, no longer delivers human relations to us").[27]
Brecht is concerned with realism as a means of production rather than
with realism as an art form, and the theatre is the site of production.
"Theater is not theory, after all, but something that actually happens."[28]
Accepting an artistic production as formalistic reality is Brecht's starting
point for theatrical recognition. Realism-as-formalism is a tool for examining social causality in a reified condition of human relationships.

Adorno and Brecht agree that to make a representation of reality
speak about reality is impossible because representation reifies human
relationships. Reification affects subjectivity at its core, which makes the
consciousness that Lukács advocates suspect. In this situation, formalism
can provide access to reality. Brecht writes: "Realistisches Schreiben ist
keine Formsache. Alles Formale, was uns hindert, der sozialen Kausalität
auf den Grund zu kommen, muß weg; alles Formale, was uns verhilft, der
sozialen Kausalität auf den Grund zu kommen, muß her" (Realistic writing is no matter of form. Everything formal that hinders us in getting to
the bottom of social causality must be gotten rid of; everything formal
that helps us in getting to the bottom of social causality must be taken
up).[29] Reversed perception, then, requires reversed production, so that
even for Brecht, who could not be more opposed to Adorno's concept of
autonomous art, the moment of production in a theatrical setting might
be the only reality one can count on.

ART AS THE SPEAKER OF HISTORY

Despite their somewhat antagonistic intentions, Brecht, Benjamin, and Adorno form a network of authors that provides an extraordinary approach to history and modernism. In this network, Benjamin is the key mediator between Brecht's concept of forgetting and Adorno's constructions of remembrance. Adorno's aesthetic theory is a meditation on history and memory in the wake of Auschwitz; Brecht's theatrical concept of *Verfremdung* (estrangement) rests on the retrospective presentation of evanescent events; and Benjamin's practice of interpretation is designed to reveal the historicity of the artifacts with which it is concerned rather than revealing history itself.[30] Numerous differences notwithstanding, Brecht, Benjamin, and Adorno all share a retrospective approach to reality. Rejecting any "realist" approach, they examine reality through a critical gesture that emerges from the tension between past and present.

What unites all three is a shared suspicion of the Enlightenment's philosophy of history, especially of its belief in progress. Marxism shares this belief through its concept of the inevitability of revolution. This rational telos affects the formation of the modern subject in that history becomes a pedagogical project in which the subject matures with historical progress.[31] By defining human virtue in terms of historical progress, an "enlightened" philosophy of history writes its own history:

> Indem Geschichtsphilosophie die humanen Ideen als wirkende Mächte in die Geschichte selbst verlegte und diese mit deren Triumph endigen ließ, wurden sie der Arglosigkeit beraubt, die zu ihrem Inhalt gehört. . . . So aber wird nicht bloß Geschichte unmittelbar in ihr Gegenteil verkehrt, sondern die Idee selbst, welche die Notwendigkeit, den logischen Gang des Geschehens brechen sollte, entstellt. Die Gefahr des Seitensprungs wird abgewandt. Die als Macht verkannte Ohnmacht wird durch solche Erhöhung noch einmal verleugnet, gleichsam der Erinnerung entzogen.

> [By attributing humane ideas as active powers to history, and presenting them as history's culmination, the philosophy of history stripped them of the naivety inherent in their content. . . . But not only is history thereby turned into its direct opposite, but the idea, which was supposed to break the necessity, the logical course of events, is itself distorted. The danger of the "freak event" is averted. Impotence mistaken for power is denied a second time by such elevation, as if erased from memory.][32]

Adorno insists that the Enlightenment writes history by viewing its own teleological projections through a retrospective lens. By transforming "virtuous" ideas into irresistible historical forces, the past is made to appear backward and the future progressive. For Adorno, this entails a denial of history's contingency because any true genealogy of the present will fall victim to the privileging of expectation over the experience of the past. The Enlightenment's philosophy of history rests upon amnesia—an amnesia that Adorno thought equally implicated in the project of a progressive subjectivity and in the catastrophes of twentieth-century German history.

The split between Lukács on the one side, and Brecht, Benjamin, and Adorno on the other takes place along the lines of the philosophy of history. Lukács considers reversed perception to be a constitutive part of capitalism but remains committed to a teleological philosophy of history whose Marxist concept of revolution is rooted in Christianity. In contrast, Brecht, Benjamin, and Adorno, in different ways and to different degrees, consult history to reflect on the present. The *memoire involuntaire* (involuntary memory) that has become famous as the nucleus of Benjamin's approach to mass culture and revolution also plays a fundamental role in Adorno's approaches to art and history. While Brecht does not follow Benjamin in taking his cues from either Proust or Baudelaire, his dynamic of remembering and forgetting involves something similar to Benjamin's notion of "chock" (shock) as the moment when one awakes to an unexpected reality.

According to Adorno's understanding of *memoire involuntaire* (involuntary memory), the subject can perceive true history, the history of the object, only in "bewußtlose Geschichtsschreibung" (unconscious writing of history). Adorno's model for this is found in Proust, and this *Bewußtlosigkeit* (unconsciousness) ties art to reality: "Proust, bei dem genaueste ›realistische‹ Beobachtung mit dem ästhetischen Formgesetz unwillkürlicher Erinnerung so innig sich verbindet, bietet das eindringlichste Beispiel der Einheit pragmatischer Treue und—nach Lukács'schen Kategorien—unrealistischer Verfahrensweise" ("Proust, in whose work the most precise 'realistic' observation is so intimately connected with the formal aesthetic law of involuntary memory, provides the most striking example of the unity of pragmatic fidelity and—in terms of Lukács' categories—unrealistic method").[33] Involuntary memory as a form of remembrance occurs independently of subjective intention, which makes it a truer approach to reality than immediate observation. This, of course, brings to mind Freud's insistence that repressed memories are truer than conscious ones. Adorno bases his concept of experience *(Erfahrung)* on *memoire involontaire* (involuntary memory) despite the fact that Proust applies the term only to memories of things that the subject never experienced. Both represent memory as the construction of something new that remains beyond the subject's control.

Adorno roots involuntary memory as "bewußtlose Geschichtsschreibung" (unconscious writing of history) in the autonomous work of art, a work of art free from the intention of the artist and the recipient. The finished artwork differs from that intended by the artist because "intention" is pure thought, whereas art is thought materialized through labor and matter. In addition, autonomous works of art embody the contradiction between genealogy and appearance. Through the production process, the material can emancipate itself from subjective intention, thus rendering the completed work of art unpredictable and freeing it from the intention of the subject who produced it. Art highlights the separation between subject and object and challenges the subject's need for identification. By resisting identification, autonomous art challenges both subjective meaning and objective rationality because art stands neither for itself nor for something else. It disrupts the *Verblendungszusammenhang* (context of blindness) and opens the possibility both for experience and for historical cognition based on remembering. Experience requires a distinction between the "identical self" and the subject: "Die subjektive Erfahrung wider das Ich ist ein Moment der objektiven Wahrheit von Kunst" (The subjective experience *[Erfahrung]* directed against the I is an element of the objective truth of art).[34] This distinction allows the subject to experience its own negativity, and through this true experience, the subject perceives itself as "objektiv vermittelt" (objectively mediated). This then allows the subject to recognize that the wholeness of the self can only be achieved by dominating the object:

> Ergriffen wird das Ich von dem unmetaphorischen, den ästhetischen Schein zerbrechenden Bewußtsein: das es nicht das letzte, selber scheinhaft sei. Das verwandelt die Kunst dem Subjekt in das, was sie an sich ist, den geschichtlichen Sprecher unterdrückter Natur, kritisch am Ende gegen das Ichprinzip, den inwendigen Agenten von Unterdrückung.

> [The I is seized by the unmetaphorical, semblance-shattering consciousness: that it itself is not ultimate, but semblance. For the subject, this transforms art into what it is in-itself, the historical voice of repressed nature, ultimately critical of the principle of the I, that internal agent of repression.][35]

Bewußtsein (consciousness) is the awareness of object-related subjectivity, an awareness that invalidates the false image of the *Ich* (I) and permits the subject to perceive the artwork as the historical representation of nature. By communicating history, autonomous art allows nature to occur. Note that the destruction of the self is tied to the subject's experience of art's language, which works as the "geschichtlicher Sprecher unterdrückter Natur" (historical voice of repressed nature). Through the destruction of the self, the subject can perceive language as historical and thus recognize that history refers to *das Lebendige* (the living; that which is alive).

Understanding the connection between *das Lebendige* (the living; that which is alive) and history requires criticism that permits the unfolding of the artwork's essential center, the truth content *(Wahrheitsgehalt)*, and links it to historical cognition. "Die geschichtliche Enfaltung der Werke durch Kritik und die philosophische ihres Wahrheitsgehalts stehen in Wechselwirkung" (The historical development of works through critique and the philosophical development of their truth content have a reciprocal relation).[36] Here Adorno reveals the connections between his aesthetics and his concept of history by implicating history in one of the most abstract concepts of his aesthetics—the *Wahrheitsgehalt* (truth content). Truth content cannot be determined; instead, it provides a point of reference and a locus for reflection. Reflection upon the truth content links art to philosophy and to what Adorno calls *begreifen*—an untranslatable verb whose meanings range from intellectual understanding or comprehension to more physical grasping, touching, and feeling—thus presupposing critique, the task that links art to history. While reflection preserves the unknowable, labor constructs the historical inversion.[37]

According to Brecht the main task of his theatre is to construct historical inversion that produces *begreifen* (to grasp; to comprehend), a concept closely related to Adorno's vision of comprehension through labor. For Brecht, *begreifen* (to grasp; to comprehend) becomes possible through *eingreifen*, which encompasses several English verbs such as the physical "to interfere" and the social "to engage." Brecht writes, "Wir können den andern nur begreifen, wenn wir in ihn eingreifen können. Auch uns selbst können wir nur begreifen, indem wir in uns eingreifen" (24:182) (We can only grasp others when we are able to engage in them. We can also only grasp ourselves while we engage in ourselves).[38] The result is not consistency, but rupture, a rupture that allows the emergence of unpredictable history in place of the Enlightenment's coherent historical narratives. Brecht inserts the pain of the past into the staging of the present in order to signify the way that historical trauma constitutes reality. For Brecht, experience is the awareness of violent rupture that destroys the consistency of the historical narrative.

According to Adorno, productive aesthetic theory must follow the rules of the work of art—rules that necessarily remain implicit—because the work of art stands against historical narrative as "ihrer selbst unbewußte Geschichtsschreibung" (self-unconscious historiography of their epoch).[39] Aesthetics must construct a historical experience out of art. Here, the presence of the subject is essential because "Kunstwerke lassen desto wahrhaftiger sich erfahren, je mehr ihre geschichtliche Substanz die des Erfahrenden ist" (Artworks may be all the more truly experienced the more their historical substance is that of the one who experiences it).[40] For Adorno, history is a substantive reality in the present that needs to be mediated through the subject's experience of the past. The artwork, as "sedimentierte Geschichte" (sedimented history), produces historical snapshots for the subject; Adorno's critical work seeks to do the same by combining contradictory elements such as intellect and material. Works of art are material producers of historical images, and images are not merely self-existent facts; they must be manufactured by men. The subject, according to Adorno, can only perceive history through images that come from the subject's history: "Auf jeder ästhetischen Stufe erneuert sich der Antagonismus zwischen der Unwirklichkeit der imago und der Wirklichkeit des erscheinenden geschichtlichen Gehalts" (At every aesthetic level the antagonism between the unreality of the *imago* and the reality of the appearing historical content is renewed).[41] The contradiction between image and reality secures the artwork's autonomy; thus, the historical narrative that emerges from the perception of art, while derivative of the subject, is out of its final control.

In *Negative Dialektik (Negative Dialectics)*, Adorno insists that the images produced by art must be translated. Negative dialectics provide a reading that reveals "jedes Bild als Schrift" (every image as writing). Thus, as Rolf Tiedemann points out, Adorno's *Bilder* (images) are not *Abbildungen* (facsimiles). Instead, the work of art functions as a kaleidoscope that produces ever-new constellations that break the domination of the subject: "Das Schriftähnliche solcher Konstellation ist der Umschlag des subjektiv Gedachten und Zusammengebrachten in Objektivität vermöge der Sprache" (What resembles writing in such constellations is the conversion into objectivity, by way of language, of what has been subjectively thought and assembled).[42] Language, as constellation, can condense into a monad that allows the object to emerge. The object needs to open itself to "einer monadologischen Insistenz" (a monadological insistence),[43] and it is because of its monadological insistence that the object reveals history in general. The monad reveals the object's nonidentity, and history expresses itself through this negative revelation: "Solche immanente Allgemeinheit des Einzelnen aber ist objektiv als sedimentierte Geschichte. . . . Der Konstellation gewahr werden, in der die Sache steht, heißt soviel wie diejenige entziffern, die es als Gewordenes in sich trägt" (But such an immanent generality of something individual is objective as sedimented history. . . . Becoming aware of the constellation in which a thing stands is tantamount to deciphering the constellation which, having come to be, it bears within it).[44] The critical unfolding of language as constellation recognizes both the object and its history, a suppressed history that emerges for a moment through the subject's mediation. The subject's intention is to reflect on the object, but the object actually reflects upon the subject. The self becomes subject by thinking itself object, and the subject based on the object is the product of abstraction and alienation. As a result, the object's specific history reveals the history of the subject.

The history of the subject via the history of the object takes more concrete shape in poetry, where language can reach society:

> Die spezifische Paradoxie des lyrischen Gebildes, die in Objektivität umschlagende Subjektivität, ist gebunden an jenen Vorrang der Sprachgestalt in der Lyrik, von dem der Primat der Sprache in der Dichtung überhaupt, bis zur Form von Prosa herstammt. Denn die Sprache ist selber ein Doppeltes. Sie bildet durch ihre Konfigurationen den subjektiven Regungen gänzlich sich ein; ja wenig fehlt, und man könnte denken, sie zeitigte sie überhaupt erst. . . . Die Selbstvergessenheit des Subjekts, das der Sprache als einem Objektiven sich anheimgibt, und die Unmittelbarkeit und Unwillkürlichkeit seines Ausdrucks sind dasselbe: so vermittelt die Sprache Lyrik und Gesellschaft im Innersten.

> [The paradox specific to the lyric work, a subjectivity that turns into objectivity, is tied to the priority of linguistic form in the lyric; it is that priority from which the primacy of language in literature in general (even in prose forms) is derived. For language is itself something double. Through its configurations it assimilates itself completely into subjective impulses; one would almost think it had produced them. . . . The unself-consciousness of the subject submitting itself to language as to something objective, and the immediacy and spontaneity of that subject's expression are one and the same: thus language mediates lyric poetry and society in their innermost core.][45]

For Adorno, poetry as autonomous art, with its reduced referentiality, brings literature as close as it can go to language as matter, as script, and thus to social relevance. Adorno and Brecht both see language as the essential mediator between poetry, society, and history. Brecht, like Adorno, develops concepts of microhistory through poetic inquiry, and he inserts history in his plays through his concept of *gestus*, a concept he explains most clearly in his essay "Über reimlose Lyrik mit unregelmäßigen Rhythmen" (On Rhymeless Verse with Irregular Rhythms):

> Es handelte sich, wie man aus den Texten sehen kann, nicht nur um ein »Gegen-den-Strom-Schwimmen« in formaler Hinsicht, einen Protest gegen die Glätte und Harmonie des konventionellen Verses, sondern immer doch schon um den Versuch, die Vorgänge zwischen den Menschen als widerspruchsvolle, kampfdurchtobte, gewalttätige zu zeigen. (22.1:359)

> [It was, as one can see from the texts, not only a matter of a "swimming-against-the-current" in a formal sense, a protest against the smoothness and harmony of conventional verse, but always-already of the attempt to show the affairs between men as full of contradictions, conflict-ravaged, violent.]

Brecht may have developed the concept of "gestisches Sprechen" (gestic speaking) primarily for his poetry, but he did so while constantly thinking about theatre. Accordingly, he describes his concept of *gestus* as "die Sprache sollte ganz dem Gestus der sprechenden Person folgen" (22.1:359) (the language should entirely follow the *gestus* of the person speaking). Brecht's struggle with the historical material for his play *Leben Eduards des Zweiten von England (The Life of Edward the Second of England)* led him to develop a language that signifies the complexities and contradictions inherent in historical events. "Gestisches sprechen" (gestic speaking) poses difficulties for reading and writing because it moves them into the realm of labor. Brecht, moving his discussion back and forth between Marlowe and Shakespeare, gives an example:

> Statt zu schreiben:
>
>> Seit sie da Trommeln rührten überm Sumpf
>> Und um mich Roß und Katapult versank
>> Ist mir verrückt mein Kopf. . . .
>
> schrieb ich:
>
>> Seit diese Trommeln waren, der Sumpf, ersäufend
>> Katapult und Pferde, ist wohl verrückt
>> Meiner Mutter Sohn Kopf. Keuch nicht! (22.1:358–59)

[Instead of writing:
>Since they there beat drums over the swamp
>And around me sank steed and catapult
>My head is mad to me. . . .

I wrote:
>Since there were drums, the swamp, drowning
>Catapult and horses, is probably deranged
>My mother's son's head. Don't gasp!]

Note that the rewrite eliminates the grammatical "I" and breaks with the past tense. It also adds another historical dimension—that of the mother—and complicates the meaning of "verrückt" (deranged) by including the possibility of physical displacement. Finally, Brecht adds an imperative that transforms the stanza from monologue into dialogue. To the macrohistorical presentation of Edward's life, Brecht adds an array of microhistories that become significant in the moment of performance.

Adorno's surprisingly similar concept of natural history takes shape in his essay on Hölderlin entitled "Parataxis" in which he analyzes a process that he calls "parataktische Zerrüttung" (paratactical disorder) in terms that resemble the Brechtian *gestus*. "Parataktische Zerrüttung" (paratactical disorder) rests upon a notion of *Fügsamkeit* (obedience, submission, docility); as in all autonomous poetry, the subject follows the language: "Losgelassen, freigesetzt, erscheint sie nach dem Maß subjektiver Intention parataktisch zerrüttet" (Set free, language appears paratactically disordered when judged in terms of subjective intention).[46] The destruction of the hypotactical, and thus hierarchical, order of a sentence in order to equate all syntactical elements is familiar from Brecht's concept of "gestische Sprache" (gestic language). The "parataktische Zerrüttung" (paratactical disorder) happens despite the subject's intention to establish coherent meaning. In Hölderlin, language-as-object creates the subject—"Das Subjekt wird es erst durch Sprache" (The subject becomes a subject only through language)[47]—a subject mediated through language-as-object rather than through individual-as-agent.

The destruction of traditional notions of subjectivity and history is essential to Hölderlin's work, but it is the way in which one can trace the formation and destruction of the traditionally unified subject through Hölderlin's stanzas that makes his poetry unique for Adorno: "Hölderlin hat die Ideale, die man ihn lehrte, . . . zur Maxime verinnerlicht. Danach mußte er erfahren, daß die Welt anders ist als die Normen, die sie ihm einpflanzte" (Hölderlin believed in the ideals he was taught; . . . internalized them as maxims. Later he was forced to learn that the world is different from the norms that had been implanted in him).[48] The historical experience that one witnesses in Hölderlin's poetry is the experience of difference between the interiority of the subject and the "reality" of the outside world. Parataxis, as Adorno observes, creates "Korrespondenzen" (correspondences) rather than consistency and allows one "Zeiten durcheinander zu schütteln, Entlegenes und Unverbundenes zu verbinden" (to mix eras together, to connect things that are remote and unconnected).[49] Hölderlin's experience builds along *Fügsamkeit* (obedience; submission; docility) toward pedagogy, at first constituting a virtuous *Innerlichkeit* (inwardness) that faces destruction through his *Fügsamkeit* (obedience; submission; docility) toward language. His poetry thus consists of one of the great contradictions of modern subjectivity: the denial of genealogy for the sake of a consistent pedagogical project of self-formation. Hölderlin presents this process in reverse: the virtue of pedagogy is disguised as violence in the reality of the world.

Fügsamkeit (obedience; submission; docility) and confrontation also create the dialectic in Brecht's theatre. In contrast to Adorno, however, Brecht draws these insights from the culture of mass society that Adorno seeks to overcome. Brecht's starting point for theatrical dialectics is the "Zertrümmerung der Person" (shattering of the person), which he considers the historical destruction of bourgeois subjectivity "aus ihrer Ausdehnung in ihre kleinste Größe, . . . und eigentliche Unentbehrlichkeit im Ganzen" (21:320) (from its enlargement to its smallest size, . . . and actual expendability within the whole). The effect, for Brecht, is liberating because it denies the subject its fictional control of history, a denial he seeks to replicate in his concept of epic theatre: "*Die epische Form*, als den Vorgängen folgend und sich den Kurven der Realität anpassend, die solche Kurven »macht«, indem sie sie *mitmacht*" (21:320) (*The epic form*, in following the events and adapting itself to the curves of reality, "makes" such curves by *participating in* them). Brecht's theatre articulates the moment in which the subject experiences *Fügsamkeit* (obedience; submission; docility) and confrontation, a moment marked by violence. Brecht's concept of *gestus* seeks to articulate this moment that, as he explains, "ist wohl verrückt / meiner Mutter Sohn Kopf" (22.1:359) (is probably deranged / My mother's son's head). The moment we cease to be in agreement with ourselves, we become able to agree with the historical reality around us. For Brecht, *Einverständnis* (consent) is the entrance into the multiple facets of any historical reality, an entrance available only through a commitment to intersubjective activity. This can only occur through language in which the *Ich* (I) emerges as an answer because it is always-already someone else. The *Ich* (I) as someone else derives from *gestus* as Brecht's technique of signification. On Brecht's stage this allows the actor citing her or his role to stress the arbitrariness of this signification while simultaneously emphasizing the physical reality of the body on stage. Brecht uses repetition to signify *Vergänglichkeit* (transitoriness), but signification is always a negative form of representation. By rejecting representation, Brechtian *gestus* signifies what it is not.

The history that Brecht's theatre presents is thus unpredictable. Brecht's technique of insertion blocks the construction of a historical narrative, opting instead to signify the negative side of dramatic representation, and in this way Brecht fulfills Adorno's demand for the construction of historical experience. Adorno's "Was aber wäre Kunst als Geschichtsschreibung, wenn sie das Gedächtnis des akkumulierten Leidens abschüttelte" (But then what would art be, as the writing of history, if it shook off the memory of accumulated suffering) is answered by Brecht with the destruction of memory in order to unfold the historical event.[50] Brecht's theatre lives within the confrontation between the theoretical model and the theatrical play; he does not attempt to translate one into the other. Adorno's mediating subject differs from Brecht's subject-in-performance, but it is precisely this difference that enables Brecht's theatre to open the stage for the aesthetic, social, and historical truth content so essential to Adorno's philosophy and to do so for a much broader range of people than Adorno could ever speak to.

NATURAL HISTORY

Adorno, Benjamin, and Brecht are most closely linked in their pursuit of new ways to comprehend industrialized mass society, a pursuit that led each to develop a new concept of natural history. This is not surprising if one considers the importance natural history had gained in the arts and social sciences during the late nineteenth century through the emergence of Social Darwinism and naturalism. Brecht's *Hauspostille (Manual of Piety; Devotional for the Home)* and his early plays, Benjamin's *Ursprung des deutschen Trauerspiels (Origin of German Tragic Drama)* and his Baudelaire essays, and Adorno's 1932 essay "Die Idee der Naturgeschichte" (The Idea of Natural History) and his and Max Horkheimer's 1947 book *Dialektik der Aufklärung (Dialectic of Enlightenment)* all seek to defy naturalistic and Darwinian approaches to moder-

nity by undercutting the concept of the "natural" as an uncritical reference to a history that identifies its development as progress in order to
define the status quo as modern (rather than contingent and historical).[51]
They all oppose what Adorno calls the myth of Enlightenment. The concepts of natural history that they develop overcome the problems with
the philosophy of history that Adorno points out in *Dialektik der Aufklärung (Dialectic of Enlightenment)* in two related ways: by integrating
myth and substance, natural history breaks with the telos that shapes
classic historical narrative; and by escaping the telos, the subject can
engage in constructive remembering that begins to uncover that which
coherent narratives have excluded from memory.

Thus, Adorno seeks a notion of natural history that potentially
emerges "wenn es gelingt, *das geschichtliche Sein in seiner äußersten
geschichtlichen Bestimmtheit, da, wo es am geschichtlichsten ist, selber als
naturhaftes Sein zu begreifen, oder wenn es gelänge, die Natur da, wo sie als
Natur scheinbar am tiefsten in sich verharrt, zu begreifen als ein
geschichtliches Sein*" (if it is possible *to grasp the historical being in its most
extreme historical certainty—there, where it is most historical—as natural
being itself; or, if it were possible, to grasp nature as a historical being—there,
where it appears most deeply persistant in itself as nature*).[52] For Adorno, natural history occurs in the artwork, an approach that corresponds in part
with the aesthetic theories of Lukács and Benjamin because all employ
Lukács's concept of first and second nature. According to Lukács's *Theorie des Romans (The Theory of the Novel)*, "first nature" refers to living matter and sensuality, while "second nature" refers to technology in an alienated world in a state of "transzendentale Obdachlosigkeit" (transcendental
homelessness).[53] By invoking the term *second nature* for something that is
historically produced, Lukács objects to calling only the nonindustrialized
world natural.[54] Adorno objects, however, to the teleological and thus fictional quality of historical totality with which Lukács endows "second
nature." Adorno insists instead upon the application of history to "first
nature." But whereas Lukács remains in the Hegelian system of transcendence, Benjamin remains close to the insights he gained by examining the
fragmented and transitory object in his study of the baroque play of
mourning *(Trauerspiel).*[55] In doing so, Benjamin moves history from the
"unendliche Ferne" (infinite distance) of transcendence into the
"unendliche Nähe" (infinite nearness) of philosophical interpretation.

A history that is subject to interpretation results, of course, from the
notion of allegory that Benjamin develops in his reading of the German
baroque play of mourning: "Wenn mit dem Trauerspiel die Geschichte in

den Schauplatz hineinwandert, so tut sie es als Schrift. Auf dem Antlitz
der Natur steht ›Geschichte‹ in der Zeichenschrift der Vergängnis"
(When, as is the case in the *Trauerspiel*, history becomes part of the setting, it does so as script. The word "history" stands written on the coun-
tenance of nature in the characters of transience).[56] This transience of civilization also becomes essential for Adorno's concept of nature: "Der
tiefste Punkt, in dem Geschichte und Natur konvergieren, ist eben in
jenem Moment der Vergänglichkeit gelegen" (The deepest point at which
history and nature converge is lying precisely in that moment of transitoriness).[57] Nature, presented as transitory, becomes history. In 1950,
Adorno writes that Benjamin's

> gesamtes Denken ließe als »naturgeschichtlich« sich bezeichnen. . . .
> Der Hegelsche Begriff der zweiten Natur als der Vergegenständlichung
> sich selbst entfremdeter menschlicher Verhältnisse, auch die Marxische
> Kategorie des Warenfetischismus gewinnt bei Benjamin eine Schlüssel-
> position. Ihn fesselt es nicht bloß, geronnenes Leben im Versteinten—
> wie in der Allegorie—zu erwecken, sondern auch Lebendiges so zu
> betrachten, daß es längst vergangen, »urgeschichtlich« sich präsentiert
> und jäh die Bedeutung freigibt. Philosophie eignet den Warenfetischis-
> mus sich selber zu: alles muß ihr zum Ding sich verzaubern, damit sie
> das Unwesen der Dinglichkeit entzaubere. So gesättigt ist dies Denken
> mit Kultur als seinem Naturgegenstand, daß es der Verdinglichung sich
> verschwört, anstatt ihr unentwegt zu widersprechen.

> [totality of . . . thought is characterized by what may be called "natural
> history." . . . The Hegelian concept of "second nature," as the reifica-
> tion of self-estranged human relations, and also the Marxian category of
> "commodity fetishism" occupy key positions in Benjamin's work. He is
> driven not merely to awaken congealed life in petrified objects—as in
> allegory—but also to scrutinize living things so that they present them-
> selves as being ancient, "ur-historical" and abruptly release their signif-
> icance. Philosophy appropriates the fetishization of commodities for
> itself: everything must metamorphose into a thing in order to break the
> catastrophic spell of things. Benjamin's thought is so saturated with cul-
> ture as its natural object that it swears loyalty to reification instead of
> flatly rejecting it.][58]

According to Adorno, Benjamin's concept of natural history unites
Hegel's concept of second nature (the reification of alienated human relations) with Marx's concept of the commodity. Benjamin's philosophy
embraces reification and fetishism to create a long-term perspective on
the history of events, whose archaeological traces persist from the past

into the present. The allegorical image created by those traces then becomes subject to interpretation. Benjamin's concepts of allegory, reification, and fetishization become the producers of the corpse (or archaeological trace) that remains in the present and lends itself to interpretation. According to Benjamin, allegory is the medium through which the transience of life and history can be comprehended, a definition that moves allegory into an intimate relation to dialectics. In one of his Baudelaire essays, he considers total reification to be the unifier between "'man and thing, man and nature.'"[59] Benjamin, who sees Brecht's theatre as a reappropriation of allegory, also considers in his *Ursprung des deutschen Trauerspiels (Origin of German Tragic Drama)* that from the perspective of death, life is nothing other than the production of the corpse. Reification, as a form of death produced by capitalism, thus provides the retrospective stance from which the historical materialist can decipher life as a prehistorical condition of modern culture. Through reification, Benjamin commits philosophy to both historical materialism and philological interpretation. The present is placed into an allegorical constellation with the past and lends itself to philosophical interpretation.

Allegory puts nature and history into a constellation that constantly shifts between meaning and transience. Brecht uses the same constellation in his astonishing treatments of death in which he shows that questions of life and death depend equally on perspective and on economy and distribution:

Und ich sah, daß auch nichts ganz tot war, auch nicht das Gestorbene. Die toten Steine atmen. Sie verändern sich und veranlassen Veränderungen. Selbst der totgesagte Mond bewegt sich. Er wirft Licht, sei es auch fremdes, auf die Erde und bestimmt die Laufbahn stürzender Körper und verursacht dem Meerwasser Ebbe und Flut. Und wenn er nur einen erschräke, der ihn sieht, ja wenn ihn nur einer sähe, so wäre er nicht tot, sondern lebte. Dennoch, sah ich, ist er in bestimmter Art tot; wenn man nämlich alles zusammengetragen hat, worin er lebt, ist es zu wenig oder gehört nicht her, und er ist also im ganzen tot zu nennen. Denn wenn wir dies nicht täten, wenn wir ihn nicht tot nennten, verlören wir eine Bezeichnung, eben das Wort tot und die Möglichkeit, etwas zu nennen, was wir doch sehen. Da er aber doch, wie wir ebenfalls sahen, auch nicht tot ist, müssen wir eben beides von ihm denken und ihn so behandeln wie ein totes Nichttotes, aber doch mehr Totes, in gewisser Hinsicht Gestorbenes, in dieser Hinsicht ganz und gar und unwiderruflich Gestorbenes, aber nicht in jeder Hinsicht. (18:73–74)

[And I saw also that nothing was quite dead, also not the thing that had died. The dead stones breathe. They change themselves and instigate changes. The moon itself, declared dead, moves. It casts light, even if it is alien, on the earth and determines the course of falling bodies and causes the ebb and flow of the ocean. And if it would only shock one who sees it, yes if only one would see it, it would thus not be dead, but would live. Nonetheless, I saw, it is dead in a certain way; when one has namely gathered everything in which it lives, it is too little or does not belong here, and so it is on the whole to be called dead. Because if we did not do this, if we did not call it dead, we would lose a designation, specifically the word dead and the possibility of naming something that we certainly see. But since it, as we likewise saw, is also not dead, we must simply think both of it and treat it like a dead not-dead-thing, but really more a dead thing, in a certain respect a thing-that-has-died, in this respect entirely and irrevocably a thing-that-has-died, but not in every respect.]

Here, life and death are relative, for they depend on a body's state of animation and its effect on the environment. Further, animation is a matter of perception—if something can be seen, it is to some degree alive. However, in order to see a dead object, one might have to depend on *Verfremdung* (estrangement) to cast a different light on that object—the way the sun casts its light onto the dead moon, which then becomes visible to us by reflecting that sunlight (the moon's own light from our point of view) onto the Earth. Life and death, then, are not absolute conditions in the spirit of "to be or not to be," but matters of distinction that depend on quantity and, above all, perspective.

In making the perception of death a matter of visuality and perspective, Brecht appears to reconnect with a rather traditional notion of aura of the kind Benjamin describes in one of his Baudelaire essays: "Die Erfahrung der Aura beruht also auf der Übertragung einer in der menschlichen Gesellschaft geläufigen Reaktionsform auf das Verhältnis des Unbelebten oder der Natur zum Menschen" (Experience of the aura thus arises from the fact that a response characteristic of human relationships is transposed to the relationship between humans and inanimate or natural objects).[60] Brecht is not, however, out to revitalize the cultic experience of aura in our perception of art; he seeks to employ visual interaction between man and nature to arrive at the signification of death.

Brecht seeks to use the perception of nature to arrive at what Rainer Nägele calls "Umkehrung der Blickrichtung" (the reversal of perspective). Reversing perspective is also Brecht's approach to theatre and film, as illustrated in his epic theatre in which a *Schauspielerin* (actress) becomes

an *Anschauspielerin* (watched actress), a subject that acts out of the awareness of being seen.[61] According to Brecht, this awareness combines cognition with political action and control, and viewers of this *Anschauspielerin*
(watched actress) are supposed to grasp how to learn in everyday life as if
they are being watched constantly. In fact, the major element of epic theatre, *gestus*, can be described as a gesture that is aware of its own status
because it is seen by others, which is to say that the gesture constitutes *gestus* through its awareness of its status as a social act.

Yet, this social aspect undergoes an unexpected twist in the mass
media. In his film *Kuhle Wampe oder wem gehört die Welt (Kuhle Wampe
or To Whom the World Belongs)*, Brecht transfers *gestus* to the camera.[62]
Brecht considers the camera to be the dead eye of technology rather than
the social eye of the living observer; thus, rather than participating in a
social-visual network, it disconnects people from experience. Regarding
gestus and mass culture, Benjamin notes that the "Auffindung und Gestal-
tung des Gestischen nichts als eine Zurückverwandlung der in Funk und
Film entscheidenden Methoden der Montage aus einem technischen
Geschehen in ein menschliches bedeutet" (discovery and construction of
gestus is nothing but a retranslation of the methods of montage—so crucial in radio and film—from a technological process to a human one).[63] It
is thus the camera that generates the experimental forms of theatre predominant in Brecht's teaching plays. The construction of experience, for
Brecht, is immanently social: "Die Erfahrungen anderer Leute sind für
den Visionär entbehrlich. Das Experiment gehört nicht zu den Gepflo-
genheiten des Sehers" (22.1:307) (The experiences of other people are
dispensable to the visionary. The experiment does not belong to the habits
of the seer). The theatrical experiment communicates experience—not in
the form of knowledge or information, but by creating new experience. It
follows from this that Brecht designed the teaching plays without envisioning a separate audience, for the audience is an essential and integral
part of the plays' production. *Gestus*, then, the most essential element of
estrangement, draws life and death close together, opening an ever-renew-
ing process of reevaluation through the construction of social experience.
It is not surprising that Brecht himself calls the teaching plays a *Sterbelehre* (teaching of death) that demonstrates the social and thus ever-
changing implications of death.

Benjamin extends his allegorical outlook to Brecht's theatre when
he observes that it provides us with a long-term perspective on human
history. This long-term historical perspective ties mass culture and
Brecht's theatre to natural history, which moves Brecht's approach to

history close to Ferdinand Braudel's concept of *longue duree*, a concept that links natural, structural, and event-based history. Brecht's approach to nature combines the Marxian maxim that quantity produces quality with Hegel's insight that *Vorgänge* (events) are *Übergänge* (transitions). Brecht's early plays—such as *Baal, Trommeln in der Nacht (Drums in the Night)*, and *Im Dickicht der Städte (In the Jungle of Cities)*—and the later teaching plays examine the allegorical constellation of reification and death as these inform a vision of survival. What have often been hastily disqualified as counterrevolutionary aspects of Brecht's early plays (*Trommeln in der Nacht [Drums in the Night]*, for example) could also be considered conspiratorial adaptations to the historical process, a process that reveals its revolutionary potential in the revolving nature of events and conditions rather than through a predictable movement toward a telos.

The quality of death in Brecht's theatre is comparative rather than absolute: it is a question of being more dead than alive, a question whose answer is immanently changeable depending on perspective. Brecht shows this in his theatrical fragments, where the outcomes of life-threatening conflicts hinge on the ability to be more or less than (instead of adhering to) the traditional, absolute opposition of "to be or not to be." This closely ties the political history of revolution to natural history, with all its brutal implications, throughout the teaching plays. To put the same point another way, Brecht presents death as a question of quantity, just like politics or economics. Transferring this signification from nature to politics is, in part, the subject of Brecht's poetry in his *Lesebuch für Städtebewohner (A Reader for Those Who Live in Cities)*, where we find the intimate combination of natural and political death:

> Sprich mich
> Bitte nicht an!
> Wenn ich sehe dein Gesicht
> Erinnere ich mich an dich:
> Du bist
> Erschossen worden. (11:174)

> [Address me
> Not please!
> When I see your face
> I remember you:
> You have been
> Shot dead.]

The famous chilling effect of the poems included in the *Lesebuch für Städtebewohner (A Reader For Those Who Live in Cities)* rests on the anonymity of what Helmut Lethen calls *Verhaltenslehren der Kälte (Behavior Lessons of Coldness)* as preparation for isolation, unmet needs, and guaranteed disappointment.[64] This poem presents the shock of an involuntary memory of an execution that will take place in the future. The remembering hinges on the gaze; it is thus the gaze that locates the past in the future: ". . . direkt vom Aug / Geht ein Strang zu Furcht" (directly from the eye / Goes a line to fear), writes Brecht, "Denn immer Furcht / Zeigt an, was kommt" (10.1:465) (Because always fear / Points out what is coming). Here, Brecht applies his theatrical principle of reversed perception to history and nature. Reversed perception also affects the gaze itself:

> Während du redest, weiß jedermann
> Daß du doch nichts mehr siehst.
> Gib es zu:
> Du hast
> In die Gewährläufe geschaut. (11:174)

> [While you talk, everyone knows
> That you surely see nothing more.
> Admit it:
> You have
> Looked into the rifle barrels.]

Here, death is presented as a social rather than biological event, for if a person dies, it is through others. The confrontation contained in this direct, present-tense speech functions as the defense mechanism of a speaker who does not want to be addressed or contacted. Receiving the gaze of someone who no longer sees might prove contagious in a social setting in which subjects emerge in response to one another ("Ich entstehe in der Form einer Antwort" [21:404] [I emerge in the form of an answer], as Brecht writes in his notes on dialectics). In the poem the question does not simply go unanswered; the entire poem serves to block an initial question that would bring two speakers into being. Social death, then, precedes the organic death that will take place in the future, a future so certain to take place that it can be safely projected into the past.

By creating shock to motivate remembering, Brecht comes close to Benjamin's notion of "chock" (shock), which the latter claims is a breakthrough in experience when it distinguishes *Erlebnis* (conscious experience; isolated experience) from *Erfahrung* (unconscious experience; long experience):

> Je größer der Anteil des Chockmoments an den einzelnen Eindrücken ist, je unablässiger das Bewußtsein im Interesse des Reizschutzes auf dem Plan sein muß, je größer der Erfolg ist, mit dem es operiert, desto weniger gehen sie in die Erfahrung ein; desto eher erfüllen sie den Begriff des Erlebnisses. Vielleicht kann man die eigentümliche Leistung der Chockabwehr zuletzt darin sehen: dem Vorfall auf Kosten der Integrität seines Inhalts eine exakte Zeitstelle im Bewußtsein anzuweisen.

> [The greater the shock factor in particular impressions, the more vigilant consciousness has to be in screening stimuli; the more efficiently it does so, the less these impressions enter long experience *(Erfahrung)* and the more they correspond to the concept of isolated experience *(Erlebnis)*. Perhaps the special achievement of shock defense is the way it assigns an incident a precise point in time in consciousness, at the cost of the integrity of the incident's contents.][65]

Experience here is twofold, for it contains the Freudian distinction between the conscious and the unconscious. Conscious (or isolated) experience, *Erlebnis*, compromises the content of an event in order to create a meaningful chronology that can be remembered, but fixed time is exactly what Brecht's poem destroys. The experience of terror disrupts questions of cause and effect in a way that is in keeping with Benjamin's definition of *Erfahrung* as the emergence of content in the moment of shock. Through remembering, *Erfahrung* (unconscious experience; long experience) is thus always tied to death, as Benjamin points out,[66] and Brecht locates both death and terror in the social sphere where we can encounter them as a theatrical event.

For Brecht, visible death belongs to the social sphere and is thus part of the mimetic economy of being more dead or less dead. To die, then, is neither God's will nor a biological event, but a matter of social consent. Brecht's infamous teaching plays demonstrate the brutal implications of consensus building when, for instance, the sick boy's execution is negotiated in *Der Jasager. Der Neinsager (He Said Yes. He Said No)*, or when someone becomes unrecognizable upon refusing to join the collective and must leave the stage in *Das Badener Lehrstück vom Einverständnis (The Baden-Baden Lesson on Consent)*. The most notorious teaching play, *Die Maßnahme (The Measures Taken)*, presents an example of complete exclusion from the social sphere when a young comrade who betrays the collective must die and disappear. Here, Brecht demonstrates the process through which a memory is built, for the play itself consists of those who killed their comrade reenacting the procedure for a chorus.

The destruction of consciousness and the construction of experience through the shock of estrangement and reification unite Brecht, Benjamin, and Adorno. All three seek to explore the historical nature of modernity through constructive remembering. The commonalities among the three become clearer after considering their views on surrealism. This might be a self-evident approach to Benjamin and Adorno, who wrote directly on the topic, but examining Brecht in the context of surrealism may seem more surprising until one takes a closer look at his early plays and poetry. Adorno does not share Benjamin's appreciation of surrealism as a revolutionary art form. However, surrealism does meet Adorno's criteria for autonomous avant-garde art that provides us with an allegorical access to history:

> Das Kunstwerk selbst ist Material. Sein Bild aber wird in das betrachtende Subjekt hineingenommen. In diesem Prozeß materialisiert das avantgardistische Kunstwerk die allegorische Geschichtsbetrachtung, die in einem Herausbrechen von singulären Elementen aus ihrem ursprünglichen Kontext und der erneuten Zusammenfügung besteht.

> [The artwork itself is material. But its image is taken into the viewing subject. In this process the avant-garde artwork materializes the allegorical viewing of history, which consists of a breaking-out of singular elements from their original context and of a new construction.][67]

The surrealist collage presents the fetish "dinghaft, tot" (Thinglike and dead) as a revelation of the forgotten and repressed.[68] Adorno grants surrealism the revelatory power that he sees in Benjamin's concept of allegory as the path to natural history.

But surrealism also approaches natural history more directly. Max Ernst, for example, takes the *Histoire Naturelle*, a seventeenth-century natural history collection, as a model for establishing similarities between minerals, flora, fauna, and anthropomorphic traces. In his modernist collages, Ernst uses mixed creatures (such as his famous tree people) to present the metamorphosis of nature into technology and vice versa. Ernst claims that he creates his collages "indem das Alltägliche als ahistorisches Fundstück in seiner Fremdartigkeit enthüllt und neu gelesen wird" (in which the everyday, as an ahistorical finding, is revealed in its foreignness

and read anew), in order to take advantage of the "Vieldeutigkeit von vex-
ierenden Strukturen" (arbitrariness of vexing structures).[69] Brecht also
seeks to present the ordinary as strange, and to this end he exploits the
arbitrariness of structures—verbal and natural, but also social and economical. In *Im Dickicht der Städte (In the Jungle of Cities)*, for example,
Brecht presents a natural history of modern times by employing elements
of surrealism (most often noted are the Rimbaud citations in the play),
but he also presents metamorphosis and mixed formations. In so doing,
he presents the history of modern life in terms that anticipate Michel
Foucault's preference for a genealogy of the body over a history of events,
while also offering the form of prehistory that Benjamin locates in the
"mimetic faculty."

MIMETIC ACTIVITIES

To understand the importance of mimesis for Brecht, Benjamin, and
Adorno, we must examine how mimesis intersects with their understandings of modernity and history. All three see modernity as a specific historical moment rather than as the end product of progressive development. They also consider mimesis to be a genealogical force that
undercuts historicist notions of meaning. That Benjamin and Adorno
share this perspective might be unsurprising given that mimesis plays a
well-known key role in their respective concepts of modern subjectivity.
However, to associate Brecht with mimesis would seem to deny everything we conventionally associate with his theatre because mimesis has
become so closely associated with traditional dramatic elements, such as
identification and catharsis, that Brecht fought to destroy. This associa-
tion of mimesis with traditional theatre has led critics to perceive Brecht's
famous V-effect as radically anti-mimetic. This is an accurate appraisal of
the formal elements of Brecht's theatre, but mimesis is nevertheless crucial to other realms of Brechtian theory such as perception, apperception,
mass culture, and behavior.

   The case for reevaluating Brecht on mimesis is strengthened by recent
work done by anthropologists and intellectual historians on the role of
mimesis in complex encounters with the unknown.[70] This new work
allows, first of all, a break with conventional understandings of mimesis
as a defining element of realism and naturalism by reviving a key insight
of *Dialektik der Aufklärung (Dialectic of Enlightenment)* and "Über das
mimetische Vermögen" (On the Mimetic Faculty): mimesis can be seen as

a complex encounter with an unknown environment, an encounter that includes intellectual, sensual, and social forms of understanding. Understood in this way, mimesis provides an alternative means for diagnosing the ills of modern subjectivity that, for example, Adorno sees in the ego principle (i.e., wrong projection). A comparative reading of Adorno, Benjamin, and Brecht shows that all three reconceptualize mimesis in their respective attempts to develop an innovative concept of the history of modernity, a concept that includes art as well as politics, mass culture as well as revolution.

Adorno establishes mimesis as a key concept throughout his entire work—from his critique of enlightened rationality to his late writings on aesthetics. He invokes mimesis to break with the compulsion inherent in enlightened rationality. In *Dialektik der Aufklärung (Dialectic of Enlightenment)*, for example, mimesis (the "organische Anschmiegung ans andere" [organic adaptation to otherness])[71] refers to a prehistorical condition in which the subject, prior to separating from the object, employs imitation and repetition to master nature. Mimesis survives in Enlightenment thought as sensuality, expression, and the communication of the living substance. In this way mimesis enters into philosophical thinking, revealing that the reification of philosophy, which has grown out of insistence on coherent, holistic systems, results from the projection of the subject's "consistent" identity. By combining mimesis and rationality under the banner of philosophy, Adorno renders rationality sensual (rather than cold) and mimesis rational (rather than magical). In fact, Adorno considers mimetic activity to be inherent in humanity and insists that rationality is nothing but misguided mimesis: "Die Ratio, welche die Mimesis verdrängt, ist nicht bloß deren Gegenteil. Sie ist selber Mimesis: die ans Tote" (The reason that represses mimesis is not merely its opposite. It is itself mimesis: of death).[72] By using rationality to reverse mimesis, the subject creates a system of displacement that constructs nature and the sublime according to its own image. The consistent identity that the subject bases on rational thought is built on an artificial split between mind and object: "Einmal radikal vom Objekt getrennt, reduziert Subjekt bereits das Objekt auf sich; Subjekt verschlingt Objekt, indem es vergißt, wie sehr es selber Objekt ist" (Once radically parted from the object, the subject reduces it to its own measure; the subject swallows the object, forgetting how much it is an object itself).[73] The subject builds its identity by forgetting its own status as object. The subject, unaware of its dependence on the object, directs its attention to the teleological project of forming its identity. "Mimesis ans Tote" (mimesis of death) is, among other things,

a form of amnesia that prevents the self from perceiving its own genealogy and thus blocks it from recognizing its own status as object.

Whereas Adorno considers mimesis the way to true subjectivity, Benjamin sees it as the way to revolutionary action. Susan Buck-Morss has
traced Benjamin's ideas on revolution through his reflections on childhood and behavior.[74] Bourgeois culture distinguishes between intellectual
and physical activity, and it privileges the intellect. In contrast, revolutionary activity hinges on the conversion of thought into action—something not only corrupted by bourgeois interests, but also called into question by bourgeois modes of comprehension. In early childhood, however,
perception and creative transformation go together because the child perceives by imitating. In "Über das mimetische Vermögen" (On the
Mimetic Faculty), Benjamin describes the complexities of physical imitation: "Das Kinderspiel ist überall durchzogen von mimetischen Verhal-
tungsweisen; und ihr Bereich ist keineswegs auf das beschränkt, was wohl
ein Mensch dem anderen nachmacht. Das Kind spielt nicht nur Kauf-
mann oder Lehrer sondern auch Windmühle und Eisenbahn" (Children's
play is everywhere permeated by mimetic modes of behavior, and its
realm is by no means limited to what one person can imitate in another.
The child plays at being not only a shopkeeper or teacher, but also a
windmill and a train).[75] Here, the child adjusts to both the social and the
technological environment. What separates the working class from the
middle class—the adaptation to the machine—is what the child performs
willingly and creatively. But whereas the worker's adaptation to the
machine prevents him from comprehending the entire production
process, the child employs the drive to imitate in order to comprehend
people and processes as well as machines. The industrial revolution represents a new nature with its powers still unknown, and to master the
apparent power of this new nature over matter "we need a mimetic, not
an instrumental skill."[76] For Benjamin and, as we shall see, for Brecht, the
unification of mimesis and comprehension is an essential precondition for
any structural change that might culminate in revolution.

Benjamin clearly considers this form of sensual mimesis more fundamental than language, the asensual mimetic form. Tactile cognition
employed by the child is based on a language of gestures that we rarely
reflect upon in the course of everyday life. Among adults, mass culture
in the form of film provides the main instrument to rehearse gestural
language: *"Das Publikum fühlt sich in den Darsteller nur ein, indem es
sich in den Apparat einfühlt. Es übernimmt also dessen Haltung: es testet"*
(The audience's empathy with the actor is really an empathy with the cam-

era. *Consequently, the audience takes the position of the camera; its approach is that of testing).*[77] By adjusting both to the perspective and to the technological potential of the camera, the audience learns to observe consciously the different nature in which "an die Stelle eines vom Menschen mit Bewußtsein durchwirkten Raums ein unbewußt durchwirkter tritt" (a space informed by human consciousness gives way to a space informed by the unconscious).[78] Movements and gestures that we conventionally consider familiar and predictable turn out to contain unknown elements that become obvious through close-ups and slow motion—cinematic techniques that reveal, in the process, what Benjamin calls the "Optisch-Unbewußte" (optical unconscious).[79] Film, then, does for the optical unconscious what psychoanalysis does for the mental unconscious: it isolates fragments out of an illusory whole in order to open them up to investigation.

Brecht, whose concept of estrangement relies on a similar kind of disrupted continuity, looked to film for a new way to comprehend physical reality. As *Kuhle Wampe* shows, Brecht uses the camera to unfold human gesture in slow motion and with repetition. Like Sergej Eisenstein, whose editing techniques he adopted for *Kuhle Wampe*, Brecht studied Kabuki and Noh theatre. But while Eisenstein sought to appropriate theatrical gesture for his film work, Brecht sought to integrate film techniques such as slow motion and repetition into theatre. For Brecht, as for Benjamin, the camera—with its possibility of enlargement, repetition, and temporal variation—provides what Susan Buck-Morss calls a "new schooling of our mimetic powers."[80] Brecht adapts this to his stage in his teaching plays, which are designed to rehearse predefined mechanical gestures (for example, gestures of agreement or disagreement). In the teaching plays, Brecht seeks to redefine theatre as an institution by eliminating the separation between actors and audience and by transforming the stage into a space that exists between these various participants where individual gestures can be examined. In these theatrical experiments, Brecht uses insights he gained from his film work to transfer mass culture from passive consumption to social interaction. These insights are closely related to Adorno's and Benjamin's theories on mimesis.

Brecht, Benjamin, and Adorno all stress the "prehistoric" dimension of mimesis, something Benjamin describes as "nichts als nur ein schwaches Rudiment des ehemals gewaltigen Zwanges, ähnlich zu werden und sich zu verhalten" (nothing but a weak rudiment of the once powerful compulsion to become similar and also to behave mimetically).[81] Brecht's use of "prehistoric" mimesis begins in his first play, *Baal*, in which Baal adapts mimetically to nature by opening himself to a process of organic transformation that spirals into death. Baal, whose soul is equated with water, one of the most basic natural elements, becomes an expert in drowning and summarizes his destiny as an artist as: "Ich befreunde mich mit dem Tod" (1:54) (I am making friends with death). Brecht's use of mimesis is reminiscent of Freud's death drive. Anthropologist Michael Taussig also detects echoes of the death drive in *Dialektik der Aufklärung's (Dialectic of Enlightenment's)* identification of mimesis as a "'trend which is deep-rooted in living beings, and whose elimination is a sign of all development: the trend to lose oneself in the environment instead of playing an active role in it; the tendency to let oneself go and sink back into nature.'"[82] Brecht's early poetry *(Die Hauspostille [Manual of Piety; Devotional for the Home])* similarly presents death as the loss of subjective control and as adaptation to organic nature. However, his early plays are particularly intriguing for their staging of the confrontation between natural and social mimesis as a way of illuminating political progress and human survival.

In the plays immediately following *Baal*, Brecht's characters engage in various dynamics of imitation and resistance that result in genealogical transformation. In *Trommeln in der Nacht (Drums in the Night)*, Kragler's refusal to participate in the Berlin revolution not only reflects his counterrevolutionary longing for a bourgeois life, but also reveals the deficits of the revolutionary movement, deficits tied to the movement's failure to address Kragler in his marginalized position. The incomprehensible and ultimately senseless fight between two men who copy one another's lives that is the subject of *Im Dickicht der Städte (In the Jungle of Cities)* reveals a similar dynamic. In both plays the characters survive by giving up their initial position and adapting to the situation around them. They opt out of drama's conventional struggle for consistent character, engaging instead in a theatre of mutual imitation reminiscent of a boxing match in which the participants rely on sensuous comprehension. In his early plays, then, Brecht moves from the mimetic adaptation of the subject to its environment, which Adorno and Horkheimer locate in prehistory, to mimesis as orientation on and adaptation to the rapidly changing social relations of the twentieth century.

Mimesis reveals a connection between Brecht's theatrical concept of history and Michel Foucault's concept of genealogy. Foucault describes history as an "endless play of dominations" forming a subject's "descent" that can be traced in her or his body, something very reminiscent of what we see in Brecht's early plays. The teaching plays, then, can be read as experiments in acts of domination. For Brecht, the past spills out of historical narrative into a genealogy of bodies that can only be comprehended through mimesis. Mimesis, then, can be seen as carnal interaction with historical continuity (imitation) and change (adaptation). Brecht's theatre uses mimetic exchange to negotiate the alterations in bodies and power relations that Foucault has taught us to read as genealogy.

Mimesis as sensuous knowing illuminates both Adorno's concept of prehistory and Brecht's concept of experimental theatre.[83] Both Adorno and Brecht treat mimesis as a form of the death drive and as an adaptation to what Adorno calls "unbewegte Natur" (immobile nature).[84] Adorno treats idiosyncrasy as the moment of hysteric shock when fragments of prehistoric mimesis reappear in a way that proves that the subject's commitment to individuality is ultimately based on delusion:

> Das Ich, das in solchen Reaktionen, wie der Erstarrung von Haut, Muskel, Glied sich erfährt, ist ihrer doch nicht ganz mächtig. Für Augenblicke vollziehen sie die Angleichung an die umgebende unbewegte Natur. Indem aber das Bewegte dem Unbewegten, das entfaltetere Leben bloßer Natur sich nähert, entfremdet es sich ihr zugleich, denn unbewegte Natur, zu der, wie Daphne, Lebendiges in höchster Erregung zu werden trachtet, ist einzig der äußerlichsten, der räumlichen Beziehung fähig. Der Raum ist die absolute Entfremdung.

> [The self which experiences itself in such reactions—rigidity of the skin, muscles, and limbs—is not quite master of them. For a few moments they mimic the motionlessness of surrounding nature. But as what is mobile draws closer to the immobile, more highly developed life to mere nature, it is also estranged from it, since immobile nature, which living creatures, like Daphne, seek with utmost agitation to become, is capable only of the most external, spatial relationships. Space is absolute alienation.][85]

According to Adorno, all activity is mimetic. Positive mimesis is "organische Anschmiegung ans andere" (organic adaptation to otherness)[86] in which *Anschmiegung* (adaptation) refers to the subject's physical adjustment to the object, an adjustment through which the subject acquires sensuous knowledge of the object. Space, then, intervenes between subject and object, making sensuous adaptation impossible and leading the subject to turn increasingly to rational and projective modes of comprehension. Rationality becomes, according to Adorno, "Mimesis ans Tote" (mimesis of death).

Theatre is implicated in at least two ways in the notion of space as "absolute Entfremdung" (absolute alienation) and the sphere of death.

First, performance space is an essential, defining component of theatre. Second, theatre's anthropological roots lie in the death ritual. It is therefore noteworthy that, following the early "mimetic" plays, Brecht abandons the stage as a predefined, elevated performance space and makes both space and death the subjects of his teaching plays. Participants in each play create a stage of their own: *"in seinen Abmessungen der Anzahl der Mitspielenden entsprechenden Podium"* (3:27) *(podium corresponding in its dimensions to the number of players)*. Brecht begins exploring the inherently alienating effects of space in the text that has come to be seen as his first teaching play. This text explores the concept of man's adaptation to the machine by focusing on Lindbergh's flight across the Atlantic. The space in which the play takes place is thus very constrained and distant from social interaction. This alienating effect is underscored by the fact that *Der Flug der Lindberghs (Lindbergh's Flight)* is written as a radio play to be performed in a spaceless void. The pilot imitates technology to overcome nature, but this style of mimesis ultimately fails because it neglects social mimesis. Brecht returns to these themes in later teaching plays. The reliance on technology in *Das Badener Lehrstück vom Einverständnis (The Baden-Baden Lesson on Consent)* produces profound confusion and renders the fallen airmen unable to say "was ein Mensch ist" (3:30) (what a man is). Brecht directly addresses the space of Adorno's "Mimesis ans Tote" (mimesis of death) in *Der Jasager. Der Neinsager (He Said Yes. He Said No)* in which a boy who gets sick on a mountain trip is supposed to be thrown off the mountain by his fellow travelers. In all three plays, self-importance leads the characters to leave the ground and adapt to space. However, in *Der Jasager. Der Neinsager (He Said Yes. He Said No)*, the failure of social mimesis can be corrected again through physical mimesis in which tradition is broken and the boy is carried back for treatment by his fellow travelers who, as a group, form one coherent body. This physical mimesis replaces the old custom and saves the boy's life.

Notwithstanding those who continue to view the teaching plays as Brecht's most propagandistic and ideological work, the plays actually present ideological thought as a failure of the mimetic faculty. The most famous and controversial teaching play, *Die Maßnahme (The Measures Taken)* (in which three agitators report on their revolutionary work in China that included the killing of a fourth comrade) actually releases ideology into a mimetic exercise by redefining political commitment as primarily theatrical. For example, the comrades begin their subversive work with the theatrical gesture of erasing their faces and replacing them with masks that consist of empty sheets of paper on which the revolution writes its instructions. These instructions do not, however, consist of Marxist maxims or other ideological statements. Instead, the comrades must become members of the Chinese working class and live the contradictions that eventually produce revolution. When the impatient fourth comrade unmasks himself before the revolution can begin, he reveals a different face from the one that the mask first covered. By unmasking himself, the comrade separates himself from the collective, and it must then kill him. The teaching plays release ideology into staged exercises in mimesis that present ideology as mimetic failure.

Brecht's teaching plays, as experiments in the organization of mimesis, demonstrate how ideology—whether traditional or revolutionary—in practice comes down to social domination, which is the opposite of mimesis. They further show that a true change in power relations has to be mimetic (an insight that Brecht sadly abandoned in his later epic theatre). Mimetic change unites body and intellect, and it unites all those involved in the change, in part because it never fully leaves behind the condition from which it changes. Brecht calls the historical conditions that determine our thoughts and actions "Erbmasse" (inheritance), and that is "vorhanden im Zusammenleben der Menschen selber, feudale Verhaltensarten beim Proletariat neben bürgerlichen usw" (22.1:140) (present in the social life of men themselves, feudal modes of behavior by the proletariat next to bourgeois etc). Theatrical mimesis secures the performative incorporation of that which is already there—the material economy of the status quo. Imitation, then, is a fundamentally theatrical form of resistance that opens up imitation's opposite—alterity—which, in turn, encompasses sameness.

Imitation for the purpose of alteration evolved as a formative principle both of Brecht's theatre and of his social thought, making his social concepts of mimesis more complex than the traditional notion of imitation. In his notes on Chinese acting called "Die Beibehaltung der Gesten durch verschiedene Generationen" (The Retention of Gestures Through Different Generations) Brecht asserts that imitation is an essential component of estrangement. "Daß der junge Schauspieler zunächst gezwungen wird, den alten zu imitieren, besagt nicht, daß sein Spiel zeitlebens eine Imitation sein wird" (22.1:127–28) (That the young actor is at first forced to imitate the old is not to say that his playing will be an imitation all his life). In order to defamiliarize, one must know and present the familiar, and the longer and more thoroughly the familiar is presented, the more radical is the change. *Gestus*, then, one of the most essential elements of defamiliarization, rests on imitation and familiarity. "Tatsächlich interessiert die Techniker des epischen Theaters nicht die Beibehaltung der Gesten, sondern ihre Änderung, genauer gesagt, die Beibehaltung im Hinblick auf die Änderung" (22.1:127) (The retention of gestures does not actually interest the technician of epic theatre, but rather their change, more precisely, retention in view of change). Imitation plays an integral role in change, an insight at the core of Brecht's concept of *gestus*, and one central to Brechtian thought on topics ranging from theatre to politics. The more consistent the imitation, the more radical the change.

Mimesis, then, becomes an active part of Brecht's concept of *gestus* through a process that Taussig, in another context, calls "active yielding." This twofold concept includes both the comprehension of an environment and the physical adaptation to it. What Taussig calls the "bodily copying of the other," in which "one tries out the very shape of a perception in one's own body,"[87] finds its political counterpart in Brecht's notion of "unerbittliche Nachgiebigkeit" (unrelenting flexibility), which represents the survival of historical and natural unrest. This constitutes the essential core of any revolutionary activity. What makes active yielding so important for both Brecht and Taussig is that it offers a strategy for survival and action that overcomes our inability to comprehend the history that is emerging around us. Brecht explains this when writing about the theatrical presentation of events: "Wie das immer liegen mag, hinter dem Vorgang liegt noch ein anderer Vorgang. Der gespielte Vorgang allein enthält nicht den Schlüssel. . . . Der Vorgang ist nicht wirklich zu verstehen, und das muß gezeigt werden" (22.1:521) (However that may lie, behind the event lies yet another event. The event played does not alone contain the key. . . . The event is not really to be understood, and that must be shown). To access the incomprehensible, one must accept one's limitations. For Brecht this means staying close to the ground and accepting the discomfort and limitations created by the interests of others. "Das Schicksal des Menschen ist der Mensch" (the destiny of man is man) is, according to Brecht the only lesson worth learning, for it is the one most easily forgotten in situations of individual accomplishment that are, in his eyes, moments of devastating delusion. But what makes social recognition so paramount (for Brecht and Taussig) is that it is a recognition that takes place outside the subject's control. Taussig calls it the "mirroring of the knower in the unknown, of thought in its object,"[88] a process that gives the subject access to unintentional knowledge through adaptation to the other.

Viewing mimesis as the dynamic of mutual understanding establishes contingency as an integral part of that understanding. Thus, mimesis is a key element in Brecht's theatre of estrangement and in his politics of revolutionary change. Change opens the door to the unknown, and mimesis gains importance as what Taussig calls "alternative science," a term that applies equally to Brecht, Benjamin, and Adorno in their readings of mimesis. Through theatrical materialism, Brecht reads historical change to make sense of an already-known future: "Also erkennen die Menschen an gewissen Merkmalen die wahrhaftigsten Bilder ihres Lebens, an den Zusammenstellungen von Figuren in bestimmten Haltungen, welche die wahrhaftigen Interessen der Menschen dieser Zeit zeigen" (10.1:516) (Thus, men recognize the truest pictures of their life by certain features, in the arrangements of figures in certain dispositions, which signify the true interests of the men of this time). These true interests become obvious not in what we intentionally communicate, but through the way we unconsciously relate to one another. Mimetic knowledge is thus not translatable into facticity, but depends on ever-changing social relations. Brecht writes, "Das Nichtgewusste ist der zugrundeliegende Gestus" (21: 357) (The not-known is the basic *gestus*). What has not reached the realm of conscious knowledge can become a matter of experience through mimetic activity.

Here, Brecht's concept of dialectic theatre opens an avenue of recognition to which Adorno himself might have been sympathetic: it creates a central position of critique that has a decidedly physical component. In "Dialektische Kritik" (Dialectical Criticism), Brecht defines "to criticize" as releasing something into crisis and "crisis" as the state in which we are able to act (*eingreifen* [to interfere; to engage]) and thus to comprehend (*begreifen* [to grasp; to comprehend]). Mimesis, as carnal knowledge combined with intentional estrangement through theatrical space, makes for a specifically Brechtian form of dialectics. Brecht's dialectical theatre produces a "Kräftefeld der widersprechenden Interessen" (21:512–13) (field of forces of contradictory interests) in which a critique of the mimetic activity can take place.

Brecht's reappropriation of mimesis in a defamiliarized theatrical setting repeatedly undermines any consistent ideological message. Two very different scholars make complementary observations in this regard. On the semantic level, Hans Mayer notes that one of the most challenging aspects of Brecht's Marxist theatre is the tenderness with which he explores the betrayal of revolutionary projects. On a semiotic level, Roland Barthes notes that Brecht's theatre rehearses that which it actually attacks. It caresses ideology by adding history rather than using one ideology to demolish another or to shape history.

By following Adorno's concept of mimesis as an antidote against projections and as the adaptation to the other, Brecht engages in what he called his loving intimacy with treason, which leaves many who long for final answers frustrated. On the other hand, this sort of corruption makes Brecht the powerful social critic that he remains in the postcommunist world.

2

Prehistories

In the middle of his career, Brecht issued what became a famous theoretical aphorism that numerous critics have linked to his commitment to Marxism. "Verfremden" (To estrange), he claimed, "ist historisieren" (is to historicize), and with this statement he linked his concept of theatrical estrangement to a broad and self-consciously revolutionary concept of human history. If, however, critics have tied this approach to Brecht's Marxism, they have also been careful to show how Brecht imported modernist aesthetic principles into his historical vision, thus developing a political and philosophical concept that grew out of Marx but rejected simplistic orthodoxies of any sort.[1] What is sometimes implied in these critical appraisals, but which has never been adequately traced or theorized, is the way in which Brecht's aesthetic modernism shaped his approach to history prior to his turn to Marxism. This chapter traces Brecht's struggle to stage human history in *Trommeln in der Nacht (Drums in the Night)* and *Im Dickicht der Städte (In the Jungle of Cities)* and shows the way he developed a "theatrical materialism" that would shape and enrich his later turn to historical materialism.

If we consider Brecht's work in the context of theatrical materialism, it becomes obvious that his relationship to history must be understood to have been shaped by modernist skepticism toward any historiography that believes in truthful representations of the past. Brecht presents the 1918 revolution in Berlin and "den Kampf zweier Männer in der Riesenstadt Chicago" (the fight of two men in the giant city of

Chicago) as historical events that defy categories such as historical cau-
sation and subjective agency.[2] In *Trommeln in der Nacht (Drums in the
Night)*, Brecht destroys subjectivity and history in order to present a
marginalized historical perspective that sheds new light on the nature of
bourgeoisie and revolution in Germany. In *Im Dickicht der Städte (In
the Jungle of Cities)* he seeks the destruction of traditional historical narrative by subjecting the validity of character and events to constant dispute. The second part shows how the no-longer-coherent narrative
opens one's eyes to the role instinct plays in understanding social interaction, a process Brecht presents through bodily transformation.

By presenting revolution and conflict as causeless and inexplicable,
both plays undermine subjective agency and comprehension. As a result
Brecht's concept of history falls somewhere between that of Michel Foucault, with his genealogies of bodies and systems of power, and that of
Walter Benjamin, who sees mimesis—the drive toward similarity—as the
most powerful force in human history. Placing Brecht's vision of the unintentional making of history within this philosophical constellation shows
that he developed a theatrical materialism before studying Marx, and it
directly challenges conventions regarding the primacy of Marxist ideology
throughout his work.

THE THEATRICAL DESTRUCTION
OF SUBJECTIVITY AND HISTORY

Wie macht man Revolution, wie macht man keine, war es eine?

[How does one make revolution, how does one make none, was it one?]

—Brecht

Brechtian scholars have traditionally read *Trommeln in der Nacht (Drums
in the Night)* as a representation of one of two post–World War I conflicts
in Berlin—the November Revolution of 1918 or the January 1919 battles. Brecht's story is told through the homecoming of Andreas Kragler, a
soldier who has been missing in action and presumed dead for four years
when the play begins. He returns from being a POW in Africa on the eve
of his fiancée's engagement to another man. She rejects him, after which
he goes to a bar and joins a group of rebels preparing to leave for the revolution. Anna, his former fiancée, changes her mind, follows Kragler, and
reunites with him. He then withdraws from the other rebels and goes

home with Anna. This thumbnail sketch of the plot should reveal why many critics have seen Kragler as moving from helpless-victim status at the beginning of the play to revolutionary action in the middle, before finally giving in to a counterrevolutionary search for the comforts of a bourgeois home. Brecht himself had some investment in this reading, a reading that limits the play's "message" to an evaluation of Kragler as a supporter and then betrayer of the revolution.[3]

This chapter argues against interpretations of the play that have placed it within a discourse of political commitment and individual agency, and it extends recent departures in Brechtian scholarship that have criticized overly simplistic "political" readings of the early plays and the later *Lehrstücke* (teaching plays).[4] Reiner Steinweg's research has been crucial in this regard. By uncovering the consistent theoretical basis for the radically new concept of theatre that informed Brecht's teaching plays, Steinweg rendered readings of the teaching plays as the products of an experimental propagandistic phase preceding Brecht's later epic theatre unconvincing. Rainer Nägele builds on this insight by showing Brecht's use of theatrical and corporeal elements in the teaching plays to demonstrate pedagogical violence; and Andreas Huyssen and David Bathrick show that, in the teaching plays, history emerges as a product of interaction among actors on the stage rather than existing as a lesson to be presented to the audience.[5] My reading of *Trommeln in der Nacht (Drums in the Night)* shows that the concerns with subjectivity, history, and representation, which have attracted so much attention from Brecht scholars of the teaching plays, were already central to Brecht's early theatre.

Trommeln in der Nacht's (Drums in the Night's) importance lies not in the political position of the protagonist Kragler, but in Brecht's demolition of subjectivity. When Kragler returns late from the war as a "Negro" from Africa, he enters the play in a spatially and temporally disjunctive position. With the discourse on race, Brecht makes the body central to Kragler's position in the play. But race also demonstrates social contradiction and domination. This entails a break from the traditionally unified subject, and this chapter explores the implications of that break for the poetics of drama.

Rejecting the play as a portrayal of specific historical events and seeing it instead as a theatrical event that produces its own history—a history informed by a distinct notion of revolution—opens a variety of previously ignored cultural and historical perspectives. Brecht indirectly suggested such an approach when, settled in the GDR in the 1950s, he offered a half-apology for having failed to write a more committed political play:

Gleichwohl konnte man an diesem Stück sehr gut sehen, woran die deutsche Revolution verlorenging: nicht nur an einem Verrat der Führer, sondern auch an der Interessenverschiedenheit der revoltieren-den Volksmassen (der Verrat setzte erst da ein, wo diese Interessenver-schiedenheit weggelogen wurde, damit jene Massen, deren Interessen überhaupt nicht befriedigt werden sollten, mitkämpften).[6]

[All the same, one could see very well in this play where the German revolution was lost: not only in a betrayal by the leaders, but also in the differences of interest of the revolting masses of people (the betrayal first began where these differences of interest were flatly denied so that those masses whose interests were not even supposed to be satisfied fought as well).]

This reading takes up Brecht's suggestion that the play should be viewed as a presentation of differences among the characters. It defines the central trope of "betrayal" as the concealing of difference and shows that Kragler can be reduced neither to a representative revolutionary nor to a counter-revolutionary. Instead, his figure points to a fragmented subjectivity that can neither be integrated into established social categories, nor, to approach the same point from a different perspective, can it represent a continuous narrative. Thus, history emerges not through Kragler as subject, but through the presence of the body and the stage, through a dynamic of for-getting and remembrance, and through the temporality of belatedness.

The "history" in the play undermines subjectivity in order to open a new perspective on revolution. During the 1940s, Brecht explicitly artic-ulated his position on the historicization of the individual:

Vor dem Historisierenden hat der Mensch etwas Zweideutiges, Nicht-zu-Ende Komponiertes. Er erscheint in mehr als einer Figur; er ist zwar so wie er ist, da es zureichend Gründe dafür in der Zeit gibt, aber er ist, sofern ihn die Zeit gebildet hat, auch zugleich ein anderer, wenn man nämlich von der Zeit absieht, ihn von einer anderen Zeit bilden läßt. . . . Sein his-torisierter Mensch spricht wie mit vielen Echos, die gleichzeitig gedacht sein müssen, aber mit immer abgeändertem Inhalt. (22.2:689–90)[7]

[For the historicizer, man has something ambiguous, not-composed-to-the-end. He appears in more than one figure; he is just as he is since there are enough reasons for it at the time, but he is, insofar as the time has shaped him, also simultaneously another, namely, if one refrains from the time, lets him be shaped by a different time. . . . His histori-cized man speaks as if with many echoes that must simultaneously be thought, but always with modified content.]

Here, he treats both man and the historical process as arbitrary constructs that can only be approached through the equally arbitrary medium of language. "History," in the play, is produced through a process of forgetting and remembering, but the version of history thus presented lacks facticity. Such a presentation undermines the play's ties to specific revolutionary movements in post–World War I Berlin and produces an alternative notion of revolution.

This chapter extends Brecht's historicization of *der Mensch* (man) to encompass the slightly more abstract *Subjekt* (subject) by linking subject formation to both Enlightenment discourse and dramatic representation. Bourgeois tragedy, in which the subject represents enlightened virtue within the pedagogical telos of the play, constituted the greatest normative force in German dramatic tradition, and thus the norm within and against which Brecht wrote.[8] Within that tradition, history creates meaning by revealing the way to achieve enlightened subjectivity, and the subject's history is its identity. In *Dialektik der Aufklärung (Dialectic of the Enlightenment)*, Adorno and Horkheimer describe this as the genealogy of the subject, in which enlightenment "Zusammenhang, Sinn, Leben ganz in die Subjektivität zurück[nimmt] und sich in solcher Zurücknahme eigentlich erst konstituiert" (takes continuity, sense, life entirely back into subjectivity and actually constitutes itself for the first time in such withdrawl).[9] The history of Enlightenment stands as the *Urgeschichte*—the metahistory—of the subject, and history, internalized, builds the subject's identity. But as Horkheimer and Adorno mention, and as Foucault has shown more explicitly, the formation of subjectivity requires either the exclusion of the body or the control of the body according to the subjective image.[10] In *Trommeln in der Nacht (Drums in the Night)*, Brecht approaches the body in a supposedly concrete historical context. In doing so, he demonstrates that the body, as living matter, interrupts subjective and historical representations of the Berlin uprising by presenting its own history of suffering and pleasure against the conventional history of both World War I and "the revolution."

In *Trommeln in der Nacht (Drums in the Night)*, subjectivity's metahistory constitutes the identity of the war-profiteering bourgeoisie, who are represented by Anna's parents (Karl and Amalie) and by her lover (Murk). They owe not only their social and economic position to World War I, but also their identity and value system. They perceive history as a continuous success story and thus see the war as a stimulus to economic growth and bourgeois self-determination rather than as a human catastrophe.

The figure of Kragler, who experiences the war as a trauma that fragments the apparent continuity of history, carries a critique of the traditional Enlightenment subject. He externalizes his past in a theatrical spectacle through which his present and past decontextualize each other. This
reverses the classic process of subject formation, for his history leaves him
with a carnal existence but no identity. His physical presence disrupts the
principle of representation—creating fragmentation, surprise, and
uproar—and frees characters from the shackles of representation.
Through this, the play presents contradiction as the motivating force of
its characters: Kragler as both supporter and betrayer of the revolution;
Anna as both forgetful of and committed to Kragler; the people in the
"Zibebe" as both petit bourgeois and rebellious. These contradictions play
out against a spatial context made more complicated and less "national"
by Kragler's presence as a "Negro" from "Africa."

This break with dramatic representation, through which history and
subjectivity are redefined in *Trommeln in der Nacht (Drums in the Night)*,
precedes Brecht's theoretical elaboration of these issues in what later
became his concept of epic theatre. Nonetheless, *Trommeln in der Nacht
(Drums in the Night)* already contains a complex network of epic components that simultaneously support and interrupt the fable of the play.[11]
The stage directions, for example, call for signs bearing the title of each
act to serve as part of the set. These titles produce alienating effects
when, for example, the title of Act I, "Afrika" (Africa), appears on a sign
above the Balicke's bourgeois Berlin living room. The sign simultaneously announces the title of the act and imports Kragler's fragmented
past into the bourgeois present. Brecht also uses what he later called the
principle of "Gestus" *(gestus)* in *Trommeln in der Nacht (Drums in the
Night)*. According to later Brechtian theory, the *gestus* is corporeal and
shows the social aspect of speech—it shows the relation of people to one
another. Each play has a basic *gestus* that dominates each individual sentence, even though the composite of those sentences helps constitute that
basic *gestus*. Brecht uses this technique to make contradiction a part of
each scene and thus to make contradiction determine the entire play.[12] In
doing so, he also signifies contradiction within the subject by demonstrating that one's perception of oneself differs from the way one is perceived by others.[13] As Walter Benjamin has shown, the *gestus* is the
moment of interruption in a play when historical cognition becomes
possible.[14] Epic components and *gestus* combine in a system of internal
quotation that constitutes both Kragler's presence and the presentation
of his past.

Brecht wrote *Trommeln in der Nacht (Drums in the Night)* without having explicitly articulated a theory of drama, but the different versions of the play create a theatrical intertext that illuminates Brecht's understanding of theatre at that point. The first printed version of the play appeared in 1922, but an earlier manuscript version, the "Augsburger Fassung" (Augsburg version), was recently uncovered.[15] In the Augsburg version, which privileges theatricality and corporeality relative to the printed text, Kragler's final decision for Anna appears more complex than it does in the printed version because Kragler's past and present are shown in a cultural context that undermines any clear-cut political message. This perspective renders the term *betrayal* especially misleading, for one can only betray a group or an idea to which one has made a commitment. Reading the two versions of the play against one another reveals Brecht's recognition that political commitment requires cultural awareness.[16]

Brecht calls the printed version of *Trommeln in der Nacht (Drums in the Night)* a "Glosse für die Bühne" (gloss for the stage), but he labeled the Augsburg version a comedy. This change in genre both reflects and contributes to a changing presentation of subjectivity and history. *Trommeln in der Nacht (Drums in the Night)* appears as an inversion of bourgeois tragedy. It replicates tragedy's five-act structure but reverses conventional expectations of tragedy.[17] These reversals range from the setting—the action occurs at night rather than during the day—to more complicated questions of content. Anna's virtue, for instance, is presented as the self-interested product of mass culture, rather than as sublime; it is a quality that her parents and lover consider only in terms of their economic strategies. Brecht parodies tragedy in order to undermine the concept of representation upon which bourgeois tragedy is built. These reversals culminate in the final act of the Augsburg version, which presents Kragler's decision for Anna as the rejection of both heroism and tragedy.

The move to "Glosse für die Bühne" (gloss for the stage) already suggests the introduction of structural elements that would later become central to Brecht's epic theatre. The word *Glosse* (gloss) comes from the Greek word for "tongue" or "expression," both of which highlight Brecht's insistence upon language's sensuality. He brings together flesh and language, for example, by having Kragler refer to his "Negersprache im Hals" (Negro language in the throat). The pleasure and physicality of expression in the play should not be mistaken for Expressionism, a movement with which Brecht's early plays are sometimes connected. Language, in *Trommeln in der Nacht (Drums in the Night)*, does not express characters' subjective emotional condition as it does in expressionist theatre; instead, it takes the form of quotations whose exchanges produce pleasure, conflict, even linguistic violence. Brecht also plays on the modern German meanings for *Glosse* (gloss)—short polemic newspaper commentaries and malicious, mocking, colloquial comment.[18] Throughout *Trommeln in der Nacht (Drums in the Night)*, the characters invoke the "revolution" in short, polemical, self-interested exchanges. These mocking glosses reflect self-referentially upon a revolution found only in the "newspapers." Characters refer to the battles occurring "in the papers," and in Act IV, two people engage in an allegorization of revolution by throwing newspapers at each other. Brecht's stage directions add another level of self-referentiality by providing epic commentary on the performative parts of the text. The structural qualities of this new genre (*Glosse* [gloss]) reinforce the fable of the play, complicating revolution as a historical event by throwing it onto the playground of language.

Trommeln in der Nacht (Drums in the Night) repeatedly undermines any attempt to tie its revolution to historical events. The story takes place in Berlin, a hotbed of political unrest in 1919, but the play's Berlin is fictional. Instead of using the city's distinctive urban dialect, residents speak in the Bavarian accent characteristic of Brecht's native Augsburg. In this imaginary Berlin, the newspapers write about a revolution that everyone has heard of but no one has seen, a revolution supposedly occurring in the newspaper quarters. As the final act shows, however, the site of the revolution remains literally beyond the reach of all the characters.

Instead, "revolution," in *Trommeln in der Nacht (Drums in the Night)*, serves as a medium of both confirmation and dispute among the characters. Karl and Amalie Balicke cite the revolution to reaffirm domestic life, thus justifying the arranged engagement of their daughter Anna to Murk, who has made Anna pregnant. Both father and prospective groom claim the marriage will create a private sphere protected from outside threats such as the revolution. But the revolution does not come. The real threat to their arrangement enters in the guise of a man of uncertain identity who arrives from Africa. He announces himself as Andreas Kragler— Anna's first fiancé, who had fought in World War I and was reported dead four years earlier.

The question of Kragler's identity propels the early action of the play. Before Kragler even appears, his character has begun to emerge out of gestures and quotations rooted in other people's interests. Thus, Amalie Balicke negotiates with Karl regarding the finality of Kragler's death, asking:

Und w e n n er kommt, der Leichnam, der jetzt fault, wie du sagst, aus dem Himmel oder aus der Hölle? Mein Name ist Kragler—wer sagt ihm dann, daß er eine Leiche ist und die Seine einem andern im Bett liegt? (1:177)

[And if he comes, the corpse that now rots, as you say, from Heaven or from Hell? My name is Kragler—who will tell him then that he is a corpse and his (woman) lies in bed with another?]

Here, the announcement of Kragler's name unifies the disjunctive elements that constitute presence: first she labels him a corpse, even while questioning his death, and she holds open the possibility of his return from spiritual spheres. But the incongruous introductory phrase that she inserts into her speech—"Mein Name ist Kragler" (My name is Kragler)—is a direct quotation of the phrase with which Kragler later reenters the Balickes' living room. Kragler uses this introductory phrase despite having been so beloved by Amalie and Anna that no such introduction should be needed. The stage directions reinforce the anonymity of the figure entering the Balicke's living room by calling him "Mann in kotiger dunkelblauer Artillerieuniform" (1:186) (Man in feculent dark blue artillery uniform) until he claims his "Name ist Kragler" (name is Kragler). Only then does the text refer to him by name.

The play's theatricality creates barriers to determining Kragler's identity. David Bathrick has shown that *Trommeln in der Nacht (Drums in the Night)* is antidramatic by virtue of its antidialogic structure.[19] In place of the dialogue that conventionally reaffirms characters, Brecht offers an array of discourses, and each character gets caught up in her or his own talk rather than creating meaningful conversation. Instead of building character through dialogue, the play relates plot and character through a montage of shifting references and quotations. Kragler is brought into being by memory and by repeated announcements of his name, but this disrupts the emergence of a full-blown "character." As Walter Benjamin wrote on epic theatre, "Einen Text zitieren, schließt ein: seinen Zusammenhang unterbrechen" (Quoting a text entails interrupting its context).[20] Kragler's appearance depends on a principle of rupture based on mutual quotation. This principle breaks with subjectivity, and adherence to that principle produces the play's break with dramatic representation.

The question of Kragler's identity remains crucial throughout the play. First, Anna's parents question it in order to exclude him from their sphere. They and Murk have economic interests in Murk's marriage to Anna, and Anna, pregnant by Murk, is committed to marry him. They all feel haunted by Kragler—first by his absence, and then by his presence. When he arrives, they perceive him as a ghost or specter whose presence they seek to efface by denying his identity: upon meeting the returning Kragler, Karl Balicke asks, "Herr Kragler, wenn Sie der sind, wie Sie behaupten, darf ich Sie bitten, mir Auskunft zu geben, was Sie hier suchen?" (1:187) (Mr. Kragler, if you are he, as you claim, may I ask you to inform me what you are looking for here?). Balicke's question reveals the way the play turns away from dialogue to create discursive space. Balicke asks Kragler what he is looking for, although Kragler has already said that he desires Anna. In addition to speaking of Anna, Kragler describes Africa in order to explain why, though he is not dead, he had been unable to write to Anna. Nonetheless, Kragler is repeatedly asked: "Was wollen Sie eigentlich?" (What do you want actually?). As Act II, which takes place in the "Picadillybar," shows, Kragler becomes subject to projection and degradation rather than developing into a character with whom others converse.

Kragler's arrival confirms for the Balickes and Murk all of their anxieties about their economic status. As a representative of the culturally uncanny, Kragler becomes the object upon which the war-profiteering bourgeois figures project the repressed. By piously mourning Kragler's reported death, the Balickes had surmounted their anxieties by treating the dead virtuously. When he reappears he brings back those anxieties, anxieties they seek to re-inter by reducing Kragler to a biological being unworthy of subjective emotion. His presence puts the lie to their understanding of the war as an economic success story and reveals the shallow and opportunistic nature of Murk's masculinity. Kragler, the uncanny male who materializes in the Balickes' living room and has a lingering influence over Anna, seems as frightening as a communist revolutionary and as mysterious as Africa.[21] Murk summarizes this when he declares his hate for Kragler:

> Gespenst! Gespenst! Was bist du denn eigentlich? Soll ich mich verkriechen, weil du die afrikanische Haut umhast? Und Trommeln auf der Gasse hast? Und in den Zeitungsvierteln brüllst? Was kann ich dafür, daß du in Afrika warst? Was kann ich dafür, daß ich nicht in Afrika war? (1:201)

> [Ghost! Ghost! What are you then actually? Should I creep away because you have on the African skin? And have drums in the street? And roar in the newspaper quarters? What can I do about the fact that you were in Africa? What can I do about the fact that I was not in Africa?]

Kragler returns from the dead as the haunting specter of communism. Murk responds with the paranoid callousness of the war-profiteering bourgeoisie, seeking to dominate his rival by invoking race and class. At the same time, he expresses irritation at Kragler's former absence. Returning from Africa in a temporal state of belatedness, Kragler misses Anna's engagement but by so small a margin that Murk must justify his status as Anna's fiancé. Kragler's absence and reemergence put him in a displaced position that creates a spectacle within the play. This spectacularity makes Kragler a representative of the historical situation in which the other characters find themselves, and thus for the absent revolution.

Kragler's identity and biography remain crucial to the play when he leaves the "Picadillybar" and takes the prostitute Marie on an odyssey through Berlin's pubs and taverns before entering the "Zibebe." Unlike the bourgeois characters in the play, who perceive Kragler as the ultimate "other," the rebels in the bar want to identify with him, or they at least attempt to erase the ways in which he and they differ. When Glubb, owner of the "Zibebe" and soon-to-become rebel leader, tries to recruit him for the revolution, Kragler's displaced position takes a different turn. The bar patrons ask him to tell, and even perform, his story so that they can identify with him.

Glubb asks Kragler to take command of the bar patrons and lead them to the newspaper quarters and the revolution. Kragler disappoints them. Long before he chooses Anna, he expresses disdain for the revolutionaries' value system by questioning the fight against injustice:

> Hast du Unrecht gesagt, Bruder roter Herr? Was für ein Wort das ist! Unrecht! Macht euch's bequem auf dem Stern, es ist kalt hier und etwas finster, roter Herr, und keine Zeit für das Unrecht, die Welt ist zu alt für die bessere Zeit und Schnaps ist billiger und der Himmel ist vermietet, meine Lieben. (1:217)

> [Did you say injustice, brother red sir? What a word that is! Injustice! Make yourselves comfortable on the planet, it is cold here and somewhat dark, red sir, and no time for the injustice, the world is too old for the better time and schnapps is cheaper and Heaven is rented out, my dears.]

Clearly then, Kragler never commits to any revolutionary project, and scholarly concern over his so-called "betrayal" of the revolution is misplaced. When he declares "die Welt ist zu alt" (the world is too old), he signals his rejection of the redemptive and teleological structure of time so central to conventional revolutionary projects. Kragler never relates injustice to his personal situation. Instead, he invokes *Unrecht* (injustice) as a trope in a way reminiscent of the nihilism of *Baal.* He only articulates commitment to the revolution in response to the newspaper woman shouting, "Wo ist das Militär? Hier, Herr Artillerist!" (1:219) (Where is the military? Here, Mr. Artilleryman!). This fleeting expression of allegiance is only one of several ways that Kragler reacts to references to his past, and it is better understood as an attempt to communicate and socialize in the bar rather than as an expression of ideological commitment. It also reflects his suicidal exhaustion: "Ich bin heiser. Das Afrika wächst mir zum Halse heraus. Ich hänge mich auf" (1:221) (I am hoarse. Africa grows out of my throat. I hang myself). Glubb seeks to transform Kragler's apathy into revolutionary action, asking: "Kannst du dich nicht morgen aufhängen und jetzt mit in die Zeitung gehen?" (1:221) (Can't you hang yourself tomorrow and go along into the newspaper now?). Even for the model revolutionary Glubb, revolutionary commitment grows, in part, out of indifference.

Trommeln in der Nacht (Drums in the Night) demonstrates this contradiction through Brecht's emerging concept of *gestus.* The commitment to man the barricades—Kragler's, but everyone else's in the "Zibebe" as well—has little to do with revolutionary ideals. When Bulltrotter, for example, enthusiastically proclaims: "Jetzt kommt die Revolution. Jetzt gibt es Freiheit" (AF:46)[22] (Now comes the revolution. Now there is freedom), the stage directions indicate that he is lounging around with his feet propped on a table. This gesture of passive affirmation dominates his revolutionary language.

The contradictions in Kragler's character complicate any attempt to see him as a simple victim of the war. Instead, Brecht uses a specific moment in Kragler's life to show the fictional nature of representational subjectivity. The Balickes exclude Kragler from their world on the basis of projection, while the rebels seek to include him in theirs on the basis of an equally fictive identification. These competing images of Kragler leave little space for the traditional dramatic subject.[23]

Kragler's fragmented subjectivity emerges from an underlying historical condition—the political and economic transition following the war—that determines the play's fable. Balicke retools his munitions factory to produce baby carriages, but he signals no corresponding ideological change. The rebels in the "Zibebe" attempt to formulate ideological change without success. These failures highlight one of the main concerns in Brecht's early work—the question of organic transition.

Kragler, associated with "Milch und Blut" (milk and blood) before the war, has degenerated into a "verfaulte Dattel" (rotted date) by the time he returns from Africa. These organic metaphors for duration and aging signify the inscription of history onto Kragler's body. These and other "natural" descriptions—"Negerkutsche" (Negro carriage), "verkrachter Elefant" (broken-down elephant), and "altes Tier" (old beast)—allow Kragler to distinguish himself from the others in the "Zibebe." His skin, whether "wie ein Hai schwarz" (like a shark, black) or "afrikanisch" (African), adapts to new environments. His ability to adjust to change protects Kragler. Glubb, when he loses his alcohol, and the farmer, when he loses his land, are described as having their skins torn off (1:215), something Kragler's chameleon-like quality prevents. Glubb, the model revolutionary, uses the same trope in his response: "Dir ist ein kleines Unrecht geschehen. Sage ja und schlucke es. Halte dich ruhig, wenn sie dir die Haut abziehen, sonst geht sie entzwei, es ist deine einzige" (1:218) (A small injustice happened to you. Say yes and swallow it. Stay calm when they tear the skin off you, otherwise it will break in two, it is your only one). Organic adjustment to circumstance becomes equated with resistance, part of Brecht's attempt in his early work to illuminate the relationships among resistance, revolution, and survival. Brecht would, in the teaching plays, work through various aspects of human and social death, but in *Trommeln in der Nacht (Drums in the Night)*, he opts for the survival of the living being.

This survival does not, however, mean that the unified subject coheres. Instead, Brecht uses organic transition to fragment history and subjectivity by denying Kragler status as a "character." We learn nothing about what he was like before the war beyond Amalie Balicke's entirely conventional claim that he was a good person. Even this description is directed at a photograph taken of Kragler before the war rather that at his physical being during the action of the play. The Kragler who reemerges in the play manifests his qualities through his theatrical presence—physically and temporally. He embodies endurance—Anna prefers him to Murk because Kragler is the one "der vier Jahre lang gewartet hat" (who has waited for four years). Yet by returning just after Anna's engagement—seemingly too late—and still ending it, he embodies something other than rational linear temporality. Rather than simple development through time, Kragler signifies a twofold temporality of suddenness and belatedness.[24]

This complex temporality manifests itself from the beginning of the play and helps introduce the play's equally complicated sense of place.

Kragler's seeming return from the dead shocks Murk and the Balickes, and they attack him on the grounds of race, class, and sexuality. He responds by telling what he remembers of Africa, offering a displaced perspective on the history he shares with his accusers, a perspective from which history appears as terror, and Kragler himself is both victim and tormentor. The trauma of his belated arrival at the Balickes' house confronts him with his past. He responds by acting out the work of remembering, decontextualizing both past and present to construct something new. No longer is he simply the "good person" Amalie recalls. The stage directions—which place the word "Afrika" (the title of Act I) in the Balickes' living room—aid the process by inserting Kragler's African past into the play's present. This bourgeois living room in "Berlin" serves as an allegory of Kragler's time in Africa. He is brought into the picture not through a memory of him, but through the citation of his name, and the labeling of space. Through these references—Benjamin calls citation a *Wieder-Holung* (bringing back)—the stage is set for Kragler.[25]

Kragler's physical presence adds a different perspective—racially, culturally, and geographically. Returning from Africa with his African skin, he speaks as the "Negro" in the "Negro language." Africa is literally inscribed on his body, signifying endurance and offering a perspective that reflects the "temporality of emergence" and the "belatedness of the black man."[26] This position allows Kragler to disrupt both the historical denial of the bourgeoisie (represented in the play by the Balickes and Murk) and the partially formed revolutionary project of the emerging proletariat (represented by Glubb and his followers, who look to Kragler's story for motivation). Brecht uses Kragler to present both the war and the revolution from the perspective of the displaced subject, a subject whose history and identity cannot be contained in a single "national" narrative.

Trommeln in der Nacht (Drums in the Night), then, provides a modernist presentation of history by virtue of its refusal to treat either World War I or the revolution as matters of historical fact. Instead, both become spectacles whose meanings arise through the distance and displacement separating the event from its spectators.[27] When Kragler enters the "Zibebe" announcing, "ich habe nicht den Durchfall" (I do not have diarrhea), the drunk responds, "Ob es eine Geschichte ist" (Maybe it is a story), and Bulltrotter replies, "Was heißt hier Geschichte?" (What does story mean here?). Kragler responds by telling his story, offering, in the process, another retelling of the history of World War I from a displaced perspective:

Ja, Afrika. *Stille.* Die Sonne, die brannte den Kopf aus wie eine Dattel, unser Gehirn war wie eine Dattel, wir schossen Neger ab, immer in die Bäuche, und pflasterten und ich hatte die Fliege im Kopf, meine Lieben, wenn ich kein Gehirn mehr hatte, und sie schlugen mich oft auf den Kopf. (1:213–14)

[Yes, Africa. *Silence.* The sun, it burned out the head like a date, our brain was like a date, we shot Negroes dead, always in the bellies, and paved and I had the fly in the head, my dears, when I had no more brain, and they struck me often on the head.]

This narrative scarcely conveys what happened to Kragler in Africa—that he was imprisoned and forced to build roads—and it provides no hint that "Fliege" (fly) is a trope for Anna. Bulltrotter praises the story nonetheless: "Das ist eine leibhaftige Geschichte. Sie ist gut gemacht" (1:214) (That is a fleshy story. It is well made). In his comment, Bulltrotter not only privileges the epic form as entertaining and informative, he also reveals that Kragler's listeners interpret the story as a literal account of his biography and genealogy. Thus, in the "Zibebe," as in the "Picadillybar," Kragler provides the perspective of historical and geographical displacement.

Kragler's position is only the most prominent of several displaced perspectives offered in the play, perspectives that force critical reflection—not only on revolution, but also on drama as a genre. Both versions of the play present a displaced feminine perspective in the final act, when Kragler splits from the revolutionaries to go with Anna. In the Augsburg edition, his decision to marry Anna entails quite elaborate negotiations. He blames her for being pregnant with Murk's child, but Marie defends Anna, saying: "Sie sollen sie anhören. Ich bin auch nicht gehört worden. Was wissen denn Sie? Sie wissen ja nichts!" (AF:62) (You should listen to her. I have also never been heard. What do you know? You know nothing!). By insisting upon the legitimacy of the neglected feminine perspective, Marie exposes the false virtue of the revolutionary project. Babusch further defends women against idealist projects: "Wenn eine Frau kaputt geht, auf die Idee kommt es nicht an!" (AF:65) (When a woman breaks down, the idea does not matter!). Glubb responds by asserting the purity of the revolutionary ideal, a purity he claims is defiled by a woman's presence. Babusch, however, rejects the revolutionary force of this idealism and simultaneously breaks with drama as a genre: "Lassen Sie sich nicht zum Helden machen, Kragler! Wenn Sie wollen, ist es keine Tragödie" (AF:65) (Do not let yourself be made into a hero, Kragler! If you want, it is no tragedy).

Brecht excludes this argument in the later version of the play, allowing Anna instead to describe her experiences during Kragler's absence,
thus narrating another history of the war: "Vater und Mutter habe ich
etwas vorgespielt und im Bett gelegen bin ich mit einem Junggesellen. . . .
Und dich habe ich ganz und gar vergessen, trotz der Photographie, mit
Haut und Haar" (1:227) (to father and mother I have pretended something and I have lain in bed with a bachelor. . . . And I have forgotten you
completely and utterly, in spite of the photograph, with skin and hair).
But in an earlier conversation with her father, Anna asserts her inability
to forget Kragler (1:179). Her false claim to have forgotten him serves as
a negotiating ploy to gain control of her relationship with Kragler. This
tense exchange explodes into an erotic battle when Kragler asks, "Soll ich
dich mit dem Messer holen?" (Should I take [get] you with the knife?),
and Anna replies, "Ja, hol mich. Ja, mit dem Messer" (1:227) (Yes, take
[get] me. Yes, with the knife). Kragler's rejection of revolutionary virtue
and refusal to play the tragic role it demands opens the possibility for this
erotic theatricality. Anna's voice brings to the surface the ways in which
both revolution and drama are conflicts on the terrain of gender politics.
    Brecht's rejection of a positivist version of history is underlined by
the way that the revolution in Berlin—supposedly the central historical
event in the play—grows shadowy and recedes into the background.
Brecht further decenters the revolution by describing it as "die grosse rev-
olutionäre Aktion, die hinter den Szenen immer stärker wird, im
Zuschauerraum nur dünn und gespenstig" (AF:12) (the great revolutionary action that grows increasingly strong behind the scenes, in the
auditorium only thin and ghostly). The journalist Babusch speaks of the
occupation of the newspapers in the *Vorortvierteln* (suburban quarters),
providing the only description of any concrete act in this revolution.
This leads the rebels from the "Zibebe" to discuss "in die Zeitungen
gehen" (going into the newspapers), but the main action in the final act
consists of the rebels missing the *Vorortviertel* (suburban quarters). This
revolution that lacks a place also lacks a goal, as Marie points out: "Was
sollen wir tun. Wir sind klein. Viele sagen: In die Zeitungen gehen. Dort
ist es, aber was ist in den Zeitungen" (1:218) (What are we supposed to
do. We are small. Many say: Go into the newspapers. There it is, but
what is in the newspapers).
    In 1953, Brecht rewrote Act IV, eliminating the arbitrariness of time
and place in the interest of historical accuracy: in this version he sets the
action in 1919 and changes the title of the act from "Schnapstanz"
(Schnapps Dance) to "Es kommt ein Morgenrot" (A Dawn Comes), a

line from the final stanza of "Die Ballade vom toten Soldaten" (The Ballad of the Dead Soldier). He also adds an "Arbeiter" (worker), who provides concrete times (such as "Elf Uhr Hausvogteiplatz" [11 o'clock Hausvogtei Square] or "Im Anhalter sitzt die Gardesschützendivision seit sechs" [In addition the Riflemen Guards Division has been sitting still since six]) and a concrete place (the publishing house of the social-democratic newspaper "Vorwärts" [Forward]) (1:233). In addition, the drunk's song inserts knowledge that the revolution failed into the play's text:

> Meine Brüder, die sind tot
> Und ich selbst wär's um ein Haar
> Im November war ich rot
> Aber jetzt ist Januar. (1:236)

> [My brothers, they are dead
> And I myself were to but by a hair
> In November I was red
> But now it's January.]

Kragler also sings the full text of "Ein Hund ging in die Küche" (A Dog Went Into the Kitchen) instead of just the fragments he sings in earlier versions. As Hans Mayer shows, Kragler's performance of this song in its eternal repetition marks him as a self-pitying petit bourgeois.[28] By rooting the play in a specific time and place and tying it to specific historical events, this late rewrite creates a historical perspective from which, unfortunately, the earlier Kraglers are ideologically dismissed.[29]

This late, concretely historical version of the play emphasizes the contingent and negotiated nature of revolution in the earlier texts. Halfway through the play, Murk and Anna find themselves midway between the seemingly stable bourgeois world of the "Picadillybar" and the proletarian "Zibebe" of the rebels discussing the revolution and their future.[30] Anna tells Murk that she is leaving him to pursue Kragler, opening up the following exchange:

MURK: Und du willst hinunter? In die Vorstädte, in das Finstere, in das Nichts?

ANNA: Ja. Zum Nichts will ich.

MURK: Nichts als ein Schnapsrausch! Nichts als ein Zeitungsroman! Nichts als ein Schnee vom vorigen Jahr!

ANNA: Nichts sonst . . .

MURK: Das ist es: Nichts sonst! Jetzt weiß sie es: Für das Nichts! (1:209)

[MURK: And you want to go down there? Into the suburbs, into the darkness, into the nothing?

ANNA: Yes. I want to go to the nothing.

MURK: Nothing but a schnapps rush! Nothing but a newspaper novel! Nothing but a snow from the previous year!

ANNA: Nothing else . . .

MANKE: That's it: Nothing else! Now she knows it: For the nothing!]

Das Nichts (The nothing) functions here and throughout the play as the locus of spatial, temporal, and social disjunction. In addition to separating the "Piccadillybar" from the "Zibebe," it separates Anna and Murk and invalidates all interpersonal feelings and relationships. Murk labels the revolution a fiction—a *Zeitungsroman* (newspaper novel). When he says, "Nichts als ein Schnee vom vorigen Jahr" (Nothing but a snow from the previous year), he calls into question both Kragler's relationship to Anna and his return from the past. The trope of *Nichts* (nothing) refers to both Kragler and the revolution and, in doing so, invalidates both. Through *das Nichts* (the nothing), Manke answers Marie's later question about what awaits her in the newspapers: she should expect to find nothing.

In addition to invalidating characters and events, *das Nichts* (the nothing) points to a more radical notion of revolution and the revolutionary. *Nichts* (nothing) is a recurrent trope in Brecht's work, appearing both in his poetry and in several plays.[31] Only in his teaching plays, however, does the concept of nothingness become central to Brecht's destruction of subjectivity and representative meaning. In *Trommeln in der Nacht (Drums in the Night)*, however, Brecht had already touched upon the destruction of the subject through revolution, death, nothingness, and disappearance. Anna and Murk, assuming Kragler is in the revolution, speak of nothingness. Kragler's brief moment as a "revolutionary" emerges from his temporary death wish: "Schlußmachen ist besser als Schnaps. Es ist kein Spaß. Verschwinden ist besser als schlafen" (1:219) (To make an end is better than schnapps. It is no joke. To disappear is better than to sleep). During his temporary commitment to the cause, Kragler equates his participation in the revolution with physical disappearance.[32]

Kragler's "betrayal" of the revolution is often seen as the resolution of the play's central conflict, but it is his objection to disappearance that frames the play. His theatrical presence disqualifies him from representing great ideas or acting upon primarily ethical motivations. His commitment to Anna in Act V results from Kragler's recognition of his own mortality. Characters truly committed to the revolution perform the disappearance that will become an imperative in the teaching plays. As is often the case in this play, the stage directions serve as an additional voice when Kragler separates from his friends. They become a constitutive part of the text when the disappearance of the revolutionaries is presented in the text as a role unto itself: "AUGUSTE *ist mit den andern schon verschwunden*" (1:228) (AUGUSTE *has already disappeared with the others*). The conventional direction for disappearing is *ab* (off). This epic component of *Trommeln in der Nacht (Drums in the Night)* shows that, for Brecht, revolution and organic transition are mutually dependent, and both involve the dissolution of the unified subject.

Kragler has little to do with the revolution in Berlin, but his body—transformed into that of a "Negro" in Africa—is emblematic of Brecht's notion of revolution as *Nichts* (nothing). Only by adapting organically to the ever-changing present can the limitations of the subject be overcome through a revolution without a knowable telos. Here, Brecht inscribes the concepts of nonsubjectivity and negativity that will become essential to his teaching plays. Kragler's final exchange with the model revolutionary Glubb anticipates the way that the teaching plays juxtapose death and disappearance:

KRAGLER: Du läufst an die Wand, Mensch.

GLUBB: Ja der Morgen riecht viel, mein Junge. Die Nacht vergeht wie schwarzer Rauch. Einige freilich bringen sich wohl in Sicherheit. *Er verschwindet.* (1:228)

[KRAGLER: You are running to the wall, man.

GLUBB: Yes the morning smells much, my boy. The night goes by like black smoke. A few of course probably bring themselves to safety. *He disappears.*]

Glubb equates revolutionary activity with death and vanishing. "Revolution," in *Trommeln in der Nacht (Drums in the Night)*, entails both social contradiction and organic transition. Glubb vanishes with the night; Kragler opts for survival, rejecting anonymous sacrifice: "Mein Fleisch soll im Rinnstein verwesen, daß eure Idee in den Himmel kommt?" (1:228) (My flesh is supposed to decompose in amber so that your idea gets into Heaven?). Rejecting Glubb's identification with an idea, Kragler regresses to himself: ". . . aber ich liege im Bett morgen früh und vervielfältige

mich, daß ich nicht aussterbe" (1:229) (. . . but I will lie in bed early
tomorrow morning and reproduce myself so that I do not die out). He
offers no rational justification for this regression because his subjectivity
is not defined according to ideas rooted in the Enlightenment. He insists
only on carnal needs, pleasure, and social contact. His rejection of revolutionary sacrifice grows out of his recognition that death is inevitable, a
recognition that creates his commitment to life.

Kragler chooses more than the comfort and shelter of bourgeois existence, and his choice represents something more complicated than a simple "betrayal" of the revolution. He opts for life and flesh in a desperate
attempt to escape the fate of the soldier in the "Ballade vom toten Soldaten" (Ballad of the Dead Soldier). This reading is reinforced by the
Augsburg version, in which Kragler explicitly states his reasons for leaving
the rebels:

> Fort mit euch, ich bin das Gespenst. Tot bin ich, man hat mich
> begraben. Dreck! Leben will ich, ich bin da, der Wind geht an meinem
> Arm, das ist meine Frau, seht sie an, so ist sie, aber sie ist es doch! Ich
> bin dicker als ihr. Ich habe sonst nichts. Ich will Luft, ich will Fleisch,
> ich bleibe nicht allein, also fort mit euch! (AF:70)

> [Away with you, I am the ghost. Dead I am, they buried me. Filth! I
> want to live, I am here, the wind goes along my arm, that is my woman,
> look at her, so she is, but she it is after all! I am fatter than you. I have
> nothing else. I want air, I want flesh, I do not remain alone, so away
> with you!]

He commits to Anna in order to escape being victimized in Berlin street
battles just as he had been victimized in World War I. He stands against
the complex notion of revolutionary survival that Brecht presents in his
early poetry and in the teaching plays. In a poem in the "Lesebuch für
Städtebewohner" *(A Reader for Those Who Live in Cities)*, Brecht warns:

> Sorge, wenn du zu sterben gedenkst
> Daß kein Grabmal steht und verrät, wo du liegst
> Mit einer deutlichen Schrift, die dich anzeigt
> Und dem Jahr deines Todes, das dich überführt!
> Noch einmal:
> Verwisch die Spuren! (11:157)

> [Take care, when you think to die
> That no gravestone stands and betrays, where you lie

With a clear inscription, that points you out
And to the year of your death, that condemns you!
Once again:
Erase the traces!]

But Kragler follows the opposite trajectory: he vanishes and is presumed dead and lost, but he returns and reclaims his name. Kragler accepts his own mortality and still chooses to live, to be known, and to create clear traces of his existence. His choice of Anna, then, represents less a "betrayal" of the revolution than a reversal of the narrative direction of this poem, a poem which deals not with political commitment, but with the illusory nature of individuality and historical continuity.

Kragler also insists on the illusory nature of the stage: "Ich hab's bis zum Hals. . . . Es ist gewöhnliches Theater. Es sind Bretter und ein Papiermond und dahinter die Fleischbank, die allein ist leibhaftig" (1:228) (I've had it up to the neck. . . . It is ordinary theatre. It is boards and a paper moon and behind that the butcher's stall, which alone is real). The *Fleischbank* (butcher's stall), the only true place, is the site of the slaughter. Neither life nor death, but the moment when the two meet in a violent act, is called true. The emptiness of the subject coincides with the void of its death, and in the teaching plays, Brecht presents the linguistic and performative void of subjectivity and death as the language of revolution. In so doing, he brings the lesson of anonymity from the earlier poem into theatrical form, where it serves the purpose of "sterben lehren" (to teach to die; to teach dying). This radically new form of theatre can almost be seen as a direct answer to the doubts Kragler voices about the ability of theatre to represent the polarity of life and death. In *Trommeln in der Nacht (Drums in the Night)*, Brecht already introduces the central issue of the teaching plays: the role of physical violence in negotiating the reality of ideology.

In his final speech, a soliloquy, Kragler not only rejects the revolution, he also accuses the audience of counterrevolution. In doing so, he directly addresses the content of the play of which he is part. Having returned from war, death, and Africa as a "Negro," he does not fit into the revolutionary program. But he is present, nonetheless, and his presence, combined with the moments when he tells his memories of Africa, invalidates the historical narrative of revolution and counterrevolution in Berlin. This undermines what appears to be the historical context of the action in the play. Kragler reinforces this process of destruction by pointing contemptuously to the artificiality of the theatre as a performance space. The stage directions act as an epic component to highlight the tension between the play as performance and the play as text: *"Sein Gelächter bleibt stecken im Hals, er kann nicht mehr, er tirkelt herum, schmeißt die Trommel nach dem Mond, der ein Lampion war, und die Trommel und der Mond fallen in den Fluß, der kein Wasser hat"* (1:229) *(His laughter remains stuck in his throat, he can no more, he stumbles around, throws the drum after the moon, that was a Chinese lantern, and the drum and the moon fall into the river that has no water).* Like Kragler's soliloquy, this destroys the representative staging of the play. It stresses, instead, the allegorical qualities of the set, and the confluence of this allegorical landscape with Kragler's soliloquy constitutes what might be called the play's tragic moment. This moment exists not in Kragler's "abandonment" of the revolution for Anna, but in a revolution that has a time but lacks a place, that has suffering but lacks a goal. When the red moon (Brecht's overwrought symbol of the revolution) sinks into the river (an archetypal emblem of memory) the conventional picture of revolution as the culmination of human progress disappears from the play. In its place there is the possibility for the awareness of human differences that are rooted in social contradiction and for organic transformation as a precondition for truly revolutionary change.

In *Trommeln in der Nacht (Drums in the Night)*, Brecht presents History as the history of the subject. By learning about the modification of subjectivity under specific historical circumstances and the resulting fragmentation of the subject, we gain a new understanding of revolution. Brecht offers a new form of historicity in order to break the teleological production of meaning that created the enlightened subject. Kragler stands for a history of nonperception: he creates neither meaning nor morality out of his wartime experience. Instead, his body materializes them when he becomes a "Negro" returning from Africa. From this belated and displaced perspective, the revolution in Berlin is just one more misconception that perpetuates the terror of his past, a terror presented in this theatrical spectacle. History, then, appears not as a continuous narrative, but as a process that emerges in constellation with a subject that is deprived of its own sense of identity.

THE UNORGANIZED MATERIAL

In his critique of historical representation Brecht writes:

> Die Geschichte der Menschheit ist ein Haufen ungeordneten Materials. Schwer erkennbar ist es, wer immer die Veranwortung trug für seine

Zeit. Das Hervortreten der großen Typen, die Kreierung der großen Ideen und jene Zusammenstöße zwischen den Typen und Ideen, die nicht immer in Schlachten und Revolutionen deutlich wurden, müßten zusammengefaßt werden. Jener Typus, der im Jahre 1923 den ersten Kampf aus Kampfeslust führte, jenen ersten uninteressierten Kampf, C. Shlink, ist eine historische Person. (21:180)

[The history of mankind is a pile of unorganized material. It is hard to recognize who always bore the responsibility for his time. The emergence of the great types, the creation of the great ideas and those collisions between the types and the ideas, which did not always become clear in battles and revolutions, would have to be grasped together. That type, who in the year 1923 led the first fight for the pleasure of fighting, that first disinterested fight, C. Shlink, is a historical person.]

Lamenting the disorderly nature of human history seems to fit neither the "anarchic" nor the "Marxian" Brecht. We should not read Brecht's comment as a complaint about the state of historiographical narratives because we know from other sources (including his own theatrical practice) that Brecht was suspicious of imposed order as a disguise for conflict. As the passage continues, it reveals Brecht's suspicion of written history's ability to present the forces that "are responsible for their times." The emergence of the "great types" and the "creation of great ideas" are not always recognizable in what is conventionally considered a historical event such as a war or a revolution. Brecht assumes a disjunction between human actions and ideas and the way that both influence historical reality and historiography. He rejects any simple causal relationship between "progressive" and "conservative" thought and the direction of social change. Historical insight, then, depends on what Brecht calls *zusammenfassen* (to gather together; to summarize), the recognition that coherent narratives can only be created when imposed upon a chaos of historical reality. The emphasis on *fassen* (to grasp) underscores the active distortion inherent in seizing events in order to perceive them as history. What Brecht suggests here is a reorganization of the production and perception of history, and he seeks to replace the traditional narrative of character and events with a theatrical presentation that focuses on inconsistencies and contradictions.

With this approach to history Brecht comes remarkably close to Michel Foucault who, in his essay "Nietzsche, Genealogy, History,"[33] examines Nietzsche's critique of historicism in light of his own critique of power and knowledge. Foucault describes Nietzsche's concept of

"wirkliche Historie" (effective history) as a history that "introduces discontinuity into our very being—as it divides our emotions, dramatizes
our instincts, multiplies our body and sets it against itself."[34] With this
discontinuity any reassurance regarding cause and effect in historical
events, identity in historical characters, or meaning in historiography
ceases to exist. Moreover, a history that considers itself to be a genealogy
of bodies, instincts, and emotions reveals meaningful historiography to
be the product of the "passion of scholars." Here, Foucault asserts that
scholars use academic discourse to disguise "the personal conflicts that
slowly" became transformed into "weapons of reason."[35]

In *Im Dickicht der Städte (In the Jungle of Cities)*, Brecht takes the
opposite trajectory. Reason and the meaningful narratives that it creates
are destroyed, and what remains is the bare reality of social and physical
conflict. Shlink, the "historical person" that Brecht introduces in the quotation above, emerges from the disorganized material of society as a historically significant figure who is set against himself because of the disinterested pleasure he takes in fighting. Shlink's importance, according to
Brecht, lies less in his achievement as a fighter than in his indifference
toward winning or losing compared to the simple pleasure he takes in the
fighting. Shlink's fight for pleasure—and his pleasure in fighting—is
played out in *Im Dickicht der Städte (In the Jungle of Cities)*. In this play,
Shlink publicly attacks Garga, an impoverished clerk in a Chicago library,
for no apparent reason. He gets the clerk fired, forces his girlfriend into
prostitution, and gains access to Garga's family by hiring his sister as a
housemaid. Garga responds to this challenge, and the two men take turns
bankrupting and criminalizing one another. Each ends up isolated from
his original social network—Garga from his family and Shlink from his
gang. They finally withdraw from society completely and spend three
weeks hiding out together, having sex, and talking before Garga hands
Shlink, a Malayan, over to a lynch mob. Shlink forestalls the lynching by
committing suicide, and Garga retreats to New York.

The play explores the fight between Shlink and Garga as an example
of the unorganized material of life that creates various histories: social history is created when Garga's family is destroyed; economic history arises
through various business transactions involving Garga and Shlink; cultural history is produced when they experience changes in class and sexual orientation; and even natural history can be perceived through their
physical transformation. The lack of organic comprehension that Brecht
observes in historiography's desire to divide the aspects of a single set of
events appears in the play itself because the play lacks clarity of plot and

character. The foreword announces the play as the unexplainable
"Ringkampf zweier Menschen" (wrestling match of two people) and
directly addresses the audience with the words: "Zerbrechen Sie sich nicht
den Kopf über die Motive dieses Kampfes, sondern beteiligen Sie sich an
den menschlichen Einsätzen . . ." (1:438) (Do not rack your brains for the
motive of this fight, but take part yourselves in the human stakes). Instead
of searching for meaning and motivation, the audience is encouraged to
participate in the fight—either by taking sides or by betting on the winner. This brings to mind Brecht's address to the audience in another play,
Das Elefantenkalb (The Elephant Calf), where he explicitly invites people
to talk and smoke during the performance and to visit the bar to bet on
the winner of the play (2:158).

By presenting these plays as boxing matches, Brecht moves the cultural setting of the theatre where *Im Dickicht (In the Jungle)* takes place to
the street.[36] The public life of the streets is especially emphasized in the
first of the two versions of the play where "Stimmen von Zeitungsweibern
und Zeitungsjungen" (voices of newspaperwomen and newspaperboys)
shout out headlines that relate to the play's fable, such as "Verbrechen des
Malaiischen Mörders" (Crimes of the Malayan Murderer), and
"Lynchjustiz der anständigen Bevölkerung" (1:345) (Lynch Justice of the
Decent Population). Brecht demonstrates the chaos of social reality by
revealing that Shlink is not a murderer and then rendering unsuccessful
the mob's attempt to murder him. But we also know that newspapers are
a major source for historiography, and Brecht further complicates the
question of sources when he says in the foreword that *Im Dickicht (In the
Jungle)* presents "lediglich die wichtigsten Sätze, die hier an einem bestimmten Punkt des Globus zu bestimmten Minuten der *Menschheits-
geschichte* fielen" (1:345) (merely the most important sentences, which fell
here on a certain point of the globe at certain minutes in the *history of
mankind*). Brecht confronts the concept of transcendent historical importance with the specificity of an individual event's time and place. In the
jungle of Chicago, Brecht presents the transformation of two people
through a variety of economic, cultural, and sexual transactions. Such
microcosmic transformations are presented as the key to understanding
social change.

For Brecht, history is neither a coherent narrative nor a body of
knowledge, but an accumulation of events that may or may not be
recorded and that may or may not produce meaning for those involved.
Im Dickicht der Städte (In the Jungle of Cities) does not provide us with
meaningful developments or interactions, but with interests, actions, and

reactions that are subject to constant dispute. In this dispute the sides taken do not remain constant, and each contestant appropriates the opponent's arguments in different settings. The fight presented in the play can also be read as a fight for representation not only between Shlink and Garga, or among all characters in the play, but also between the play and the audience when Brecht suggests that what really happened is a matter of betting (winning or losing). The characters dispute while they are interacting because they find themselves in a chaos of action and meaning rather than as "representatives" of transcendent historical forces.

Such is the case at the very beginning of the play when Shlink enters "C. Maynes Leihbibliothek in Chicago" (C. Mayne's lending library in Chicago). Garga, who works there as a librarian, understands this to be a place for books and readers, while Shlink considers it, like any other public place, to be a site where he can pick a fight with anyone he chooses. Garga's conviction that the library is his domain is destroyed when Shlink declares war on him: "Und an diesem Vormittag, der nicht wie immer ist, eröffne ich den Kampf gegen Sie. Ich beginne ihn damit, daß ich Ihre Plattform erschüttere" (1:441) (And on this morning that is not the same as always, I open the fight against you. I begin it by shaking your platform). Shlink shakes the ground on which Garga stands by staging a performance in the library that throws Garga's life into pandemonium and culminates with Garga losing both his job and his girlfriend. Garga had firmly and unreflectively believed in the stability of his professional and private life: that he was the rightful employee of C. Maynes, the responsible lover of Jane Larry, and the caring son of his parents; that he lived up to his responsibilities as an agent who acts according to his position; and that he fulfilled his responsibility by handling books, visiting his lover, and earning a living for his family. Shlink upsets this coherent picture by presenting Maynes as a rigid businessman, Jane as an alcoholic who readily rejects her impoverished lover, and, eventually, Garga's parents as greedy exploiters who would accept any breadwinner as their son. The play's opening combines with the turn of events it presents to destabilize the identities of the characters and undermine the possibility of any coherent recording either of the historical events presented in the play or, by extension, of any social process.

The play's critique begins in the economic realm, then moves to the social, and finally extends to the cultural when Shlink upends Garga's value system. Shlink begins the attack on Garga's economic position. He offers to buy the librarian's judgment about the quality of different books. In the course of the argument, Shlink belittles Garga for his poverty and insists that he should gladly accept money for his literary opinions. Garga refuses: "Ich verkaufe Ihnen die Ansichten von Mister V. Jensen und Mister Arthur Rimbaud, aber ich verkaufe Ihnen nicht meine Ansicht darüber" (1:439) (I will sell you the views of Mister V. Jensen and Mister Arthur Rimbaud, but I will not sell you my view on that). According to Garga, a book is a materialized thought that can be sold as a commodity, whereas his opinion about the book is a subjective achievement—something that should be excluded from market relations and public dispute. His opinion is part of himself, so selling it would be prostitution (1:440).

In the fight that follows, Shlink destroys Garga's belief that intellectual freedom is more important than social and economic bondage. Shlink and his men consider personal opinion a luxury that is beyond Garga's social status, as shown when Skinny asks Garga, "Sind Sie aus einer transatlantischen Millionärsfamilie?" (1:440) (Are you from a transatlantic millionaire's family?). Skinny then introduces the split between moral principles and social life that Brecht traces throughout the entire play: "Daß Sie Ansichten haben, das kommt, weil Sie nichts vom Leben verstehen" (1:440) (That you have views, that comes because you understand nothing of life). Skinny shows that Garga tries to rise above social struggle by assigning superior value to thought, and in rejecting that effort, Skinny hints at the incompatibility of life and thought. The tension between life and thought also provides the perspective from which Shlink and his men mock authorship: "Die Schriftsteller! Sie rächen sich am Leben durch ein Buch. Das Leben rächt sich dadurch, daß es anders ist" (1:353) (The writers! They avenge themselves on life through a book. Life avenges itself by being different). They reject the notion that anyone can comprehend life through the inanimate medium of print or through abstract intellectual inquiry. The revenge that they foresee (revenge never refers to the battle between Shlink and Garga because they are not motivated by revenge, but by the pleasure of fighting) arises out of this tension that is produced by an author's attempt to reduce social life in its material complexity—a complexity that includes the corporal existence of the author as well as that of his subjects—to the abstract thought embodied in print. Material life takes revenge on the intellectual life of print by contradicting its narrative presentations of coherent meaning. The cruelty we perceive in nature arises from the intellectual imposition of supposedly rational moral meaning on the amoral process of life. By presenting this conflict to the civilized social body, Brecht shows the city to be a jungle, and he shows that the jungle is home to the contradictions between thought and life—both the "individual's" life and the life of the social body.

Garga builds his identity as a librarian by conceiving of thought as separate from life, a belief he shows by asserting that material goods are less important than and unrelated to immaterial goods. Shlink reveals his desire to unite the material and the immaterial worlds by calling his fight with Garga a "metaphysische Aktion" (metaphysical action): "Sie haben nicht begriffen, was es war. Sie wollten mein Ende, aber ich wollte den Kampf. Nicht das Körperliche, sondern das Geistige war es" (1:493) (You have not grasped what it was. You wanted my end, but I wanted the fight. It was not the physical, but the spiritual). While Shlink insists that his impulse to fight is spiritual (*das Geistige* [the spiritual]), he merges the spirit with the realm of physical action by speaking of understanding as *begreifen* (to grasp; to comprehend) rather than *verstehen* (to understand). Shlink's approach to fighting is informed by Brecht's notion of *das Geistige* (the spiritual) as a social interaction that receives and records its experience and the knowledge produced by that experience through and upon the body. Garga ultimately proves unable to learn this lesson.

Brecht thinks *das Geistige* (the spiritual) is achieved through physical contact and contrasts it with "understanding," which is an artifact of language. Following their three-year fight, and before Garga's final retreat to New York, the two men spend three weeks together living off the fruits of their struggle and trying to making sense of it. Ultimately, as Garga notes, they fail: "Ich habe Ihnen jetzt drei Wochen zugehört. . . . Warum sitze ich und verliere meine Zeit? Sind wir nicht drei Wochen hier gelegen?" (1:492) (I have now listened three weeks to you. . . . Why do I sit and lose my time? Have we not been lying here three weeks?). Shlink, recognizing that they have gained neither sense nor a reliable bond from their three weeks together, asks, "Und niemals, George Garga, wird ein Ausgang dieses Kampfes sein, niemals eine Verständigung?" (1:492) (And there will never, George Garga, be an end to this fight, never an understanding?). Garga's negative response reflects his earlier comment: "Die Sprache reicht zur Verständigung nicht aus" (1:491) (Language is not sufficient for understanding). Understanding, or the acceptance of its impossibility, reaches an impasse when Garga proves unable to follow Shlink to a less conventional approach. Shlink says:

> Ich habe die Tiere beobachtet. Die Liebe, Wärme aus Körpernähe, ist unsere einzige Gnade in der Finsternis! Aber die Vereinigung der Organe ist die einzige, sie überbrückt nicht die Entzweiung der Sprache. (1:491)

[I have observed the animals. Love, warmth from bodily closeness, is our only mercy in the darkness! But the unification of the organs is the only one, it does not bridge the division of language.]

Shlink's commitment to fighting derives from his observation of animals, and a relationship based on animalistic enmity does not entail understanding.

Like antagonistic animals, Shlink and Garga have tracked one another during their battles. Fighting has kept them close for, as Shlink remarks early in the play, to possess one's hate (as Garga does) is the same as to possess one's love, and in either case one is loath to lose contact. Shlink defines love physically, as warmth produced by the closeness of bodies, and he distinguishes it from mere talk, which seeks ineffectually to produce understanding. Shlink has no expectations of the "meaningful" love produced by talk, and he accepts language's arbitrariness. The division between the signifier and the signified, rather than mediating between language and life, intensifies the difference between them, and it is that very difference which fuels Shlink's initial attack on Garga. The "Entzweiung der Sprache" (division of language) meets the "unendliche Vereinzelung des Menschen" (infinite isolation of man), rendering impossible any connection between people via language and understanding and making even "eine Feindschaft zum unerreichbaren Ziel" (1:491) (an enmity into an unattainable goal). With spiritual connection rendered impossible, fighting offers a way to initiate contact between bodies and thus to escape the trap produced by the gap separating life (or social reality) and thought (or writing).

Even in hindsight Shlink's causeless and senseless—literally irrational—enmity resists valid, coherent representation because, as both antagonists come to realize, the arbitrary nature of language renders all meaning fictional. Shlink accepts this and realizes that it is impossible to "make sense" of the fight. Garga, however, does apply "sense" by excluding *das Geistige* (the spiritual) and opting for survival, which he defines as success: "Und das Geistige, das sehen Sie, das ist nichts. Es ist nicht wichtig, der Stärkere zu sein, sondern der Lebendige" (1:493) (And the spiritual, you see, that is nothing. It is not important to be the stronger, but the living). While Shlink fights to produce a distinct quality of intellectual and physical comprehension, Garga fights only to win in the most conventional sense. When he knows that the lynch mob is coming for Shlink, he takes pride in the prospect of his own survival and of winning, once and for all, his contest with Shlink. Shlink comprehends life as a perpetual fight with others, and he seeks nothing else; Garga, on the other hand, longs for solitude. Garga declares victory over Shlink to achieve solitude, ending their relationship. By winning and separating himself from Shlink, Garga abandons the fight. Shlink counts this abandonment as a loss of life.

Garga desires this break in order to pursue a different form of life, and the conflicting goals of Garga and Shlink reflect their differing conceptions of time and history. When Garga opts out of the fight in order to live in solitude, Shlink perceives Garga to be opting out of history:

> Die Etappen des Lebens sind nicht die der Erinnerung. Ich habe Reis gegessen und mit vielerlei Volk gehandelt. Meine Eingebungen habe ich nicht ausgeschwatzt. Der Schluß ist nicht das Ziel, die letzte Episode nicht wichtiger als irgendeine andere. Schließlich entsprach der Gewinn genau dem Einsatz. (1:427)

> [The stages of life are not those of memory. I have eaten rice and dealt with many people. I have not blurted out my inspirations. The end is not the goal, the last episode not more important than some other one. In the end the return corresponded precisely to the investment.]

Shlink cannot understand what it would mean for the fight to come to an end and to survive only as an object of verbal memory. His whole life has taught him to distrust language as much as he trusts physical contact and conflict. Memory —reliable memory—is imbedded in the fight rather than in verbal narrative, so it is social rather than solitary, contested rather than consensual, and in the present rather than in the past. For Shlink, Garga's withdrawal from the fight—his withdrawal into verbal memory— is a withdrawal from life. Shlink "remembers" past battles—and he has engaged in many over the course of his life—only as an integral part of whatever fight currently animates and produces meaning in his life. Fights do not come to an abrupt end and then get stored safely in a memory bank; they recur and inform one another, producing ever-changing meanings precisely because the chaos of social reality ("unorganisiertes Material" [unorganized material]) resists stable and unchanging meaning.

Garga rejects Shlink's insight and longs for the solitude in which he can create a meaningful narrative, a goal he articulates retrospectively at the play's end: "Allein sein ist eine gute Sache. Das Chaos ist aufgebraucht. Es war die beste Zeit" (1:497) (To be alone is a good thing. The chaos is used up. It was the best time). Garga speaks these words while pocketing the money he made selling his sister and Shlink's business. He welcomes the solitude, but he acknowledges that, chaotic as it was, the fight with Shlink was productive—"Es war die beste Zeit" (It was the best time). Now, with the fight over, the social conflict that produced history—Brecht's "unorganized material"—grinds to a halt. Progressive memory can no longer be produced through contestation; instead, the once productive fight between Garga and Shlink is consumed, ordered, and tamed by memory. When Garga interprets the fight in accordance with his interests, he domesticates it and drains it of its potential for change. This, Brecht's play insists, is the way historical narratives consume social reality.

This involvement, more than any fictional "outcome" that Garga envisions, creates what Foucault calls "effective history":

> An event, consequently, is not a decision, a treaty, a reign, or a battle, but the reversal of a relationship of forces, the usurpation of power, the appropriation of a vocabulary turned against those who had once used it, a feeble domination that poisons itself as it grows lax, the entry of a masked "other." The forces operating in history are not controlled by destiny or regulative mechanisms, but respond to haphazard conflicts.[37]

The fight between Shlink and Garga is an "event" in Foucault's concept of genealogy because both men engage in a fight that enriches and impoverishes them, transforms them, and sacrifices their social networks. The fight alters "a relationship of forces." By presenting the two men's shared struggle as driven by the desire for intimacy, Brecht enables us to witness the perpetual reversal of rules and domination that Foucault sees as historical change. Some of the changes produced by the struggle between Shlink and Garga are intended; however, other unintended changes occur that also affect the participants of the fight.

INSTINCTS AND TRANSFORMATIONS

> Die Zeiten ohne Instinkte haben das Mißtrauen gegen den Kopf. . . .
> [U]nd es sind die Leute ohne Leiber, die sich etwas erwarten von der
> Unterbindung des Kopfes. Es gibt eine Phantasie des Körpers und eine
> Phantasie des Geistes (das heißt, es gibt eher zweierlei Art von Phantasie
> als die Grenze von Körper und Geist), beide aber sind mehr wert als die
> dunklen Mischungen in den Venen, die man Gefühle nennt. (21:239)

> [The times without instincts distrust the head. . . . [A]nd it is the peo-
> ple without bodies who expect something for themselves from the
> undercutting of the head. There is a fantasy of the body and a fantasy

of the spirit (that is, rather, there are two kinds of fantasy as the boundary of body and spirit), but both are worth more than the dark mixtures
in the veins that one calls feelings.]

Instinct can be defined both as the drive to survive and the means by
which a particular species exercises that drive, and it is conventionally
considered more the province of animals than humans. Brecht, however,
considers instinct and intellect to be mutually dependent human qualities. Though Brecht refuses to consider one without the other, he nevertheless keeps them separate and distinct. In their conflictual dependence—their dialectical relationship to one another—each serves as a
reminder of the other's difference and incompatibility. Brecht uses them
together to sharpen the perception of what is physical and what is intellectual. In *Im Dickicht der Städte (In the Jungle of Cities)*, Brecht presents
the instinctive fight for survival as a means of intellectual comprehension
with surprising results. While the fight between Shlink and Garga is without reason, it produces unexpected physical and mental changes. The
fight takes place in a racist context—Garga even exploits racism to "win"
the fight—and yet, both men come to realize and then embody their
sameness by transforming into one another.

Shlink instinctively chooses Garga as his opponent and discovers to
his delight that he has found a fighter (1:440). Garga survives the initial
assault— in spite of his inexperience—by abandoning any attempt to find
the reasons behind Shlink's attack and employing his instinct for survival.
Shlink initiates the fight out of his need for human contact and succeeds
in establishing this contact: he invades Garga's work place and his relationships. Through a variety of moves, Shlink keeps in touch with Garga
without bonding—their contact remains impersonal not only during the
three years of their fight, but also through the three weeks of their love
affair. Throughout the play they address one another as "Sie" (you [for-
mal]) rather than "Du" (you [informal]). At the end of the play, Garga
and Shlink meditate on different varieties of contact in which no traces of
bonding can be detected. According to Shlink, "Unsere Bekanntschaft
war kurz, sie war eine Zeitlang vorwiegend, die Zeit ist schnell verflogen"
(1:490) (Our acquaintance was short, it was for a time predominant, the
time has flown by quickly). Acquaintance—pure, simple, and persistent
acquaintance—is the fruit of the contact between Garga and Shlink.

The fight that initiates this acquaintance begins, according to Garga,
with a catch: "Ich weiß nicht, was man mit mir vorhat. Man hat mich
harpuniert. Man zog mich an sich. Es scheint Stricke zu geben. Ich werde

mich an Sie halten, Herr" (1:447) (I do not know what is planned for me. I have been harpooned. I was drawn in. There seem to be cords. I will adhere to you, sir). Garga describes his encounter with Shlink as an attempt to make contact rather than simply as an attack. Garga uses passive terms to describe his connection to his attackers. By accepting his inferiority, Garga enters the fight with the prospect of surviving. He uses *Herr* (sir), a public and hierarchical signifier, when addressing Shlink, and he signals a commitment to staying in contact with his antagonist through the term *sich halten an* (to adhere to; to rely on; to stick close to), which in German entails not only holding onto something, but also accepting someone as a role model. Committed to staying close to his attacker, watching him, and acting responsively, Garga enters the fight.

By instinctively staying in touch with one another, each man transforms himself. After destroying Garga's economic livelihood, Shlink makes his antagonist more like himself by turning his lumber business over to Garga; Garga accepts this gambit and continues to move toward Shlink by immediately donating the business to the Salvation Army. Garga becomes, like his enemy, a former owner of the lumber business. Both men experience extreme physical changes over the course of the play. In the first scene, Shlink's men "skin" Garga by frightening him out of his clothes; the clothes are returned, but when Garga once again dons his outward "skin," he notices that Shlink's men are dressed just like him. They have entered his skin. Shlink, in turn, assimilates to Garga's class status by working in the coal mines, and this alters his body. In this way the antagonism between these men is something other than purely personal. It brings two social spheres into contact. This process continues throughout the play. When, for example, Garga is imprisoned for business fraud, Shlink replaces him within his family and becomes the breadwinner. Shlink transforms himself from millionaire businessman to coal-mining family member. Garga gains a lucrative business and a life of economic ease but loses a family. Following this exchange of places, each moves on, but they remain in antagonistic contact and continue to take social and economic positions in response to one another. Brecht roots their transformations in a thoroughgoing materialism even though he wrote the play years before turning to Marxism.

Physical and social economies structure not only the fight between Shlink and Garga, but also their love interests. Both men articulate their erotic interest in one another through detached physical and verbal means. For example, neither man's connection to women is rooted in sexual interest; women are simply a medium through which they express homosocial interest in one another. When Shlink says to Garga, "Ich belade Sie mit dem Schicksal Ihrer Schwester. Sie haben ihr die Augen geöffnet darüber, daß sie in alle Ewigkeit ein Objekt ist unter den Männern!" (1:471) (I burden you with the fate of your sister. You have opened her eyes to the fact that she is for all eternity an object among men!), he points out that both men are using women to stay in touch with one another. Women are a site for their struggle and a disguise for homoerotic attraction rather than a cause for fighting, a reward for victory, or an independent force in either man's life.

Their mutual attraction cannot be traced in terms of cause and effect, but it is obvious long before Shlink articulates his love for Garga in the last scene; Garga is, in fact, the one who suggests it earlier in the play (1:447). Garga's comment undercuts the primacy critics have conventionally attributed to Shlink's desire and provides a genealogy for their attraction that extends to the fight itself rather than to individual desire. When Garga arrives at the Chinese hotel inhabited by Shlink's gang, Wurm observes, "Die Harpune sitzt fester, als wir glaubten. . . . Jetzt liegt er drinnen in Shlinks Zimmer und leckt seine Wunden" (1:463–64) (The harpoon is fixed more firmly than we believed. . . . Now he lies inside in Shlink's room and licks his wounds). Garga originally used this metaphor of penetration to describe Shlink's actions in initiating the fight. Thus, while it is Wurm who makes this metaphor explicitly sexual, it echoes Garga's description of his interactions with Shlink: "»Ich nenne ihn meinen höllischen Gemahl in meinen Träumen, Shlink, den Hund. Wir sind von Tisch und Bett geschieden, er hat keine Kammer mehr. Sein Bräutchen raucht Virginias und verdient sich was in die Strümpfe.« Das bin ich!" (1:464) ("I call him my hellish consort in my dreams, Shlink, the dog. We are divorced from table and bed, he no longer has a chamber anymore. His little bride smokes Virginias and earns something for herself in stockings." That is me!). Garga anticipates Shlink's homoerotic longing precisely because he recognizes his own homoerotic interests. This allows him to render Shlink's death as an erotic allegory when he says, "Ich werde einmal seine Witwe sein" (1:464) (I will be his widow one day). By calling himself Shlink's widow, Garga anticipates winning the fight, but he does even more. "Witwe" (widow) also invokes his status as Shlink's surviving lover after their three-week honeymoon. In their longing for one another, the men become interchangeable. Garga calls Shlink a dog while behaving like one himself; he calls Shlink his hellish consort in order to affirm his own identity.

The interchangeability of Garga and Shlink is dependent on the symbolic economy of their physical and mental existence. Both men take account of their past and their fight by comparing themselves to each other in genealogical terms. The play remains in the privileged realm of the external by examining different genealogies of the skin. In Shlink's case, the skin develops through the hardships of social and racial injustice that he, as the older man, has endured over long periods of time, as the growing thickness of his skin shows:

> Die Menschenhaut im natürlichen Zustande ist zu dünn für diese Welt, deshalb sorgt der Mensch dafür, daß sie dicker wird. Die Methode wäre unanfechtbar, wenn man das Wachstum stoppen könnte. Ein Stück präpariertes Leder zum Beispiel bleibt, aber die Haut wächst, sie wird dicker und dicker. (1:462)

> [The human skin in its natural condition is too thin for this world, therefore man takes care to make it thicker. The method would be incontestable if one could stop the growth. A piece of prepared leather remains, for example, but the skin grows, it becomes thicker and thicker.]

Shlink's skin has grown progressively thicker through numerous humiliations over long periods of time. This is the sign that Garga has found himself in battle with a professional fighter, and it explains why Shlink and "Skinny" begin the fight by "skinning" the thin-skinned librarian. According to Garga, "Sie haben Prärie gemacht. Ich akzeptiere die Prärie. Sie haben mir die Haut abgezogen aus Liebhaberei. Durch eine neue Haut ersetzen Sie nichts" (1:448) (You have made prairie. I accept the prairie. You have torn off my skin for pleasure. With a new skin you replace nothing).

Garga survives the fight by adapting to the situations that others create for him: "Ich verstehe nichts, Sir, bin dabei wie ein Neger, bin mit einer weißen Fahne gekommen, jetzt entfalte ich sie zur Attacke" (1:451) (I understand nothing, sir, am in that like a Negro, have come with a white flag, now I unfurl it to attack). Brecht presents Garga's organic adaptation to new social circumstances with various tropes of changing skin: Garga's loss of his clothes is a "skinning" and leaves him, in his own estimation, a "Negro." Losing his work clothes is far more than a superficial and temporary embarrassment for Garga; it is essential and transforming: "Ich hatte meine Kindheit noch vor mir. Die Ölfelder mit dem blauen Raps. Der Iltis in den Schluchten und die leichten Wasserschnellen" (1:490) (I still had my childhood ahead of me. The oil fields with the blue rape. The polecat in the ravines and the light water skippers). The natural metaphors Garga uses to describe his loss of childhood

underscore the rapid acceleration of evolutionary change that he experiences. According to Shlink, "Richtig, das alles war in Ihrem Gesicht! Jetzt
ist es hart wie Bernstein, man findet mitunter Tierleichen in ihm, der
durchsichtig ist" (1:490) (Correct, all of that was in your face! Now it is
hard like amber, one sometimes finds animal corpses in it, which is trans-
parent). The changes through which Garga is rushed are preserved, however, like fossils in amber ("Bernstein"). The long duration of evolution has
been condensed for Garga into three years and three weeks. The amber
face with its preserved fragments of Garga's life also resembles Shlink's "yellow" Malayan skin. Shlink recognizes this transformation. In the course of
the play, Shlink and Garga turn into one another, a process they can only
perceive by observing and tracing one another as their fight requires.

Brecht defines race not in biological, but in historical terms—in
terms of the life a person lived. History, for him, materializes in the
body; it is the social relation based on instinct that overcomes racial division for the sake of being human. But this awareness is not the result of
a "shared humanity," a concept that Brecht destroys in the play's first
scene. Instead, this assurance emerges out of a combination of physical
instinct and the intellectual recognition of two opposite concepts equally
employed in the struggle.

In his "Metaphysisch-Geschichtsphilosophischen Studien" (Studies
in Metaphysics and the Philosophy of History), Walter Benjamin writes
that mimesis, by which he means the creation of similarity, is the driving
force of human history: "Die Gabe, Ähnlichkeit zu sehn, die wir besitzen,
ist nichts als nur ein schwaches Rudiment des ehemals gewaltigen
Zwanges, ähnlich zu werden und sich zu verhalten" (Our gift for seeing
similarity is nothing but a weak rudiment of the once powerful compulsion to become similar and also to behave mimetically).[38] If we consider
the fight between Shlink and Garga from this perspective, it becomes
obvious that instead of creating meaning and responding to motivation
according to the conventions of traditional theatre, both men follow a
drive to become similar to one another, and the similarity that emerges
does so in spite of, or at least without reference to, their intentions. Here,
Brecht moves from social history as disorganized material to natural history as it plays out in the fast-paced urbanity of the twentieth century.
The urban jungle invalidates traditional forms of living, forms that the
play presents as empty shells. These forms—the family, romantic part-
nerships, traditional modes of employment—force those who seek to ful-
fill them to reactivate the drive for mimesis in order to adapt and form
new and unpredictable social units. Attraction and enmity tie together

those who succeed in provoking one another. The battle that ensues is a shared collective activity whose effects can be traced through the antagonists' bodies.

Through the attraction between and transformation of Garga and Shlink, Brecht presents the history of their fight in terms congruent with Foucault's concept of genealogy. There, Foucault distinguishes identity as a result of traditional historiography, whereas genealogy traces the descent of the body as "the locus of a dissociated Self (adopting the illusion of a substantial unity), and a volume in perpetual disintegration."[39] In the play, Garga and Shlink leave their environments and dissolve their own identities in order to maximize their ability to fight. Yet, in the process of relocating, both men also appropriate the other's identity and environment. Each replaces his former line of descent based on a cultural identity with the line of descent located in his opponent. According to Foucault, "Genealogy, as an analysis of descent, is thus situated within the articulation of the body and history."[40] Brecht's articulation of the past through the body bypasses meaningful representations of history, which becomes obvious when neither Garga nor Shlink can make sense of either the cause or the effect of their fight; instead, they are the living bearers of the history their fight produces.

In spite of their transformations, important differences between the two men remain, and these differences are rooted in Shlink's traumatic past. The genealogy of Shlink's skin varies in interesting ways from that of Garga's. The famous forty-year loneliness that Shlink seeks to overcome by fighting Garga is halved by his previous encounters with the lynch mob: "Das Geschrei kenne ich. Es ist 20 Jahre her, aber ich habe es nicht aus dem Gehirn gebracht. Sie werfen einen Mann wie einen Holzstamm auf den Asphalt, diese Tiere kenne ich" (1:419) (I know that cry. It is 20 years back, but I have not gotten it out of the brain. They throw a man on the pavement like a log, I know these animals). Shlink distinguishes between different sorts of fighting. He sees lynching as the absence of fighting and perceives the lynch mob as consisting of those "die nicht bezahlen wollen" (1:419) (who do not want to pay). The mob refuses a fair fight, rejecting the rules that Shlink and Garga set up for themselves. Fighting, for Brecht, depends on the mutual acceptance of the conflict as a matter both of survival and of social interaction. Shlink's previous experience with a lynch mob traumatized him because it turned him into a victim who could not fight back. By surviving that experience, he learned how to endure.

In the course of his life, Shlink brings endurance to perfection. He transforms fear and memory into action and takes masochistic pleasure in doing so. When he applies to the Garga family to take him in as their breadwinner, he not only tolerates racist treatment, but pushes matters further with his remark: "Ich habe an allem Geschmack, mein Magen verdaut Kieselsteine" (1:460) (I have a taste for everything, my stomach digests cobblestones). Enduring racist violence becomes an extension of this process when Shlink hesitates to escape the lynch mob that Garga has unleashed for the first time: "Aber es ist noch nicht das richtige Geschrei, das weiße. Dann sind sie da. Dann haben wir noch eine Minute. Horch, jetzt! Jetzt ist es das richtige! Das weiße Geschrei!" (1:489) (But it is not the right cry yet, the white one. Then they are there. Then we still have a minute. Listen, now! Now it is the right one! The white cry!). Shlink has transformed the fearful and traumatic memory of the lynch mob into a stimulant that he can enjoy because through enduring he has acquired the ability to escape and fight back. He has endured through struggle.

Transformation plays a key role in endurance. Garga explains that Shlink's superiority as a fighter—"Sie kämpfen leicht. Wie Sie verdauen!" (1:490) (You fight lightly. Like you digest!)—is the result of harmony between his way of fighting and his body. This distinction rests on the years that separate him from Shlink, years in which Shlink was victimized by racial violence, an experience he transformed into a fighting technique. Their differences in experience are overcome through further mutual transformation. Garga begins his fight with Shlink as a self-acknowledged inferior, and Shlink changes his persona to that of a humble servant who accepts the stereotype of racial inferiority by referring to his "gelbe Haut" (1:460) (yellow skin). Shlink transforms himself to match Garga, a transformation that allows the fight to continue longer than first appeared likely. Shlink finds advantage in accepting the disadvantages of self-abnegation. He works within the racist structure he has known all his life, changing himself in accordance with it in order to seek his own death in battle with a carefully chosen white man. Garga, as that white man, can and does activate a lynch mob. By engaging with a racist power structure, Shlink can exercise his strength and endurance as a fighter in a way that permits him simultaneously to fight and to submit to his chosen death.

Garga comes to fear that Shlink has learned so much that he cannot be beaten. According to Garga, Shlink has a "zu dicke Haut. Er biegt alles um, was man hineinstößt" (1:416) (too-thick skin. He repels everything that one thrusts in). This renders Shlink invulnerable because it allows him to transform attacks into counterattacks. But despite his apparent invulnerability, the memory of lynching manifests itself in Shlink's skin— his most external feature. As in *Trommeln in der Nacht (Drums in the*

Night), Brecht presents the past not through a narrative, but as an imprint on the body, as a genealogy that combines physical and social history. As Garga puts it, "Jetzt geht es also durch Ihre Haut? Die Geschichte mit den Spießen" (1:419) (So now it goes through your skin? The story with the spears). The harpoon that Shlink aimed at Garga penetrated his body and propelled him into a new public sphere. Shlink is perforated by history and memory, a perforation that provides Garga with the information he needs for the final triumph when he hands Shlink over to the mob.

But Shlink's fighting technique cannot accept Garga's attempt to organize the chaos of the fight in terms of winning and losing. In fact, both men get from the fight what they want—Shlink does, after all, want death. Herein lies the difference between the two men: Garga fights to live but Shlink to die, as he elaborates to Garga, "Ein Weißer, gemietet, mich hinunterzuschaffen, mir etwas Ekel oder Moder in das Maul zu stopfen, daß ich den Geschmack des Todes auf die Zunge kriege" (1:493) (A white man, rented to ruin me, to stuff something loathsome or decayed in my mouth so that I get the taste of death on my tongue). After engaging Garga in love and metaphysics, Shlink engages him in his death. Thought and love are conventionally perceived as immaterial and personal entities; death is considered inevitable, biological, and beyond the realm of subjective or social interference. Shlink is old and determined to transform the biological act of dying into a social event. Shlink succeeds in this goal, and the fight enables him to distill as much life out of his death as he can.

The fight as "uninteressierter Kampf" (uninterested fight) lacks meaning, but as the "Geschichte mit den Spießen" (1:419) (story with the spears), it signifies historical change. Harpoons link uninterested people through penetrated skin, and the battle that results from that link transforms them visibly and in traceable ways into one another. Brecht's later notes regarding historical transformation may well have their origins in his *Dickicht (Jungle)* plays, as underscored by his theoretical assertion that history should be seen primarily as genealogy:

> Es soll nicht bestritten werden, daß Bürger sich wie Adelige benehmen können zu einer Zeit, wo sich Adelige schon nicht mehr wie Adelige benehmen oder wie Bauern, die sich niemals so benähmen wie Bauern, wenn sie nicht Felder bearbeiteten, der bürgerliche Mensch löst den adeligen, der proletarische den bürgerlichen nicht nur ab, sondern er enthält ihn auch. (21:522)

> [It should not be contested that bourgeois are able to conduct themselves like nobles at a time when nobles already no longer conduct

themselves like nobles, or like farmers who would never conduct themselves like farmers if they did not work fields, the bourgeois man not
only replaces the noble, the proletarian replacing the bourgeois, but he
also contains him.]

Class struggle, when viewed as genealogy, becomes more complicated
than a story of political commitment within a progressive narrative of historical development. When history as genealogy produces containment,
the assurances of cause and effect, of right or wrong, are subject to constant change. If the succession of struggle produces containment, an elevated position of moral integrity becomes an illusion. From this perspective, class struggle includes cultural and physical seduction as well as
economic and political conflict. Parties to such struggle can only achieve
"victory" by accepting their antagonists and adapting to the world they
initially seek to change. The process of *enthalten* (to contain; to embody)
might be misunderstood for what is conventionally called assimilation,
but one should keep in mind that Brecht's concept of becoming similar is
based on permanent conflict and is therefore not unidirectional. It is
mutual or multidirectional. The importance of the habitual mimesis in
Im Dickicht der Städte (In the Jungle of Cities) is that dominance constantly
shifts between the two opponents.

   If we consider containment the result of habitual mimesis, we may
subsume *enthalten* (to contain; to embody) into Brecht's vast concept of
Haltung (disposition) and thus add a historical component to this concept. As one of the key terms of Brechtian theatre, *Haltung* (disposition)
contains such diverse aspects as social attitude and physical posture.
According to Brecht, *Haltung* (disposition) as an essentially theatrical
concept is the physical signification of thought; it thus needs an audience
to decipher it. In *Im Dickicht der Städte (In the Jungle of Cities)*, Garga and
Shlink come to "contain" one another as a result of their conflictual
engagement, but each man develops a different attitude, as is obvious in
their final evaluation of the outcome of their fight:

> GARGA: . . . Wenn Sie längst Kalk über sich haben, durch die
> natürliche Ausscheidung des Veralteten, werde ich wählen, was
> mich unterhält.
>
> SHLINK: Was nehmen Sie für eine Haltung ein? Ich bitte Sie, Ihre
> Pfeife aus dem Maul zu nehmen. Wenn Sie sagen wollen, daß sie
> impotent geworden sind, dann tun Sie das mit einer anderen
> Stimme. (1:493)

[GARGA: . . . When you long since have lime over you due to the natural elimination of the obsolete, I will choose what sustains me.

SHLINK: What kind of disposition are you assuming? I ask you to take your pipe out of your mouth. If you want to say that you have become impotent, then do that with a different voice.]

The German *unterhalten* (to sustain; to maintain; to entertain) as used by Garga, entails such different concepts as subsistence and entertainment. He opts out of the fight in favor of a life free of conflict, but one that is also passive, solitary, and asocial. Garga separates himself from Shlink in two ways: first, he declares Shlink expelled from the fight; then, he moves from the social commitment of fighting to the atomizing act of choosing. Garga envisions a state of luxury in which he will be able to choose his subsistence and entertainment without making any personal investment, just as when, in the beginning of the play, he insists that opinions can be held "freely." Shlink, on the other hand, is an advocate of *Haltung* (disposition) in the materialist sense when he seeks to extend the fight into the realm of intellectual cognition. Such is the case when, in the end, he seeks to combine fighting, philosophical reflection, and sex into a single conflictual interaction. Accordingly, Shlink responds to Garga's longing for entertainment with contempt. Shlink perceives Garga's desire for solitude as passivity and sexual impotence. Shlink sees this "choice" as a rejection of social and sexual opponents and partners. Sex, like thought, depends on social contact and conflict, and, like fighting and philosophical reflection, it must be performed in an appropriate manner.

Im Dickicht der Städte (In the Jungle of Cities) presents the various elements of Brecht's concept of *Haltung* (disposition). In the beginning he uses it for human contact in terms of *sich halten an* (to adhere to; to rely on; to stick close to) when Garga holds on to Shlink in order to learn how to survive the fight. Garga acts instinctively by enduring Shlink's attack, and he gains the attitude and posture of a fighter by accepting Shlink, who is a master in endurance, as a role model. By clinging to one another over time, the two men transform into one another in terms of *enthalten* (to contain; to embody) as historical containment. Finally, the fight can be understood as the demonstration that thought, as mimetic activity, hinges on social conflict and physical endurance when Brecht writes, "Freilich ist Denken ein Kampf mit Gedanken" (21:427) (Of course, thinking is a fight with thoughts).

Cognition, for Brecht, does not take place inside the subject, but emerges as the result of successful social labor. Brecht advocates a

"Philosophie der Straße" (philosophy of the street) that shares much with Shlink's conception of a fighting life: "Wenn das Volk einem eine philosophische Haltung zuschreibt, so ist es fast immer eine Fähigkeit des Aushaltens von was" (22.1:512) (When the people ascribe to one a philosophical disposition, so it is almost always an ability to endure something). The German *aushalten* includes the English verbs "to endure," "to bear," "to suffer," "to sustain," and "to stand up to." *Haltung* (disposition) is a physical, social, intellectual, and historical position, and thought gains content through physical struggle. As Brecht outlines in the Keuner story, "Weise am Weisen ist die Haltung" (The wisdom of the wise is the disposition), thought "hat keinen Inhalt" (has no content). This becomes clear when Keuner responds to the lecturing philosopher, "Ich sehe dein Ziel nicht, ich sehe deine Haltung" (18:13) (I do not see your goal, I see your disposition). While bodies are containers of historical conflicts, thought remains devoid of content. However, when acted out and released into a social context, thought can be observed by others and become subject to dispute. The exchange of thought, then, does not rely on understanding, but on physical and social imitation that results from the social conflicts and rapid cultural changes characteristic of the twentieth century. *Im Dickicht der Städte (In the Jungle of Cities)* demonstrates the genealogical re-creation of two men who progress not through intentional acts, but through their drive to stay in touch, a drive that manifests itself in their bodies. In this play, Brecht locates historical change and intellectual comprehension strictly in the social and physical realms, and in the process, he develops a distinct theatrical materialism years before turning to the historical materialism of Marx. It is through this "pre-Marxian" and distinctly theatrical materialism that Brecht challenges and enriches Marxism.

3

Man Between Material
and Social Order

Die Schauspielkunst gehört zu den elementaren gesellschaftlichen Kräften, sie beruht auf einem unmittelbaren gesellschaftlichen Vermögen, einer Lust der Menschen in Gesellschaft, sie ist wie die Sprache selber, sie ist eine Sprache für sich. (22.2:754)

[The art of acting belongs to the elemental social forces, it is based on an immediate social capacity, on a pleasure of the people in society, it is like language itself, it is a language for itself.]

Leben heißt für den Menschen: die Prozesse organisieren, denen er unterworfen ist. (26:296)

[To live means for man: to organize the processes to which he is subjected.]

Ever since the eighteenth century, when Lessing tied Enlightenment drama to social progress and public education, the discourse on theatre has, to various degrees, also been a discourse on the public sphere. Habermas has shown that the concept of the public, as expressed by thinkers from Kant to Hegel to Marx, includes discourses on economic progress and political emancipation.[1] Brecht, to some extent, partakes in both traditions by developing a concept of theatre that includes theatre as a forum for politics and theatre as a provider of a counterpublic sphere. As both his *Dreigroschenprozeß (Threepenny Trial)* and his experimental teaching plays in particular show, Brecht considers such an alternative essential in the political and economic situation of the Weimar Republic, where the negotiations of public life ranged from National Socialist attempts to eliminate "abstract society" for a reconstituting of community, or *Gemeinschaft*, (which was institutionalized as the perverted *Volksgemeinschaft* [national community] during the Third Reich) to Marxist redefinitions of the private and public spheres.

In Brecht's suspicion of the *bürgerliche Öffentlichkeit* (bourgeois public sphere) of the Weimar Republic, he perceives the public sphere not as the coherent product of a democratic state, but as a sphere consisting of parliaments, courts, and the media that remains entirely removed from the sphere of material production. Laws, lawsuits, and press commentaries are thus not equipped to resolve conflicts in production; rather, they perpetuate the democratic ideal of bourgeois culture without living up to it.[2] To reveal the contradictions of the democratic public sphere, Brecht defines it as a theatrical endeavor in which people and institutions play their assigned roles. Once the public sphere is perceived as theatrical, its forms of representation open themselves to a different kind of critique, a critique that translates into action, which then leads from the theatrical to the social. On the one hand, this presents the challenge of explaining how this can be done; on the other hand, public events taking place in Weimar Germany—especially the prospect of a theatrical state devoted to destroying the very public that Brecht sought to bring into existence—forced him to think through what distinguishes a theatre that produces a public from a theatre that destroys it.

For Brecht, as a politically committed playwright, the public is located in art and society. Rules and conditions of the public sphere are especially important to playwrights because they write for the theatre as a public institution. Brecht saw himself challenged in post–World War I Germany by several aspects of the public sphere. The legitimate democratic government of the Weimar Republic was constantly challenged by antidemocratic forces, and Brecht's writings interrogate the resulting political instability. The politically reactionary *Kaiserreich* (empire), the horrors of World War I, and the Weimar Republic's disastrous economic situation created an extremely brutalized culture that served as a breeding ground for what Brecht called "das neue Tier, das / Geboren wird, den Menschen auszulösen" (10.1:427–28) (the new animal that / Is born to redeem mankind). Here Brecht anticipates what Oskar Negt and Alexander Kluge call "materialistischer Instinkt" (materialist instinct), which refers to the rebellion—emotional, physical, or both—against rational concepts of representation.[3] On the stage of German politics, this new animal underwent several transformations before emerging in its most perverted form in 1933.

Whereas Brecht explores instinctive adaptations to circumstance and the resulting physical transformations in his early plays, in the texts discussed in this chapter, he examines the comprehension of social and political circumstances and responses to those circumstances that range from participation to resistance. In *Mann ist Mann (Man Equals Man)*, Brecht attacks the concept of the self by replacing the *Individuum* (individual) with a *Dividuum* (dividual) as the main character, a man who is incapable of saying "no" and who agrees with every change of situation by adapting to ever-changing roles. Adaptation, then, becomes participation, a concept upon which Brecht reflects in terms of political action in his *Dreigroschenprozeß (Threepenny Trial)*. In the *Dreigroschenprozeß (Threepenny Trial)*, Brecht simultaneously critiques representation in both political and theatrical terms. In reading all social action as theatrical activity, Brecht seeks to ensure participation and adaptation by those involved in or affected by judicial processes. By considering public events to be theatrical, Brecht moves from representation to demonstration, a move he develops in detail in the *Straßenszene (Street Scene)*, where the demonstration of a car accident produces evidence of social and economic power structures.

Demonstration as a means to detect an unacknowledged crime is also Brecht's concern in those texts discussed in the second half of this chapter. For Brecht, as for many leftists of his time, fascism was an extreme form of capitalism and a number of his plays and fragments examine fascism's dependency on capitalism. From *Aufstieg und Fall der Stadt Mahagonny (Rise and Fall of the City of Mahagonny)* to the fragment *Aus Nichts wird Nichts (From Nothing Comes Nothing)* to *Furcht und Elend des Dritten Reiches (Fear and Misery of the Third Reich)*, one can trace a Brechtian genealogy of fascism. In *Furcht und Elend (Fear and Misery)*, Brecht presents fascism as social passivity that results from the inability to interfere in the crimes committed by a fascist state. An inability to interfere is learned in capitalism. In *Mahagonny*, Brecht shows how social action is largely replaced by consumption, which, in turn, prevents the consumers from understanding each other or their environment. Ties of solidarity developed during hard labor in Alaska prove fatal in the context of consumption, where they acquire a different meaning. With this, Brecht applies what Marx diagnosed as the reification of human relations immediately to human relationships. The change of meaning directly affects the proletariat, but proprietors' capital creates, in Brecht's words, a *Neutralitätsgürtel* (belt of neutrality) that protects them against social interference. The inability to interfere provides the breeding ground for the social isolation that creates the appearance of an omnipotent fascist state, fostering a feeling of complete powerlessness in each subject of the state. In this separation the "Herrschaft der Lüge" (rule of lies), as Benjamin once called German fascism, can take place. The short scenes in *Furcht und Elend (Fear and Misery)*, then, can be read as exercises on how to perceive reality in the fascist order and how to interfere in that reality.

MATERIAL AGAINST IDENTITY: MANN IST MANN (MAN EQUALS MAN)

> Bevor du sie brauchst, hast du nicht gewußt
> Mein Kind, was die Menschen sind
> —Brecht, *Die Gesetze der Stadt*
> (The Laws of the City)
>
> [Before you need them, you did not know
> My child, what men are]

Brecht formulates here a law of urban life from the insight that we do not really know people until we need them. It can also be understood as a law of modern mass society. In his theatrical work as well as his political advocacy, Brecht follows his interest in people's social lives. In order to examine people in modern mass societies and explore the laws that guide their lives, Brecht produced a number of texts that explore topics that range in focus from the loss of identity, as in *Mann ist Mann (Man Equals Man)*, to failures in representation and institutions, as in *Der Dreigroschenprozeß (The Threepenny Trial)*. In his search for ways to understand ruptures in identity and representation in these texts, Brecht seeks models that are both theatrical and social: from identity to role playing, from representation to demonstration, and from protection to participation. For Brecht, the way to comprehend mass society and the way to change it are both intrinsically theatrical.

In his early plays, Brecht abandons subjective agency by releasing his protagonists into life-threatening crises that force them to abandon their identities in order to survive. In *Trommeln in der Nacht (Drums in the Night)*, Kragler adapts to the living conditions in North Africa during World War I. In *Im Dickicht der Städte (In the Jungle of Cities)*, two men engage in a fight for no apparent reason and, in doing so, they exhibit a prehistorical drive for mimesis through which they adapt to the contradictory conditions of city life. As Brecht moved on in his theatrical experiments, and as his political explorations led him toward Marxism, he increasingly tied such adaptations and transformations to social situations and subjected them to intellectual examination. Brecht's most experimental work can be understood as a prolonged intertextual exploration of human life in mass societies in which he releases adaptation and transformation into social control *(Mann ist Mann [Man Equals Man])* and ideological exploration (the teaching plays).

In *Mann ist Mann (Man Equals Man)*, a man is reassembled into a member of a military collective. In this play, Brecht's explorations reach from man's dependency on nature to the construction of a *Massenmensch* (mass man) as represented by Galy Gay. That the new *Massenmensch* (mass man) cannot be judged according to traditional morality is suggested by the genre of the play—it is less a comedy than a clown show. Brecht even transports this genre into one of his teaching plays, *Das Badener Lehrstück vom Einverständnis (The Baden-Baden Lesson on Consent)*, in which "Herr Schmidt" is destroyed by two clowns, but as a meaningless authority figure, he does not get reassembled again. *Mann ist Mann (Man Equals Man)* takes place in Kilkoa, India, during one of the British colonial wars. Galy Gay, an Irish porter, runs into three soldiers of the British army who lost their friend when he was captured by a "native trap" while trying to loot a local temple. The soldiers desperately need a replacement because their merciless commander, "Blody *[sic]* Five," will punish them if they fall below their required enlistment. They transform Galy Gay into Jeraiah Jip, according to the rules of modern mass society. They subject him to the torturous procedures of a clown show—inventing new friendships, offering him the false reward of a fake elephant, and pretending to kill and bury him so that he can be reborn as Jeraiah Jip. The symbolic shooting serves as a death threat and is intended to solidify Galy Gay's new identity so that he cannot revert to his former self. Accordingly, Galy Gay, now Jeraiah Jip, confirms his transformation by delivering his own funeral oration.

This transformation differs from those presented in *Trommeln in der Nacht (Drums in the Night)* and *Im Dickicht (In the Jungle)* in that Galy Gay's transformation is intentional and calculated. His changes in identity result not only from the new social intelligence that he acquires (the stupidity he exhibits in the tradition of the clown show is the wisest possible move in his situation), but also from the physical law of inertia that his wife outlines in the first scene when she describes him as "ein Elefant, der das schwerfälligste Tier der Tierwelt ist, aber er läuft wie ein Personenzug, wenn er ins Laufen kommt" (2:95) (an elephant, which is the most heavy-going animal of the animal world, but he runs like a passenger train when he gets going). This dynamic secures his transformation because he obeys the law of inertia and proceeds with the process of change begun by the soldiers. He ultimately surpasses all expectations as a soldier and turns out to be unstoppable as the human war machine by the play's end.

While his transformation is detailed and calculated, Galy Gay willingly changes identities for one basic reason: given his impoverished condition at the beginning of the play, he has little to lose. *Mann ist Mann (Man Equals Man)* anticipates the teaching plays in that Galy Gay's point of departure is a no-win situation, and in this situation his person is only raw material for the transforming power of the collective. He is committed to survival, and his identity is malleable. "Meine Mutter im Kalender hat verzeichnet den Tag, wo ich herauskam, und der schrie, das war ich. Dieses Bündel von Fleisch, Nägeln und Haar, das bin ich, das bin ich" (2:141) (My mother in the calendar marked the day when I came out, and it screamed, that was me. This bundle of flesh, nails and hair, that is me, that is me). This description fits both Galy Gay and "Jeraiah Jip," the person he impersonates from then on. To retain his physical existence, Galy Gay gladly trades names.

The relationship between the carnal identity and the constructed identity in *Mann ist Mann (Man Equals Man)* can be read as a Brechtian version of Hegel's master-slave discourse in which Hegel defines the master as a man of honor and representation and the slave as materialist and survivor.[4] Brecht juxtaposes Galy Gay's determination to survive with sergeant Blody Five's defense of honor. Galy Gay's willingness to stuff himself with rice for sustenance and to trade names finds its opposite in Blody Five, who destroys himself and others in order to stay true to his name: "Daß ich esse, ist nicht wichtig, sondern daß ich Blody Five bin" (2:149) (That I eat is not important, but that I am Blody Five). Blody Five seeks to defend his reputation as the merciless conqueror discussed in history books, which are "mit diesem Namen dreimal übereinander vollgeschrieben" (2:150) (written full with this name three times over). The sergeant castrates himself in order to remain undistracted by the sexual desires that sometimes delayed his brutal attacks. Blody Five is the master who willingly risks his life in order to secure his honor; Galy Gay represents the slave who has nothing but his life to lose and thus does everything to defend it.[5]

In *Mann ist Mann (Man Equals Man)*, Brecht presents a basic lesson of modern mass society—"Einer ist keiner" (one is none)—that the soldiers in the play learn from their military experience: in mass society the individual remains unrecognized, and in the military, one's value is calculated according to the perspective of losses en masse. The soldiers demonstrate their understanding of the radicalness of this change by naming the army "Mama." This fundamental lesson abolishes the humanist version of subjectivity and replaces it with simple social mechanics. If one is none, he needs others to need him. One emerges not as an individual person, but as a member of a collective through social labor that includes the change of identities and the production of the *Dividuum* (dividual), as Brecht calls it in his fragment *Galgei*. Galy Gay describes his own transformation thus:

> . . . denn vielleicht
> Bin ich der Beide, der eben erst entstand . . .
> Einer ist keiner. Es muß ihn einer anrufen. . . .
> Ihr, seht ihr mich denn überhaupt? Wo stehe ich denn? (2:142–43)

> [. . . because maybe
> I am the Both, who just now emerged . . .
> One is none. One has to call him up. . . .
> You, do you even see me at all? Where do I stand then?]

Here, *Mann ist Mann (Man Equals Man)* anticipates the challenges to subjectivity and ideology that will become more prominent in Brecht's later texts such as *Die Straßenszene (The Street Scene), Der Dreigroschenprozeß (The Threepenny Trial)*, and the teaching plays. Social validity is achieved only when one is addressed by another and is able to emerge in the shape of an answer, as Brecht once said of himself.

But to experience oneself as divided also opens the possibility of a theatrical experience, just as Galy Gay comprehends his transformation through theatrical means. Galy Gay arrives at the self-perception that Brecht's later epic theatre requires from the actor: when Brecht asks the actor to be demonstrator and demonstrated at the same time, then the actor (or the person) is asked to enter into a social relationship with her- or himself. Because Galy Gay understands this, he requires an audience, for his understanding of himself relies on the perception of others. This vision of social existence informs Brecht's changing political vision and becomes a formative element in his teaching plays, in which every question is negotiated in a strictly defined space. This renders political problems as questions of social positioning: "Wo stehst du und wie stehst du zu uns?" (2:138) (Where do you stand and how do you stand toward us?) then becomes the ultimate subject of investigation.

That social positions are unequal to political positions is a fact that Brecht illustrates in *Mann ist Mann (Man Equals Man)*. He rewrote the play numerous times, struggling with what he calls the "bad collective," that is, the abolition of bourgeois subjectivity through the growing fascism in Germany.[6] Galy Gay's reassembly becomes more and more a man-as-machine problem. Although Brecht later denounced *Mann ist Mann (Man Equals Man)* as a failure along the lines of prescribed Marxist ideology, I would argue that the play, together with all of its failed rewrites, is an effective representation of what Negt and Kluge call "materialistischer Instinkt" (materialist instinct): "Die Massen leben mit Erfahrungen über Gewalt, Unterdrückung, Ausbeutung und, in weiterem Sinne, Entfremdung. Für sie hat die Einschränkung ihrer Lebensmöglichkeiten, ihrer Bewegungsfreiheit materielle, sinnliche Evidenz" (The masses live with experiences of violence, oppression, exploitation, and, in the broader sense of the term, alienation. They possess material, sensual evidence of the restriction of possibilities in their lives, of their freedom of movement.)[7] Galy Gay's change is an act that comes out of experience, an experience that literally leaves no space for the freedom of subjectivity. Galy Gay's wisdom is founded on his inability to say no, which guaranties him continuous participation. As Walter Benjamin observes, "Denn damit läßt er die Widersprüche des Daseins da ein, wo sie zuletzt allein zu überwinden sind: im Menschen. Nur der »Einverstandene« hat Chancen, die Welt zu ändern" (. . . for he lets the contradictions of existence enter into the only place where they can, in the last analysis, be resolved: the life of a man. Only the "consenting" man has any chance of changing the world).[8]

BRECHT'S CONCEPT OF THE PUBLIC SPHERE

Brecht had few illusions about the increasing strength of German fascism during the 1920s. His theatrical work examines the public as a breeding ground and site of accommodation for antidemocratic forces. He also seeks to establish his work publicly to find out how the new animalism that grew out of economic need and political suspicion could be redirected for revolutionary purposes. Brecht deals with the public sphere explicitly in only a few texts. One, *Der Dreigroschenprozeß (The Threepenny Trial)*, directly comments on the public sphere during the last years of the Weimar Republic, a comment that explores the law, the media, the production and consumption of mass culture, and artistic freedom of expression. In the following, I will juxtapose *Der Dreigroschenprozeß*'s

(The Threepenny Trial's) criticism of the public sphere with Brecht's short treatise *Die Straßenszene (The Street Scene)*, which I read as a theatrical response to *Der Dreigroschenprozeß (The Threepenny Trial)*. Whereas Brecht presents a complex critique of representation and political tools in *Der Dreigroschenprozeß (The Threepenny Trial)*, in *Die Straßenszene (The Street Scene)* he develops his concept of demonstration as an alternative political action that (as it turns out) also becomes one of the major elements of his theatre.

The lawsuit that Brecht presents in *Der Dreigroschenprozeß (The Threepenny Trial)* took place between himself as the author of the screenplay of the *Dreigroschenoper (Threepenny Opera)* and the Nero Film AG as the producer and distributor of the film. Brecht never made this film; the company gave the project to Georg Wilhelm Pabst when Brecht delivered a script that was significantly different from the original stage version of the *Dreigroschenoper (Threepenny Opera)*. Brecht then sued the company for depriving him of the author's rights over the film production. In the end the company settled and Brecht wrote his *Dreigroschenprozeß (Threepenny Trial)*, which was not just an account of the trial and the reaction of the mass media, but also a complex reflection on mass culture and the public sphere.[9] Brecht claims that by suing the film company, he intended to unmask democratic institutions such as the judicial system and the press as essentially antidemocratic tools of capitalism. Bourgeois ideology argues for the equal protection of material and intellectual property, but Brecht insists that his trial reveals that capital ultimately triumphs over artistic freedom in Weimar's courts. While the trial itself is of no interest here, Brecht's retrospective justification sheds light on his concept of the public sphere.

As a man of the theatre, Brecht rewrote the trial and the media's reaction, turning these events into a public and theatrical demonstration that he called "ein soziologisches Experiment" (a sociological experiment):

Man konnte ihn (den Prozeß) nicht von Anfang bis Ende mit dem Bestreben führen, ihn zu gewinnen, oder dem Bestreben, ihn zu verlieren—er hätte dann nichts ergeben. Man mußte sich ihm anvertrauen und lediglich darauf bauen, daß er in irgendeiner Weise etwas Klarheit über die Art und Weise, wie heute geistige Dinge sich materiell umsetzen, schaffen würde. Man mußte sich mit anderen Worten auf die tiefen Antagonismen unserer Gesellschaftsordnung verlassen. (21:462)

[One could not conduct it (the trial) from beginning to end with the intent to win it, or the intent to lose it—it would have yielded nothing

then. One had to entrust oneself to it and simply trust that it would create in some way some clarity about the manner in which today intan-
gible things transform themselves materially. In other words one had to
rely on the deep antagonisms of our social order.]

According to Brecht, courts of law are unfit to decide what is right or
wrong; instead, Brecht views the judicial system as a prop to economic
and political power structures in the Weimar Republic. By presenting the
deep antagonisms within German society, Brecht hoped to reveal the class
relations behind bourgeois "natural" and civil rights through a narrative
of experience, an approach that he believed would be more effective than
expository arguments. Brecht's account stages the trial as a theatrical event
designed to present to the public the transformation of ideas into action.
For Brecht as a Marxist, bourgeois culture's main contradiction consists of
the one between ideology and material life: "Diese ideologischen Unstimmigkeiten müssen erfaßt werden. Die bürgerliche Kultur ist nicht das,
was sie über die bürgerliche Praxis denkt. . . . Diese Kultur steht keinen
Millimeter über ihrer Praxis" (21:510) (These ideological inconsistencies
must be grasped. The bourgeois culture is not that what it thinks about
bourgeois practice. . . . This culture stands not one millimeter above its
practice). The gap between thought about reality and reality itself contains the deep antagonisms that Brecht seeks to explore in his trial.

This exploration transforms the *Dreigroschenprozeß* (*Threepenny
Trial*) from a presentation of legal proceedings into a presentation of historical experience that uses terms such as "just" and "unjust" as signifiers
for the condition of German society rather than as timeless qualities.
Brecht's trial is an experiment in tracing how abstract concepts manifest
themselves in real life: "Man muß sich hüten, die großen gedanklichen
Dinge, wie Gerechtigkeit oder Persönlichkeit, nur zu suchen, wo man sie
findet—in einigen mittelmäßigen Köpfen oder Mäulern—man muß
ihnen nachgehen in der gemeinen Wirklichkeit . . ." (21:448) (One must
take care not to seek the great intellectual things like justice or personality only where one finds them—in a few mediocre heads or mouths—one
must pursue them in the common reality . . .). Justice and personality, as
abstract concepts, have no meaning for Brecht. Meaning is constructed by
reality as "gemeine Wirklichkeit" (common reality), a reality shared by
everyone. In other words, it is constructed by public reality. Brecht seeks
the genealogical traces of two cornerstones of democratic society—the
court system and the media—in a public sphere shaped by social action
rather than disembodied intellectual discourse.

Tracing such concepts, however, is less an intellectual endeavor than social labor for Brecht: "Das soziologische Experiment zeigt die gesellschaftlichen Antagonismen, *ohne sie aufzulösen.* Die Veranstalter müssen also in dem Kräftefeld der widersprechenden Interessen selber eine Interessenstellung einnehmen, einen durchaus subjektiven, absolut parteiischen Standpunkt" (21:512–13) (The sociological experiment shows social antagonisms *without resolving them.* The organizers themselves must thus take up an interested position in the field of forces of contradictory interests, a thoroughly subjective, absolutely partial [biased] standpoint). Brecht's sociological experiment performs conflict, revealing in the process the persistence of social antagonisms rather than offering solutions to them. The participants represent their own interests and refuse to compromise. The political means through which compromise is reached in a democratic society is representation, where selected people act for other people. But here Brecht already finds a conflict of interest. Representatives not only defend the interests of their constituents, they also defend their own interests, which may or may not be the same. They represent these various interests to others whose motives are equally compromised by the principle of representation. The theatre magnifies these tensions by focusing them temporally and spatially. Brecht's sociological experiment consists of showing the general public the illusory nature of the bourgeois public sphere.

Die Straßenszene (The Street Scene), a short piece that Brecht calls a miniature version of epic theatre, presents the way in which residents in a bourgeois society can overcome the contradictions of representation by engaging in direct action. In *Die Straßenszene (The Street Scene),* Brecht presents witnesses of a car accident narrating or recounting the incident in order to determine precisely how it happened. The narrative elements employed are well known; they include *Episierung* (epicization), citation, estrangement, delay, and disruption. But Brecht not only argues that public demonstrations are the origin of epic theatre, he also points in the opposite direction and asserts that public life should itself be perceived as "angewandtes Theater" (applied theatre):

> Es müßten einige Grundbeispiele des Einander-etwas-Vormachens im täglichen Leben beschrieben werden sowie einige Elemente theatralischer Aufführung im privaten und öffentlichen Leben. . . . Wichtig die auch im privaten Leben geübte Gruppierung in den verschiedenen Situationen. Wie werden die Distanzen gewechselt bei einem Ehekrach— bei welchem Satz entfernt sich der Mann von der Frau, wann setzt er sich usw.? (27:126)

[A few basic examples of the showing-one-another-something in daily
life would have to be described, as well as a few elements of theatrical
performance in private and public life. . . . Important the grouping also
practiced in private life in various situations. How are the distances
exchanged in a marital spat—with what sentence does the man distance
himself from the woman, when does he sit down etc.?]

Reading public life as theatre underscores the degree to which institutional acts and hierarchies should be understood as performance. In his
Dreigroschenprozeß (Threepenny Trial), Brecht seeks to drag unacknowledged theatre into the realm of acknowledgment. In response to the social
and economic structures of the bourgeois culture in which he finds himself, Brecht locates theatre as social action occurring not within the cultural superstructure, but in society's base—meaning the street, the place
where public life is at its most direct and physical.

In *Die Straßenszene (The Street Scene)*, a car accident, as a public
event, becomes a theatrical demonstration. In order to clarify the question
of damages, the witnesses to a car accident become actors demonstrating
the course of events that led up to the accident. As in the social experiment of *Der Dreigroschenprozeß (The Threepenny Trial)*, the demonstrators
perform from the standpoint of certain interests; they themselves provide
the setting for the performance with their own bodies: "das Feld, auf dem
der Demonstrant seine Charaktere aufbaut" (22.1:374) (the field on
which the demonstrator constructs his character). Here, Brecht emphasizes his opposition to Aristotelian poetics by insisting that a character is
the product rather than the agent of action. The character does not
develop in any general sense; he or she emerges in a determined setting:
"Innerhalb gewisser Grenzen kann er so und so sein, das macht nichts aus.
Den Demonstranten interessieren seine unfallerzeugenden und unfallver-
hindernden Eigenschaften" (22.1:375) (Within certain boundaries he can
be one way or another, that does not matter. His own accident-causing
and accident-preventing characteristics interest the demonstrator). By
employing a concept of character that results from action, condition, and
situation, Brecht defies any generalizations about "humanity" just as he
seeks to defy any generalizations about ideas.

Brecht establishes "demonstration" as the link between theatre and the
public. Actors are enjoined to borrow techniques of street demonstrators:

Ein wesentliches Element der *Straßenszene* besteht in der natürlichen Haltung, die der Straßendemonstrant in doppelter Hinsicht einnimmt; er
trägt ständig zwei Situationen Rechnung. Er benimmt sich natürlich als

Demonstrant und er läßt den Demonstrierten sich natürlich benehmen. Er vergißt nie und gestattet nie, zu vergessen, daß er nicht der Demonstrierte, sondern der Demonstrant ist. Das heißt: was das Publikum sieht, ist nicht eine Fusion zwischen Demonstrant und Demonstriertem, nicht ein selbständiges, widerspruchloses Drittes mit aufgelösten Konturen von 1 (Demonstrant) und 2 (Demonstriertem), wie das uns gewohnte Theater es uns in seinen Produktionen darbietet. (22.1:377–78)

[An essential element of the *Street Scene* exists in the natural disposition that the street demonstrator takes up in two respects; he constantly takes two situations into account. He conducts himself naturally as a demonstrator, and he allows the demonstrated to conduct itself naturally. He never forgets and never permits it to be forgotten that he is not the demonstrated, but the demonstrator. That means: what the audience sees is not a fusion between demonstrator and demonstrated, not an independent, consistent Third with dissolved contours from 1 (demonstrator) and 2 (demonstrated) like that which the theatre we are used to offers us in its productions.]

By playing out the contradiction between the performer and the performed, demonstration problematizes representation. The demonstrator represents that which is demonstrated but negates the act of representation at the same time. Actors must rely on an epic component to signify the difference between demonstrator and demonstrated: ". . . er darf bei seiner Darstellung nicht das »*er* tat das, *er* sagte das« auslöschen" (22.1:376) (he may not obliterate the "*he* did that, *he* said that" with his performance). The epic component prevents the fusion between demonstrator and demonstrated and places that which is demonstrated into a retrospective context. A demonstration, according to Brecht, is always a *Wiederholung* (bringing back) that is achieved through the recitation of words or deeds. The tension between present and past, and between demonstrator and demonstrated, creates the performance space—the stage—in Brecht's concept of the public, and his theatre is created the moment someone perceives her- or himself as demonstrator. If we consider all public and social life as theatre, the demonstrating subject cannot help but create a public sphere because the demonstrative act unavoidably establishes a distance between demonstrator and demonstrated. The act thus creates a social relation between the demonstrator and her- or himself. The public demonstration depends on competing interests that make the demonstrator extremely changeable.

A social experiment that publicly examines opposing interests can only occur once a stage has been created. In developing a concept of the stage, Brecht worked closely with his friend, stage designer Caspar Neher. Concerning Neher's approach to the stage, Brecht once remarked that "Neher geht immer von den Leuten aus" (21:102) (Neher always starts out from the people). *Leute* (people) can also be translated as "general public," a term that refers to the audience both in- and outside of the theatre, as well as to the actors and stage workers. Consistent with this perspective on the public, Neher defines the stage as a "Gelände auf dem die Leute etwas erleben" (21:103) (terrain in which the general public experiences something). The stage as location is considered incomplete and dependent on social action. For Brecht, the stage as a site or terrain depends less on the theatre as an institution than on the presence of a public: "Das gute Spielfeld darf erst fertig werden durch das Spiel der sich bewegenden Figuren" (22.1:230) (The good playing field is only allowed to become complete through the play of the figures in motion). The stage results from the presence of the actors of a play or the participants of a demonstration and the positions they assume toward each other. Brecht's imperative for social experiments—that every participant should take a position according to his own interest in a terrain of opposing interests—is, therefore, essential for the stage as the very foundation of his theatre.

Brecht's belief in direct demonstration instead of representation has a fundamental impact on his concept of freedom. In his notion of the public sphere, freedom can only exist in newly determined social and spatial limitations that give every member of the public an equal chance to observe and participate. The participants negotiate their freedom from a position of constraint and discipline instead of universal ideas. Negt and Kluge follow a similar trajectory by comparing bourgeois and proletarian concepts of freedom in their reading of Hobbes:

> Wenn Hobbes als Freiheit den tatsächlichen physischen Bewegungsspielraum eines Menschen bezeichnet, so trifft das genau die materielle Erfahrungsweise der Massen. Ein Mensch im Gefängnis hat so viel Freiheit, wie er sich bewegen kann. Seine Gedanken mögen ihn trösten, sie geben ihm keinen Schritt mehr Freiheit. Der Schillersche Satz »Der Mensch ist frei geschaffen, ist frei, und wär' er in Ketten geboren« ist für die Massen absolut unverständlich, sobald sie sich auf ihre eigene Erfahrung stützen. Er drückt lediglich die radikale Trennung von geistiger und körperlicher Arbeit aus.

> [When Hobbes describes freedom as a human being's actual physical sphere of movement, he captures precisely the masses' material mode of experience. The extent of a person's freedom in prison is measured by how

much he is able to move. His thoughts may offer him consolation, but they do not give him one extra yard of freedom. Schiller's line, "man is created free, is free, even if he were born in chains," is absolutely incomprehensible to the masses in relation to their own experience. All it does is express the radical division between intellectual and physical labor.][10]

Instead of unlimited freedom, Brecht creates flexible concepts of the theatre and the public. However, they also carry strict limitations. The participants' interests may vary from situation to situation, and an absolute opposition is not always presented. This accounts for Brecht's most famous concept of theatre: the epic, or narrative, component. The situation under which the participants position themselves toward one another must be carefully staged. Brecht introduces his poetic and social concept of epic theatre in *Die Straßenszene (The Street Scene)* and declares epic theatre to be a theatre of the street. This establishes its political and social commitment as well as revealing its origins.

THE CAPTURED MATERIAL
(EXPLOITATION/IMPLOITATION)

Anschließend an die Untersuchungen der »Straßenszene« müßte man andere Arten alltäglichen Theaters beschreiben, die Gelegenheiten aufsuchen, wo im täglichen Leben Theater gespielt wird. In der Erotik, im Geschäftsleben, in der Politik, in der Rechtspflege, in der Religion usw. Man müßte die theatralischen Elemente in den Sitten und Gebräuchen studieren. Die Theatralisierung der Politik durch den Faschismus habe ich schon ein wenig bearbeitet. Aber dazu müßte das alltägliche Theater studiert werden, das die Individuen ohne Publikum machen, das geheime »eine Rolle spielen«. So müßte man das »elementare Ausdrucksbedürfnis« unserer Ästhetiken einzirkeln. Die »Straßenszene« bedeutet einen großen Schritt entgegen der Profanisierung, Entkultisierung, Säkularisierung der Theaterkunst. (26:443)

[Following the investigations of the "Street Scene," one would have to describe other kinds of everyday theatre, to consult the occasions where theatre is played in daily life. In eroticism, in business life, in politics, in the administration of justice, in religion etc. One would have to study the theatrical elements in manners and customs. I have already dealt a little with the theatricalization of politics through fascism. But in addition to that, the everyday theatre that individuals make without an audience, the secret "playing of a role," would have to be studied. Thus, one would have to encircle the "elemental need for expression" of our aesthetics. The "Street Scene" constitutes a great step against the profanation, decultization, secularization of theatrical art.]

According to Brecht, theatre's necessity consists of training in methods of
presentation and perception. In a theatrical context, doing becomes acting and seeing becomes observing. As he was developing these ideas, the
rise of film as a medium of mass communication opened up completely
new possibilities of observation for Brecht. It is certainly no coincidence
that at the same time that Brecht turned toward film, he grew increasingly
interested in Chinese and Japanese acting traditions, an interest he shared
with the Soviet director Sergej Eisenstein. Film and theatre, then, can
cooperate in tracing the consequences of politics and economics as they
show themselves in human gestures such as those shown in the rejected
screenplay of Brecht's *Dreigroschenoper (Threepenny Opera)*. Brecht takes
advantage of film as a new medium by envisioning a scene that would not
have been possible to stage in the theatre. In the screenplay, Mackie's
gangsters do not rob the bank as they do in the stage play; instead, they
take it over. As "bankers" the gangsters become legitimate, and Brecht
sought to present this change:

> Die eigentliche Übernahme der altehrwürdigen National Deposit
> Bank durch die Macheathplatte läßt sich am besten durch ein Bild
> vergegenwärtigen: Aussteigend aus ihren gestohlenen Autos, zugehend
> auf das Vertrauen erweckend bescheidene Tor dieses altrenommierten
> Hauses, überschreiten etwa 40 Herren eine illusionäre Linie auf dem
> Bürgersteig. Vor dem seinem Auge nicht trauenden Beschauer verwan-
> deln sie sich im Moment des Überschreitens aus den bärtigen Räubern
> einer versunkenen Epoche in die kultivierten Beherrscher des moder-
> nen Geldmarktes.
>
> [The actual takeover of the worthy old National Deposit Bank by the
> Macheath routine is best realized through an image: climbing out of
> their stolen cars, approaching the trust-awakening, unassuming gate,
> about 40 gentlemen cross an imaginary line on the sidewalk. In front of
> the onlooker who does not believe his eyes, they metamorphose in the
> moment of crossing from the bearded robbers of a fallen epoch into the
> cultivated rulers of the modern money market.][11]

Brecht envisions this process as a superficial change of costume rather
than an economic or historical achievement. The "gangster" metamorphosis occurs entirely on the public streets when the gangsters cross an
imaginary line on the sidewalk. The locale (the presence of the bank) and
the specific interests that come with such an institution turn gangsters
into bankers without altering their essence. Brecht hoped the audience
would realize that the transformation from gangsters to bankers (or the

reverse) relied not on personal ethics, but on the historical and institutional setting in which the figures were located. Brecht writes, "Prozesse kommen in Wirklichkeit überhaupt nicht zu Abschlüssen. Es ist die Beobachtung, die Abschlüsse benötigt und legt" (21:523) (In reality, processes do not come to conclusions at all. It is observation that needs and locates conclusions). In order to relate ideas to historical change, we must employ what Brecht calls the "filmische Sehweise" (filmic perception), a perspective that allows us to see epochal transformation—like that of robbers into respectable bankers—in compressed time.

"Filmische Sehweise" (filmic perception), the compression of real time into much shorter temporal segments, is exercised in film production by the eye of the camera and in film perception through the eye of the audience. Film as an art form employs a revolutionary technology capable of presenting long historical developments in a single scene while remaining the product of capitalist production and consumption. With his *Dreigroschenprozeß (Threepenny Trial)*, Brecht examines the contradictions of mass culture as exemplified in the film industry along with the contradictions of modern subjectivity.

Thus, the immediate transformation in the screenplay opens for Brecht a theatrical and political concept with widespread and unpredictable implications for the subject. By positing social life as theatre and theatre as social life, Brecht seeks to destroy the cultural and economic forms of bourgeois subject formation where the subject can create her- or himself through various forms of identification and projection. The most important of these forms for Brecht is the process of identification through which the subject understands her- or himself to be moral or ethical because she or he experiences compassion for others. This fuels the catharsis that Aristotelians consider the goal of tragedy. Brecht developed his poetics of epic theatre in opposition to this concept of drama. His trained eye captures these theatrical transformations in their historical significance not only in the theatre, but also in film.

"Filmische Sehweise" (filmic perception)—time compression—whether on film or on the Brechtian stage, underscores the transience of everything that traditional theatre treats as immutable character. Viewing social labor from this perspective informs Brecht's critique of bourgeois perception in a way that sheds new light on the question of who exploits whom:

Aber hauptsächlich der der kapitalistischen Produktionsweise eigentümliche scharfe Gegensatz zwischen Arbeit und Erholung trennt alle geistigen Betätigungen in solche, welche der Arbeit, und solche, welche

der Erholung dienen und macht aus den letzteren ein System zur
Reproduktion der Arbeitskraft. Die Erholung ist im Interesse der Produktion der Nichtproduktion gewidmet. Ein einheitlicher Lebenstil ist
so natürlich nicht zu schaffen. Der Fehler liegt nicht darin, daß die
Kunst so in den Kreis der Produktion gerissen wird, sondern darin, daß
dies so unvollständig geschieht und daß sie eine Insel der »Nichtproduktion« schaffen soll. Wer sein Billett gekauft hat, verwandelt sich vor
der Leinwand in einen Nichtstuer und Ausbeuter. Er ist, da hier Beute
in ihn hineingelegt wird, sozusagen ein Opfer der Einbeutung.
(21:475–76)

[But primarily, the opposition between work and recreation belonging
to the capitalist modes of production separates all mental activities into
that which serves work and that which serves recreation and makes a
system of the reproduction of labor out of the latter. Recreation is
devoted to nonproduction in the interest of production. A unified
lifestyle is naturally not to be achieved this way. The mistake does not
lie in the fact that art is thus dragged into the circle of production, but
in the fact that this happens so incompletely and that it is supposed to
create an island of "nonproduction." He who buys his ticket metamor-
phoses before the screen into a do-nothing and exploiter. He is, since
here plunder is put into him, so to speak a victim of imploitation.]

For Brecht (and here he agrees with Horkheimer and Adorno), the film
industry is the product of capitalism's division of labor and its separation
of work and leisure.[12] The exploited become exploiters once they leave the
realm of production and enter that of consumption, with the important
difference that they do not profit monetarily from their role as cultural
consumers/exploiters. The consumer of film exploits insofar as he or she
seeks to gain experience passively. Brecht's criticism of perception as part
of the cultural industry only briefly touches on film as a medium of technology and mass production, the very issues that Adorno finds so disturbing. Brecht seems to exclude the psychoanalytic and surrealist
approaches of Benjamin's essays on mimesis, artwork, and surrealism.
This is all the more surprising because Brecht uses various aspects of surrealism very effectively in his early plays. As Michael Taussig demonstrates
in his reading of Benjamin, perception cannot be reduced to a passive
form of exploitation.[13]

   According to Benjamin, technological reproduction moves the artwork closer to the audience while destroying the aura of the work of art:
"Tagtäglich macht sich unabweisbarer das Bedürfnis geltend, des Gegen-
stands aus nächster Nähe im Bild, vielmehr im Abbild, in der Reproduk-

tion, habhaft zu werden" (Every day the urge grows stronger to get hold of an object at close range in an image *[Bild]*, or better, in a facsimile *[Abbild]*, a reproduction).[14] The reproduction of art is mimetic. Mimesis, as the oldest of human faculties, gets reinvented in modernity through the technological reproduction of art. The invention of the camera opened up new ways of observing, and the industrial production and reproduction of film inaugurated new ways of sharing observations, offering a potential method of transforming an audience into a coherent public. According to Brecht, however, the audience remains excluded from the production process. By introducing the term *Einbeutung*, or imploitation, Brecht likens the consumption of cultural products to the exploitation of production; the cathartic effect "imploits" the dramatic experience to justify the viewing subject as an ethical individual.

The distinction between social reality and bourgeois culture can, according to Brecht, be understood as the product of economic exploitation and cultural imploitation, a combination that warps social exchange while enervating social thought. For Marx, it is the commodification and reification of men's social labor that makes things appear to be objects that exist independently of human labor and social relations; thought also becomes reified, but in a different way. When reification results from the objectification of labor, it arises out of the subjectification of thought. Of course, this subjectivity is fictional because it is just one step in the circle of exploitation, the step that is necessary to reproduce labor. Film, then, is potentially both progressive and regressive: progressive insofar as it introduces new modes of representation that allow a filmmaker to present vast historical developments and changes in a single scene, and regressive in that it reinforces traditional modes of perception that maintain the audience as a passive entity that expresses its opinion only when deciding whether to purchase a ticket.

Brecht's concept of the public sphere transforms intellectual processes into action in order to show the impact of ideas on human life. Furthermore, Brecht seeks to reduce economic processes to elements that can be acted out as a public enterprise. Brecht explores the inconsistencies in capitalist ideology in his *Dreigroschenprozeß (Threepenny Trial)*. "Der Kapitalismus ist konsequent in der Praxis, weil er muß. Ist er aber konsequent in der Praxis, dann ist er inkonsequent in der Ideologie" (21:509) (Capitalism is consistent in practice because it has to be. But if it is consistent in practice, then it is inconsistent in ideology). In parts of his theatre work, Brecht presents and celebrates the consistency of capitalist practice. Works such as *Aus Nichts wird Nichts (From Nothing Comes Nothing)* and *Aufstieg*

und Fall der Stadt Mahagonny (Rise and Fall of the City of Mahagonny) are
teaching plays depicting capitalist practice as social interaction. Other
teaching plays explore capitalist laws in the social realm, and it is these
teaching plays that have become infamous for their brutality.

To present capitalism in performance, Brecht privileges some elements over others. In *Aus Nichts wird Nichts (From Nothing Comes Nothing)*, Brecht presents a genealogy of bourgeois subjectivity according to
the law of supply and demand. In *Mahagonny*, Brecht shows how a judicial system emerges in congruence with the capitalist laws of consumption. His plays grow hazy, however, when he seeks to present the workings of capitalism outside of social interaction by staging the workings of
capital itself. Brecht's claim that it is incomprehensible how, exactly,
money and wealth are traded on the world market also implies that these
processes are not presentable on stage. In *Die heilige Johanna der
Schlachthöfe (Saint Joan of the Stockyards)*, the trading of money and meat
is mentioned, but it never becomes part of the performance. The places
where Brecht most thoroughly confronts capitalist laws with human
life—*Der Brotladen (The Breadshop), Dan Drew, Jae Fleischhacker in
Chikago (Jae Fleischhacker in Chicago)*—all remain incomplete. The confrontation of the visible with the invisible may explain why these extraordinary texts remain fragments.

One radical aspect of Brecht's fragments and teaching plays is the
application of economic laws to human interaction. The ups and downs
of the business cycle are presented as group dynamics, especially in the
fragment *Aus Nichts wird Nichts (From Nothing Comes Nothing)* and in the
opera *Aufstieg und Fall der Stadt Mahagonny (Rise and Fall of the City of
Mahagonny)*, where power and influence result from demand and descent
from oversupply. Each play explores a single aspect of the business cycle:
Aus Nichts wird Nichts (From Nothing Comes Nothing) presents various
forms of demand and explores how they shape a social structure;
Mahagonny is entirely concerned with supply and consumption.
Mahagonny, the "Netzestadt" (net city) confines itself solely to the topic
of consumption. Paul, the main character, comes to Mahagonny to spend
his hard-earned money on "Ruhe, Eintracht, Whisky, Mädchen," (2:353)
(rest, peace, whisky, girls) after seven years of work and hardship in
Alaska. In the end he is sentenced to death after betting on a friend in a
boxing match and losing both his money and his legal status in
Mahagonny's consumer structure. The play recalls Baal's perspective on
consumption by portraying Paul and the other men drinking, fighting,
and pursuing sex. But in *Mahagonny*, unlike *Baal*, these activities are

unambiguously pleasurable, which denies the painful aspects of pleasure seeking. Paul's support of his friend, a decision to combine human solidarity with the pursuit of pleasure, leads to his downfall and underlies Brecht's belief that this pursuit is antithetical to social and political commitment. This lesson is one of Brecht's most persistent: it appears in *Im Dickicht der Städte (In the Jungle of Cities)*, where Garga sacrifices his family for the pleasure of the fight, and in *Leben des Galilei (Life of Galileo)*, where the great man's pleasure in reason leads him to betray the community of progressive scientists.

In *Mahagonny*, Brecht goes beyond simply pointing out this tension and shows how commodification obscures the conflict between pleasure and commitment. As Begbick says, "Denn es ist die Wollust der Männer / Nicht zu leiden und alles zu dürfen" (2:336) (Because it is the lust of men / Not to suffer and to be allowed [to do] everything). The consumer need not pay for an act of betrayal because the money does, but there is a price for this safety: the consumer is excluded from the production of pleasure because that takes place between people and requires commitment. In *Mahagonny*, even the consumption of pleasure proves an empty satisfaction, as Paul's refrain of "Aber etwas fehlt" (But something is missing) clearly shows. The missing link between people is something that the sphere of consumption cannot provide, as Negt and Kluge show:

> Erfahrungen werden in dem Maße zu Waren, in dem sie auf einen Generalnenner zu bringen sind. Alle Erfahrungen des Proletariats sind spezifisch. . . . Sie werden als qualitative Momente produziert. Die Aufarbeitung der proletarischen Erfahrung ist deshalb so schwer, weil sie nicht die Kommensurabilität der Warenbeziehungen hat. Sie verändert sich mit jeder Veränderung der Situation.
>
> [Experiences become commodities to the extent that they can be reduced to a common denominator. All experiences of the proletariat are specific. . . . These experiences are produced as qualitative moments. It is difficult to work through proletarian experience because it lacks the commensurability of commodity relations. It changes with each situation.][15]

In this circle of frustration, the one remaining conflict is that between unlimited consumption and unrestrained behavior, a conflict mediated by a handful of regulations created by the providers of sex and alcohol. This conflict is resolved when Paul sings his "Du darfst" (You may) song in the face of death during a hurricane. With his "Du darfst" (You may), Paul discovers "die Gesetze der menschlichen Glückseligkeit" (the laws of human happiness), and the legal system of the town changes accordingly; from now on, "Du darfst" (You may) becomes the law of human happiness.

With this law of consumption comes isolation from others, a separation that ends in self-consumption. In four short scenes, the play demonstrates how unlimited indulgence leads to dissatisfaction and self-destruction. "Jakob der Vielfraß" (Jakob the Glutton), for example, eats two calves and complains: "Alles ist nur halb / Ich äße mich gerne selber" (2:362) (Everything is only half / I would like to eat myself). Consumption here leads to a form of self-absorption that has significance only as exhibitionism which causes Jakob to ask others to watch him eat. Jakob, as "ein Mann ohne Furcht" (2:363) (a man without fear), deludes himself that he is free because he can eat without limitations, a delusion that causes his premature if "natural" death. Paul, on the other hand, receives a death sentence because of his lack of money. He becomes a criminal by importing a solidarity rooted in the realm of labor in Alaska into Mahagonny's realm of pure consumption. Hard work and social commitment fuels Paul's ascent in Alaska, but they destroy him in Mahagonny.

While *Mahagonny* is not considered one of the teaching plays, it contains many of their defining elements. It withholds the obvious contradictions (here, those between capital and labor and between production and consumption) from the scene in order to show the conflict of interest that occurs any time an agent represents interests other than her or his own. Brecht does this by ignoring the contradiction between capitalist practice and bourgeois values and presenting a moral completely in tune with consumption. This is displayed on the signs that are carried around the stage at the end of the play: "Für die Liebe" (For love) is followed by "Für die Käuflichkeit der Liebe" (2:387) (For the commercialization of love); two other signs can be read as a direct reference to the *Dreigroschenprozeß (Threepenny Trial)*: "Für die gerechte Verteilung der überirdischen Güter" (For the just distribution of spiritual goods) and "Für die ungerechte Verteilung der irdischen Güter" (2:387) (For the unjust distribution of earthly goods). These signs are paraded during Paul's execution, and they demand a continuance of the status quo: "Für den Fortbestand des goldenen Zeitalters" (2:387) (For the continuance of the golden age). This constitutes the fall of Mahagonny that is mentioned in the title, a fall inherent in its rise, for the town lacks the production necessary to maintain consumption. The consistency between base and superstructure in the field of consumption makes progressive change impossible.

Whereas in *Mahagonny*, Brecht demonstrates the rise and fall of an economy based on consumption, in *Aus Nichts wird Nichts (From Noth-*

ing Comes Nothing), the vagaries of the business cycle are applied to the emergence and decline of a single subject in his interactions with others. Bogderkahn is hired by shepherds to do their work because they are frightened by robbers who threaten their herds. They choose Bogderkahn over others because he is "der Nichtsigste" (the most nothing) in his lack of food, shelter, and work. Entering the realm of employment, Bogderkahn acquires substance by earning three bread crusts a day and the right to live in a tent. Bogderkahn's own fear simultaneously keeps him from protecting the herds and fuels his success. He ascends from nothingness to shepherd to skin trader—a rise that culminates when he becomes a dictator who rescues himself and others from a snowstorm. At the pinnacle of his success, Bogderkahn withdraws from social intercourse and begins to rely on pure intellect to perpetuate his career, but the isolation this entails renders him useless to others, and he recedes back into nothingness.

It is Bogderkahn's initial ability to adapt to any given situation and to satisfy the needs of others, rather that any specific work-related skill, that increases his worth in the social economy: "Wenn einer nichts ist, so kann er etwas werden—wenn nur die Leute etwas von ihm halten" (10.1:690) (If one is nothing, he can thus become something—if only the people think something of him). When others mistakenly credit him for things such as dead tigers and robbers found outside his tent, Bogderkahn accepts the assumption that he must be a great shepherd because his perceptions of himself are based upon the vision that other people have of him. His transformation from nothing to something depends on a social rather than an economic law of supply and demand. As long as Bogderkahn meets demand, he can rise to become *Etwas* (something). When he satisfies others' demands, their satisfaction makes him feel successful, leading him to become careless and inattentive. Because he loses his social responsiveness, he ceases to meet the demand: "Wenn einer nun etwas ist, so kann er wieder nichts werden—wenn nur die Leute nichts von ihm halten" (10.1:690) (If one is now something, he can thus become nothing again—if only the people think nothing of him).

Brecht's notes on dialectics, written at roughly the same time, indicate that *Nichts* (nothing) and *Etwas* (something) should not be understood as essential opposites, but as quantifiers that signify the validity of the subject in interaction with others: "Es stellt sich heraus, daß dieses »Ich-bin« nichts besonders Gleichbleibendes ist, das nur ein anderes kennt, nämlich das »Ich-bin-nicht«, sondern eine unaufhörliche Aufeinanderfolge von Mehroderwenigersein" (21:425) (It turns out that this "I-am" is nothing especially unchanging which only knows one other, namely that "I-am-not," but a never ending succession of being more or less). For Brecht, existence is not an essence. He replaces the existential question of "to be or not be" with an economy of being either more or less in interaction with others.

The never ending succession of being more or less is the basis of Brecht's social economy, an economy that affects his ideas of subjectivity, history, and revolution. By moving from conventional beliefs about human qualities to measurements of human quantity, Brecht disconnects subjectivity from any abstract interaction. The subject comes into being only through interaction with others. In Brecht's social economy, no one can get lost; someone can only be more or less meaningful or influential. Brecht condemns capitalism from this perspective. His criticism is not founded on moral judgments, for concepts such as justice are left to be acted out by collectives; but by owning the means of production, capitalists exclude themselves from necessary social economies and their cycles of succession.

The major imperative of Brecht's revolutionary project, the same imperative that accounts for the brutality of his teaching plays, is the acceptance of the economic cycles of social succession. In a commentary called "Aus Nichts wird Nichts und Lehrstücke" (From Nothing Comes Nothing and Teaching Plays), Brecht comments on capitalism and exploitation:

> In »Aus Nichts wird Nichts« ist dieser Satz teils Beobachtung (Fakt), teils Forderung. Die kommunistische Forderung, der Einzelne möge seine Bedeutung von der Masse beziehen, kommt von der Beobachtung, daß in unserem (kapitalistischen) Wirtschaftssystem dies faktisch geschieht, indem der Einzelne die Masse ausbeutet und seine Bedeutung eben in der Beute liegt. Daß er seine Bedeutung lediglich an den Besitz der Produktionsmittel bindet und dadurch sich gewalttätig schützt, wieder *nichts* zu werden, ist ein Grund für die Revolution . . . (10.1:689)

> [In "From Nothing Comes Nothing," this sentence is partly observation (fact), partly demand. The communist demand that the individual draw his significance from the mass comes from the observation that in our (capitalist) economic system, this happens in fact when the individual exploits the mass and his significance lies just in the loot. That he ties his significance entirely to the ownership of the means of production, and through that violently protects himself from becoming nothing again, is a reason for the revolution . . .]

Brecht applies the business cycle to an economy of social
order to bring together the capitalist status quo, human li
munist theory in a materialist critique of bourgeois idealisr
ing capitalism, communism claims its place as part of historical necess..,

The revolutionary component of this argument is the understanding
that meaning and position are the results of exploitation. By interrogat-
ing the way ideas are produced, Brecht builds upon the observation that
the capitalist's position in society is artificially extended through the ownership of the means of production. Here Brecht suggests that thought,
like the means of production, ought to be collective property. His concept
of revolution reverses and radicalizes the Mahagonny-principle of unequal
distribution of material goods and equal distribution of immaterial goods.
He opts for the equal distribution of both and pushes even further—to
collective ownership of all.

In his *Dreigroschenprozeß (Threepenny Trial)*, Brecht shows that freedom and justice, as they occur in bourgeois culture, are meaningful only
in a certain ideological constellation that separates thought from material
and social life. Using the stage as a laboratory, he explores the invisible
forces that maintain that constellation and displays before a newly constituted public the previously concealed interests of the ruling classes. These
interests take their meaning from the historical setting in which they are
situated. For Brecht, disconnecting conceptual thought from historical circumstances renders thought ideological. To consider thought a purely
intellectual endeavor is misleading. Thought results from life, with all its
biological and social implications, and Brecht's theatre work is dedicated
to proving and exploring the implications of this view. The *Dreigroschenprozeß (Threepenny Trial)*, as a sociological experiment, proceeds thus:

> Öffentliches Denken wird entfesselt und findet mit verteilten Rollen
> statt. Es handelt sich beinahe im Wortsinn um einen Denkprozeß. Die
> Materie kommt hier lebend vor, sie funktioniert, ist nicht nur Gegen-
> stand der Schau. Der Sehende lebt ebenfalls, und zwar innerhalb, nicht
> außerhalb der Vorgänge. (21:510)

> [Public thinking is released and takes place with distributed roles. In a
> nearly lexical sense, it concerns a thinking process. The material appears
> alive here, it functions, is not only an object of show. The viewer like-
> wise lives, and does so inside, not outside the course of events.]

Seeing the trial about *Die Dreigroschenoper (The Threepenny Opera)* as a
sociological experiment allows Brecht to interrogate simultaneously the

social and theatrical aspects of immaterial concepts such as law and pub-
licity. He reveals that the court trial, which presented itself as a simple
civil suit about property rights, was in fact a profoundly ideological contest, and he asks readers to view the trial as a performance of that contest.
By doing so, they will create a public sphere.

Brecht's social experiment thus requires the awareness of social interaction as performance. As Brecht made clear in *Die Straßenszene (The
Street Scene)*, members of a social unit should perceive themselves and
others as actors. Brecht's teaching plays constitute the theatrical genre
that Brecht invents to create social acting in a theatrical context. By perceiving ourselves and others as actors or demonstrators, we overcome the
divide not just between thought and life, but also between production
and consumption. In turn, the theatre can break out of its traditional
institutional context. Brecht transforms the public into a theatre and the
theatre into a public—not as an institution, but as a playing field. It is
the field as experimental space, Brecht's "Kräftefeld der widersprechenden Interessen" (21:512–13) (field of forces of contradictory interests),
that proves to be essential for understanding the political situation that
surrounds us. Once thought becomes living matter, it becomes historical
because it is subject to historical change, and those who perceive it in this
way become a public.

POLITICAL DISTINCTIONS

»Wenn die Verbrechen sich häufen, werden sie unsichtbar. Wenn die Leiden
unerträglich werden, hört man die Schreie nicht mehr. . . .« . . . Gibt es kein
Mittel, den Menschen zu hindern, sich abzuwenden von den Greueln?
Warum wendet er sich ab? Er wendet sich ab, weil er keine Möglichkeit des
Eingreifens sieht. (22.1:142)

["When the crimes pile up, they become invisible. When the suffering
becomes unbearable, one no longer hears the cries. . . ." . . . Is there no means
of preventing man from turning away from the horrors? Why does he turn
away? He turns away because he sees no possibility of interfering.]

Brecht interrogates the perceived consistency both between superstructure and social practice and between intentions and outcomes in texts
other than the *Dreigroschenprozeß (Threepenny Trial)*. In his *Buch der
Wendungen (Book of Changes)* he writes, "Das Einführen der Demokratie
kann zur Einführung der Diktatur führen. Das Einführen der Diktatur
kann zur Demokratie führen" (18:88) (Introducing democracy can lead

to the introduction of dictatorship. Introducing dictatorship can lead to democracy). This rejection of conventional political interpretation raises the question of how we can know our political situation. Brecht's rejection of fascism does not inhibit his ability to observe it with interest when analyzing the politics of everyday life. He treats fascism with disdain but readily compares it to communism and acknowledges their commonalities. Political thought, while never entirely free from ideology and subjectivity, is released into the experimental field and becomes a matter of social experience that requires the intellectual and physical activity of each participant: "Das Begreifen des soziologischen Experiments ist ein »Griffe finden«. Es kommt nicht auf Grund eines Anschauungsaktes zustande, es endet nicht mit dem Zustandekommen einer Anschauung. Hier soll Erfahrung die Grundlage der Handhabung abgeben" (21:513) (Comprehending the sociological experiment is a "finding of handholds." It is not carried out on the basis of an act of viewing, it does not end with the carrying out of an act of viewing. Here, experience should serve as the basis of handling). Comprehension as "Griffe finden" (finding of handholds) is built on experience. Brecht calls this concept of thought "eingreifendes Denken" (engaged thinking), a particularly theatrical form of thought, a thought that is based on the observance of behavior.

Brecht roots his rejection of fascism less in a critique of Hitler's stated political principles than in the close observation of day-to-day politics. During his exile in Finland, he noted, "Welche Ausbeute für das Theater bieten die Fotos der faschistischen illustrierten Wochenblätter! Diese Akteure verstehen die Kunst des epischen Theaters, Vorkommnissen banaler Art den historischen Anstrich zu geben" (26:431) (What profit for the theatre the photos of the fascist illustrated weeklies offer! These actors understand the art of epic theatre to give a historical decor to events of a banal kind). Providing historic decor for banal events is a fascist technique. Brecht collects photos from illustrated magazines in his journal that present Hitler—also known as the "Anstreicher" (ordinary [house] painter)—as an integral part of the German people. One, for example, shows the Führer eating *Eintopf* (stew; hot pot) as a member of the family in a private home. Fascist propaganda sought to use these images to promote its specific *Volksgemeinschaft*, or national community.

Brecht analyzes propagandistic key terms of the Third Reich to show the differences between socialism and national socialism. By analyzing "Das wirtschaftliche Denken ist der Tod jedes völkischen Idealismus" (Economic thinking is the death of every national idealism), and the infamous "Gemeinnutz geht vor Eigennutz" (common interest comes before self-interest), Brecht shows that the fascist notion of community in *Gemeinschaft* (community) is based on exclusion and sacrifice and that fascist propaganda undermines the egoism necessary for survival as it occurs in *Eigennutz* (self-interest) and economic thought. Brecht argues against any socialist legitimation for "Gemeinnutz geht vor Eigennutz" (common interest comes before self-interest) by pointing out that the contradiction between *Gemeinnutz* (common interest) and *Eigennutz* (self-interest) is overcome in a socialist society: "Im sozialistischen Gemeinwesen ist der Satz *Gemeinnutz geht vor Eigennutz* also überflüssig und arbeitslos, und ein anderer Satz gilt, nämlich der Satz *Eigennutz ist Gemeinnutz*" (22.1:58) (In the socialist community, the sentence *common interest comes before self-interest* is thus superfluous and idle, and another sentence is valid, namely the sentence *self-interest is common interest*). Brecht assumes a correspondence between what is good for one and what is good for all. In his series of scenes called *Furcht und Elend des Dritten Reiches (Fear and Misery of the Third Reich)*, Brecht plays out these two maxims against each other to trace fascism into the private (not public) sphere.

In 1935, after the establishment of fascism in Germany, Brecht sought techniques and methods to examine fascism and the mechanics of its persistence, or, as he calls it, "Die Theatralisierung der Politik durch den Faschismus" (26:443) (The theatricalization of politics through fascism). Given that Brecht himself opts to stage politics in order to construct a public sphere and a political rationale, he seeks to clarify the distinction between the theatre of fascism and the theatre of antifascism. In *Furcht und Elend des Dritten Reiches (Fear and Misery of the Third Reich)*, Brecht uses his concept of observation and Benjamin's concept of mimesis to dissect the mechanics of fascism. The play is a montage of twenty-seven separate scenes that come together as a *Gestentafel* (table of gestures), demonstrating "Gesten des Verstummens, Sich-Umblickens" (gestures of becoming silent, looking over one's shoulder): "Aber dazu müßte das alltägliche Theater studiert werden, das die Individuen ohne Publikum machen, das geheime »eine Rolle spielen«" (26:443) (But in addition to that, the everyday theatre that individuals make without an audience, the secret "playing of a role," would have to be studied). Each scene demonstrates in specific detail either the regime's violence and cruelty toward its victims, or the day-to-day complicity of "normal Germans" in the regime's survival. For example, a woman packs a suitcase in "Die jüdische Frau" (The Jewish Wife), men tell jokes in the kitchen in "Das Kreidekreuz" (The Chalk Cross), and a student and a worker dig together in a labor camp in "Arbeitsdienst" (Labour Service). In these narrowly defined settings, we observe the gestures of fascism.

Brecht's concept of the public sphere sheds light on his approach to fascism. The fear and misery he depicts in the play occur most often in private; in fact, the ascent of fascism is congruent with the withdrawal of people into greater and greater privacy, seclusion, and isolation. This regression causes disorientation, as the scene "Der Spitzel" (The Spy) shows. Mother, father, and son are assembled around a coffee table on a Sunday afternoon when they are interrupted by the maid announcing a telephone call. Her question, "ob die Herrschaften zu Hause sind" (whether the master and mistress are at home), is answered with "nein" (no) (4:391). The incident releases a chain of arguments fueled by fear and accusations ranging from, "Es ist unangenehm, daß wir uns gerade jetzt von ihnen zurückziehen, wo sich alles von ihnen zurückzieht" (4:392) (It is unpleasant that we are drawing back from them just now when everything is drawing back from them), to "Einen Judas hast du mir geboren! Der sitzt bei Tisch und horcht . . . und merkt sich alles, was seine Erzeuger sagen, der Spitzel!" (4:399) (You have born me a Judas! He sits at the table and listens . . . and notes to himself everything that his begetters say, the spy!). The realistic fear of being spied upon combines with a general feeling of exclusion to fuel paranoia. This dynamic results from the family's regression into seclusion while further encouraging that very regression.

Personal seclusion breeds public dishonesty. Walter Benjamin writes about *Furcht und Elend (Fear and Misery)*, "Jeder dieser kurzen Akte weist *eines* auf: wie unabwendbar die Schreckensherrschaft, die sich als Drittes Reich vor den Völkern brüstet, alle Verhältnisse zwischen Menschen unter die Botmäßigkeit der Lüge zwingt" (Each of these short acts demonstrates *one thing*: how ineluctably the reign of terror now swaggering before nations as the Third Reich is subjecting all human relations to the rule of falsehood).[16] The characters cannot accurately perceive their relationships to others, nor can they evaluate the situations in which they find themselves in order to determine how to behave reasonably toward others. Brecht presents this situation in gestures and speech. A husband who accuses neighbors of political subversion states behind his closed apartment door, "Ich habe doch nur gesagt, daß das Radio mit den Rußlandsendungen nicht von hier kam" (I really only said that the radio with the Russian broadcasts did not come from here). His wife answers, "Du hast doch nicht nur das gesagt" (4:344) (You did not really say only that). The characters are obsessed with erasing possible traces of what they do and say so that they cannot be held accountable. As a result they cannot know what they have said because their speech is never validated by others. Attempting to comprehend what happens by relying solely on themselves, characters become vigilant spies. Constant, secret observation renders social life private and destroys the public sphere.

The only scene that presents a way out of this dynamic is entitled "Der Entlassene" (Release). It presents a communist who, after being released from a concentration camp, visits a couple who were former comrades. In order to find out if their former comrade has revealed any information under torture, the man and the woman decide to treat him as a spy and interrogate him. While the entire scene presents cautious distrust, the characters' behavior toward one another proves to be liberating precisely because the interrogation is performed openly. The three participants create a public sphere by refusing to withdraw into privacy: the husband asks his wife not to leave the room during the conversation with their visitor. The interrogation becomes a Brechtian experiment when the man states, "Wir können es schon feststellen, wo er steht" (We can surely establish where he stands), and the woman warns, "Das kann aber dauern" (4:411) (But that can take awhile). All three seek to reveal the political positions of the others and are acutely aware that these positions can change with time and circumstance. They identify each other's political position through constant interrogation and observation.[17]

The three comrades reveal their awareness of the mutability of individual political loyalty through their distrust of one another. The released prisoner, for example, chooses not to tell his hosts that Nazi torturers mutilated his hand because he fears that the couple will believe that he cracked in the face of such pain. Paradoxically, his lie communicates the more important truth that he is strong enough to resist interrogation. This presentation of a progressive public sphere being created through open confrontation, distrust, and self-interested dissimulation directly contradicts the Nazi ideology of *Volksgemeinschaft* (national community). The fascist regime sought to perpetuate prevailing power structures by pretending to unite everyone in a harmonious and homogeneous community.

Brecht presents the fallacy of this unity in "Arbeitsdienst" (Labour Service). He sets this scene in a labor camp in which a university student and a worker appear to be digging together harmoniously. However, we soon learn that the student is forcing the proletarian into dependence. The attempt to subsume cultural and class differences rather than confronting them openly reinforces class domination rather than community formation. By presenting the rise of fascism in a variety of scenes, Brecht shows the way that a theatre of unity drives social differences off the streets and into the private realm, thus contributing to the rise of fascism.

In *Furcht und Elend (Fear and Misery)*, the desire to withdraw and survive proves to be the most powerful promoter of fascism. In the scene "Rechtsfindung" (Judicial Process), a judge loses touch with his environment by accepting fascism as a given and submitting to it, using a juridical rationale that blinds him to fascism's fundamentally different nature. His confusion becomes obvious during an argument with a friend and colleague; they ostensibly debate the merits of a case before the court, but the discussion illustrates the judge's complete social isolation. He attempts to overcome that by reminding his colleague of their friendship with the words "so, wie wir zueinander stehen" (the way we stand toward one another). His friend answers, "Was willst du damit sagen »wie wir zueinander stehen«? . . . Heute ist sich schließlich jeder selber der Nächste" (4:376) (What do you mean by that, "the way we stand toward one another"? . . . Today everyone is his own neighbor in the end). The judge, by withdrawing completely into himself, has lost the anchor of social relations and thus the ability to participate in a public sphere. Unlike the released prisoner and his two comrades in "Der Entlassene" (Release), who reestablish a true community by confronting one another, the judge tries to accommodate everyone and ends up in complete isolation: "Ich bin mir auch selber der Nächste. Ich weiß nur nicht, was ich mir raten soll" (4:376) (I am also my own neighbor. I just do not know what I should advise myself). When law under fascism ceases to decide right from wrong and becomes a promoter of fascists, the judge fails to comprehend his momentary position in the court hierarchy. He cannot discern where his colleagues stand, and so he cannot decide where he himself stands. He presides over a case, but its outcome is not determined by ordered testimony, but by the chaotic invasion of the courtroom by the SA. They rearrange the seating, so that the judge presides from the defendant's docket. Isolated from any possible defenders of his own by his earlier withdrawal from the contentious and properly public world of the court, he is doomed to perform his final appearance as a judge in terms of the new role imposed upon him.

His surrender to fascism is rooted in his original desire to withdraw from it. Only the three comrades in "Der Entlassene" (Release) avoid this, and they do so by constantly negotiating with one another their involvement in the fascist state. By challenging each other, they confront each potential compromise with the state and thus retain the ability to distinguish between accommodating and subverting fascism. Each navigates a personal position toward the state through her or his position toward the other two as individuals and toward their collective. This allows them to detect and thus resist fascism's constant shifting of power.

Staying together and creating a public sphere makes theatrical investigation possible. The fascist machinery of seclusion destroys the judge in "Rechtsfindung" (Judicial Process) because he can never at any one time assemble all those who pretend to give him advice. Remaining a participant in negotiations over what is valid is the precondition for the knowledge and social orientation necessary for a progressive life. Separating power from the public realm—one goal of fascism—makes it impossible to trace the diverse interests that motivate the various members of the social body. In his later play *Der kaukasische Kreidekreis (The Caucasian Chalk Circle)* Brecht presents a theatrical path to justice based entirely on *gestus*. The play presents a trial in which the judge, Azdak, one of the most famous Brechtian characters, contrasts completely with the *Amtsrichter* (judge). The latter spends all his energy trying to find a judicial logic to concur in an anti-Semitic case brought by a fascist administration. In contrast, Azdak does not even listen to a summary of the case. Having been beaten by the police before being reinstalled as a judge, he has learned by experience that "formal" law grows out of barbarism and dominance. Azdak is acutely aware of what the *Amtsrichter* (judge) cannot face: that there is more than one verdict at stake, and that the judge is also judged.

Realizing that what is absolute in law is relative in history, Azdak adheres to history and builds his evidence not only from case descriptions and judicial evidence, but also from gossip, lies, and happenings in the courtyard. Azdak turns the principles of bourgeois law around, using what he learns to judge sympathetically and partially. This is illustrated when he is asked to perform the Solomonic task of adjudicating between two women who claim the same child as their own: one is the wife of a governor, the biological but selfish mother, the other is a servant girl who rescued the child during a rebellion against the governor and then raised it. Azdak creates a theatrical scene in which he places the child in the center of a chalk circle and asks the women to pull it out, declaring that the true mother will have enough strength to win the contest. The outcome of the contest is easy to predict; the adoptive mother lets the child go for fear of hurting it. Azdak, contradicting his earlier declaration, announces that the rightful mother is the one who proves to be incapable of hurting her child.

Both Azdak and the *Amtsrichter* (judge) are asked come up with a verdict in no-win situations. They differ because Azdak realizes that he lives in chaotic times and that chaotic times cannot produce orderly justice. The *Amtsrichter* (judge) depends on the law but does not care where that law originates. In the midst of chaos, Azdak, in contrast, stays rooted in the social sphere and derives his wisdom from what happens around him, all the while aware that the old order is reemerging in the background. Accordingly, after announcing the verdict, he takes off the gown, pockets his bribe, and leaves town the same night. He knows that in times of chaos and the reestablishment of the old order, his victory can only be temporary. The *Amtsrichter* (judge), on the other hand, holds on to the written law and ignores the power plays around him, trying to negotiate each case separately in the privacy of his office. In what should by now be a familiar Brechtian move, this withdrawal makes it impossible for him to perceive the interactions between his colleagues and to determine his position relative to these interactions, so he cannot recognize the workings of fascism.

If recognition, for Brecht, grows out of social performance, we must ask if and how recognition is possible when one has no access to others. One instrument of fascist terror is the isolation of marginalized groups and people. How, then, can these people create theatrical and performative knowledge in isolation? This question informs Brecht's teaching plays, where an always-illegal collective is necessary for the subversive work, and, like much in the teaching plays, it was anticipated in *Furcht und Elend (Fear and Misery)*. In the scene "Die jüdische Frau" (The Jewish Wife), a Jewish woman prepares to leave her husband, a Gentile, in order to promote his career as a physician, which has come to a standstill due to his Jewish spouse. Brecht portrays her struggle to achieve social and political comprehension by having the woman rehearse possible conversations with her husband, who is absent. She seeks recognition by creating an imagined public.

The scene begins with the woman, Judith, packing her suitcases and calling various friends. She informs them that she will be vacationing in Amsterdam and that they can resume contact with Fritz, who has been shunned both professionally and privately during the last few weeks. She then burns the address book containing the phone numbers—a precaution, but also a gesture that confirms her isolation—and begins rehearsing the speech to her husband. After five attempts, she gains clarity on how fascist distortion results from what Benjamin calls "die Herrschaft der Lüge" (rule of lies). Fascists are the "Lügner, die alle zum Lügen zwingen" (4:388) (Liars, who force everyone to lie). Lying expresses itself not only in speech, but also in behavior—here, in the behavior between

husband and wife. Judith leaves "weil ich nicht mehr reden kann, wenn
ich dich ansehe, Fritz. Es kommt mir dann so nutzlos vor, zu reden. Es
ist doch alles schon bestimmt" (4:387–88) (because I cannot talk anymore when I look at you, Fritz. It seems so useless to me to talk then.
Everything is surely already determined). When Judith refers to "everything" as determined, she registers her recognition that negotiations have
become meaningless and thus impossible.

Because speech has lost reliability, Judith combines speech with the
language of gestures. With the help of her own requisites—the suitcases
and their contents—she establishes signifiers of truth that serve as a lie
detector in her subsequent conversation with Fritz. Fritz pretends that
his wife will be vacationing for just a few weeks, but the number of her
suitcases clearly indicates that she is leaving for good. The ultimate confirmation of Fritz's ignorance and approval is the performance of one of
the scenes that she rehearsed earlier: she asks Fritz to hand her the fur
coat, which he does with the words "Schließlich sind es nur ein paar
Wochen" (4:390) (After all, it is only for a few weeks) despite the fact
that it is summer.

Judith gains clarity about her situation by using her possessions as signifiers of her political and cultural position. Arranging her gloves, her lingerie, etc., she had, during the rehearsals, reflected on her situation as a
Jew, as a woman and wife, and as a future refugee:

> Ich will nicht, daß du mir sagst, ich soll nicht gehen. Ich beeile mich,
> weil ich dich nicht noch sagen hören will, ich soll gehen. Das ist eine
> Frage der Zeit. Charakter, das ist eine Zeitfrage. Er hält soundso lang,
> genau wie ein Handschuh. Es gibt gute, die halten lang. Aber sie halten
> nicht ewig. (4:388)

> [I do not want you to tell me that I should not go. I am hurrying
> because I do not want to hear you finally say that I should go. That is
> a question of time. Character, that is a question of time. It lasts only so
> long, just like a glove. There are good ones that last a long time. But
> they do not last forever.]

In this rehearsal Judith examines both sides of the problem of staying or
going; in her actual conversation with her husband she transforms this
statement into a direct question: "Soll ich denn bleiben?" (Should I stay
then?) she asks her husband (4:389). He recreates the isolation of her
rehearsal by leaving the question unanswered. As we know from "Der
Entlassene" (Release) and from Brecht's teaching plays, both *bleiben* (to

stay), by which he means staying in a given place, and *zusammenbleiben* (to stay together), by which he means remaining socially committed, are essential for effective resistance. Fritz fails this test in every respect. Like all collaborators in *Furcht und Elend (Fear and Misery)*, the husband insists on the stability of his character: "Du weißt, daß ich unverändert bin, weißt du das, Judith?" (4:389) (You know that I am unchanged, do you know that, Judith?), he asks his wife. She answers his question affirmatively, but we know from her rehearsals that she is deceiving him and that doing so is an act of resistance against her husband, who has lately come to believe that "der Prozentsatz der jüdischen Wissenschaftler sei gar nicht so groß" (4:387) (the percentage of Jewish scientists is not at all so large), thus moving steadily into an anti-Semitic rationale.

Believing his character to be stable, Fritz assumes that he remains his old self and imagines that changes in his surroundings result from his own actions. When greeted by a neighbor who previously shunned him, Fritz interprets this change as the fruit of his own effort: "Die Leute sind nicht mal so ablehnend, wenn man ihnen fest gegenübertritt" (4:390) (People are not nearly so rejecting when one faces them firmly). The audience, of course, knows the change is due to the fact that Judith informed the neighbors of her impending departure. Her husband tacitly acknowledges as much when, immediately afterward, he shows his growing impatience with his wife's lingering presence: "Wann willst du denn fahren?" (4:390) (So when do you want to go?). His superficial relationship with his neighbor is purchased at the price of a deeper relationship with his wife. His principles are analogous to his wife's thoughts on durability. Yet, in his attempt to "stay the same," Fritz misses the chance to examine their marriage in both its private and public aspects.

Judith, in contrast, changes with each additional rehearsal. From a remorseful wife, she transforms herself into a self-aware "nationalist" Jew, then into a social critic, and finally into a behavioral critic committed to using everything at her disposal—from fur coat to lingerie—to survive: "Gib mir die Wäsche. Das ist Reizwäsche. Ich werde sie brauchen" (4:389) (Give me the lingerie. That is sexy lingerie. I will need it). Her change in status from a respected doctor's wife to a persecuted German Jew unveils for her the way that the status of a bourgeois wife is analogous to prostitution. She has grown so accustomed to accepting her catastrophic situation that she is willing to exploit the victim status that prostitution entails as a means of survival. In contrast to Fritz's insistence on the stability of his character as he succumbs to fascism, Judith embraces the need to adapt in order to resist.

While *Furcht und Elend (Fear and Misery)* demonstrates the rise of fascism through the elimination of the public sphere, it also examines the different private and public means through which those living under fascism can gather information and construct reliable knowledge. Judith, in private, derives her understanding of her marital and political situation through phone calls to former friends and by packing her suitcases. She realizes that one way fascism controls people is by severing them from information and interpersonal exchange; in her final rehearsal, she explains to her husband: "Die Wände haben Ohren, wie? Aber ihr sagt ja nichts! Die einen horchen und die andern schweigen" (4:389) (The walls have ears, right? But you say nothing! Some eavesdrop and the others keep silent).

Gathering information in public proves more difficult. If all roads to a social public are blocked by the fascist state, then the public exists where the state presents itself or is represented by members of the National Socialist Party. In the scene "Das Kreidekreuz" (The Chalk Cross), Brecht demonstrates how theatrical performances in everyday life can make Nazi tactics public. The scene takes place among servants (a cook, a maid, a chauffeur), the unemployed worker Franz (the cook's brother), and an SA man (the maid's fiancé) in the kitchen of an upper-class residence. It is clear from the beginning that the presence of the SA man dominates the entire scene: it determines where people sit, how and where they move, what they talk about, and how they converse. The worker enters the scene belatedly, and his failure to offer a clear "Heil Hitler" provokes a confrontation with the SA man. This conflict sets up a chain of reactions and deceptions that culminates in the revelation that Nazis continually spy on people in public.

The secrecy that poisons the family relationship in the marriage of Judith and Fritz also creates the paranoia in this scene, and the fascists use this paranoia as an excuse for murder. Paranoia transforms suspicions into certainty. As Theo says in his conversation with the chauffeur: "Ich habe nie Verdacht. . . . Verdacht, das ist schon gradsogut wie Gewißheit. Und dann setzt es auch schon was" (4:347) (I am never suspicious. . . . Suspicion, that is already as good as certainty. And then you are in trouble.). The chauffeur, anticipating the outcome of the experiment, responds "Schlagartig" (4:347) (suddenly). Theo is eager to show himself off as a warm-hearted Nazi when he proclaims, "Leben und leben lassen. . . . Scharf sind wir nur in puncto Gesinnung" (Live and let live. . . . We are only harsh *in puncto* attitude). At this point the worker begins his interrogation by asking, "Wie ist denn die Gesinnung jetzt so?" (How is the attitude now then?). This question already suggests the existence of a dictatorship, and that is confirmed by the Nazi: "Die Gesinnung ist gut. Sind Sie anderer Ansicht?" (4:349) (The attitude is good. Are you of a different view?). To be of a different *Ansicht* (view) is to have a wrong *Gesinnung* (attitude), and the worker realizes that he himself will be subject to an interrogation.

The worker transforms the political interrogation into a theatrical one by saying, "Ich meine nur, es sagt einem ja keiner, was er denkt" (4:349) (I only mean, no one really tells anyone what he thinks). Like Judith in the earlier scene, Franz recognizes privacy and secrecy as conditions that perpetuate the fascist machine. When Theo brags that he identifies subversive elements in the unemployment line and turns them in, the worker objects that after each arrest the Nazi would be recognized and avoided. Theo then volunteers to demonstrate his fascist practice: "Soll ich Ihnen zeigen, wie man mich nicht kennt?" (4:350) (Shall I show you how one does not know me?). The worker and the Nazi then perform several scenes designed to discover one another, and in doing so they reveal each other's attitude. What they learn in the course of this exchange is not only the other's position, but also the attitude of their audience: the worker recognizes his own sister as a Nazi and the chauffeur as an opponent to the Nazis.

The structure of the various performances is hierarchical. Franz is supposed to demonstrate what he already is, an unemployed proletarian opposed to the Nazi regime, in order to enable Theo to show "was wir alles auf dem Kasten haben und daß sie unter keinen wie immer gearteten Umständen durchkommen . . ." (4:350) (how we are all on the ball and that they will not come through under any, however special, circumstances . . .). Theo's eagerness to present himself and his SA methods as superior enables Franz to dupe him into betraying his cause by divulging a key trick: how the SA identifies and arrests Nazi opponents. Franz assumes the role of an ignorant buffoon, proclaiming an entire list of Nazi crimes from rape to stockpiling food and causing starvation. In response Theo assures him of his discretion: "Kollege, was du mir sagst, ist wie ins offene Grab gesprochen" (4:355) (Pal, what you tell me is spoken as if into an open grave), he says, while slapping him on his shoulder. The seemingly friendly gesture reveals the betrayal: a white chalk cross appears on Franz's shoulder, the sign designating a political dissident among the Nazis—a sign that ensures immediate arrest. From this new perspective, Theo's assurance of discretion becomes a death threat, as does his "friendly" expression of good will when Franz finally leaves.

Theo's performance exemplifies the fascist dynamic of suspicion and certainty. The SA's major target is the unemployment office, where those without work are assigned jobs or receive benefits in an economy where neither jobs nor benefits are available. The workers' frustration is economically predetermined, and their opposition to the regime is politically confirmed: their presence at the *Stempelstelle* (stamp office) already brands them as opponents to the regime, a classification most useful to those in power. Workers are marked—without reference to ideology—for what they are: poor, without employment, part of a *Volksgemeinschaft* (national community) that does not provide for them except through the *Arbeitsdienst* (labor service), a milder version of a concentration camp. In a culture in which the regime can admit neither its surveillance practices nor its efforts to eliminate all opponents, no matter how mild their opposition, the worker engages the Nazi in a game of obfuscation that reveals these denied Nazi practices. The act of clapping the shoulder of the suspect, someone without any stake in the system, transforms suspicion into certainty—"schlagartig" (suddenly), as the chauffeur observes at the beginning of the scene.

In *Furcht und Elend des Dritten Reiches (Fear and Misery of the Third Reich)*, Brecht combines his concept of "filmische Sehweise" (filmic perception), as the perception of complex historical developments in a single scene, with that of *gestus*, as a basic element of his theatre. The play, which was originally intended to be performed by emigrant actors in exile, demonstrates political terror in reduced private settings through corporeal gesture. One recognizes the tactics of the state through the everyday, commonplace gestures of its subjects. Thus, *Furcht und Elend (Fear and Misery)* corresponds with the *Dreigroschenprozeß (Threepenny Trial)* as a reading of politics through behavior and not through political thought and expression. Brecht writes:

> Das Denken wird vom Faschismus als ein Verhalten behandelt. Als solches ist es (neu!) eine juristische, eventuell kriminelle Handlung und wird mit entsprechenden Maßnahmen beantwortet. Daran ist *nichts* Tadelnswertes. Bisher üblich: das Gedachte mit Gedachtem zu vergleichen, dahinter verschwindet der Denker. Die Nuance wird preiswert. Das Denken zielt auf »Wahrheiten«, die immer gelten, gesagt zu jedem Zeitpunkt, auf jedem Feld die gleiche Wirkung haben. Die Wahrheit hat also weder Zeit noch Ort. (21:421)

> [Thinking is treated by fascism as a behavior. As such, it is (new!) a juridical, possibly criminal disposition and is answered with appropri-

ate measures. There is *nothing* reprehensible in that. Customary up to now: to compare what is intended with what is assumed, the thinker disappears behind that. Nuance becomes cheap. Thinking aims at "truths," which are always valid, said at any time, have the same effect in every field. The truth thus has neither time, nor place.]

In *Furcht und Elend (Fear and Misery)*, Brecht places fascist thought in specific contexts in order to examine a range of gestures and the ways those gestures change as the contexts producing them alter. Fascism and antifascism result from the interaction among people in different situations. What might be intended as an antifascist act by one individual can nevertheless become a fascist act depending on circumstance. Political conviction, then, is not a matter of a subjective decision based on principles, but something to be deciphered and constructed from social reality.

It is this social reality, a reality that must be confirmed by each participant, that Brecht seeks to install in the place of a bourgeois public sphere that is based on idealistic values. According to Brecht, these values crumble all too easily in a political emergency. By accepting the role that one is about to play in a certain situation, as Galy Gay does in *Mann ist Mann (Man Equals Man)*, one is able to comprehend the situation by recognizing one's own interest—not in terms of values, but in their relation to the interests of others. Only in these limitations can obedience and resistance gain significance and thus efficacy.

4

Revolution

Change and Persistence

The Teaching Plays:
Brecht's Theatre of Poverty

In his essay "Erfahrung und Armut" (Experience and Poverty), Walter
Benjamin subsumes the political, economic, cultural, and psychological
situation in post–World War I Europe under the comprehensive notion
of poverty.[1] Benjamin sees a fundamental loss in the realm of *Erfahrung*
(experience) as the mediator between succeeding generations and the culture that surrounds them. Conventionally understood, experience links
different generations through knowledge acquired, tested, and conveyed
over long periods of time. But World War I produced "eine der unge-
heuersten Erfahrungen der Weltgeschichte" (some of the most monstrous
events in the history of the world),[2] and this experience left those who
went through it speechless. This experience, according to Benjamin,
turned out to be incommunicable, and he extends this argument about
specific wartime experiences to describe an entire historical outlook:
"Diese Erfahrungsarmut ist Armut nicht nur an privaten sondern an
Menschheitserfahrungen überhaupt. Und damit eine Art von neuem Bar-
barentum" (Indeed [let's admit it], our poverty of experience is not merely
poverty on the personal level, but poverty of human experience in general. Hence, a new kind of barbarism).[3] A new barbarism has emerged
from that period because we have become incapable of sharing our experiences with others, thus robbing society of the common experience that

unites us as humanity. The experience of World War I disconnected people from past experiences and released them into the twentieth century
severed from history. Thus begins a new prehistory in which the understanding of what is human must be reconstructed far from the achievements of humanism and in the midst of both previously unimaginable
technological progress and the emergence of mass culture.

In his early plays (beginning in 1919)—including *Baal*, *Trommeln in
der Nacht (Drums in the Night)*, and *Im Dickicht der Städte (In the Jungle
of Cities)*—Brecht, who experienced as a medical orderly in a military hos-
pital what Benjamin described, already presents twentieth-century settings in which the characters turn to prehistoric or barbaric techniques of
survival such as mimesis and organic adaptation. In *Trommeln in der
Nacht (Drums in the Night)*, Brecht presents the war as a prologue that
turns Kragler into an "other," and it is as an "other" that he enters the
play. In *Trommeln in der Nacht (Drums in the Night)*, as in *Im Dickicht
der Städte (In the Jungle of Cities)*, survival is achieved not by understanding and solving a problem (tasks that require experience), but by adapting to the conditions that created it (a prerational task). According to
Brecht, acquiring survival techniques is a theatrical skill, for the theatre
operates on the mimetic adaptation to social situations and historical circumstances. Much like Brecht, Benjamin introduces a positive notion of
mimesis as a new beginning, and he locates this beginning in the arts.
Benjamin demands an art that accepts the poverty of experience instead
of flourishing in the suffocating *Ideenreichtum* (wealth of ideas) that,
rather than revitalizing the cultural landscape, helped to galvanize it. New
barbarism starts from scratch and through this fresh start emancipates
itself from traditional art forms:

> Denn wohin bringt die Armut an Erfahrung den Barbaren? Sie bringt
> ihn dahin, von vorn zu beginnen; von Neuem anzufangen; mit
> Wenigem auszukommen; aus Wenigem heraus zu konstruieren und
> dabei weder rechts noch links zu blicken.
>
> [For what does poverty of experience do for the barbarian? It forces
> him to start from scratch; to make a new start; to make a little go a
> long way; to begin with a little and build up further, looking neither
> left nor right.][4]

Among those who start constructing something from nothing, Benjamin
lists Brecht, who first approached Marxism with the simple lesson that
"Kommunismus sei nicht die gerechte Verteilung des Reichtums sondern

der Armut" (Communism is the just distribution of poverty, not of wealth).[5] Redistributing poverty instead of material goods or positive knowledge, as we shall see, fundamentally shapes Brecht's theatrical and theoretical work.

Brecht considers poverty to be the raw material not only for Marxism as a political system, but also for a new, allied, barbaric theatre. His *Lehrstücke* (teaching plays) are affected by barbarism and poverty in form and content, and they combine archaic and modernist elements of theatre. In fact, all of the plays that fall under the narrowest definition of teaching plays mix these elements.[6] They are *Der Flug der Lindberghs (Lindbergh's Flight)* (also known as *Der Ozeanflug [The Flight over the Ocean]*), the *Badener Lehrstück vom Einverständnis (The Baden-Baden Lesson on Consent)*, *Der Jasager. Der Neinsager (He Said Yes. He Said No)*, and *Die Maßnahme (The Measures Taken)*. The plays stand out due to shared formal elements: they are very short and feature a reduced fable in a reduced setting (with very few exceptions the stage is almost entirely empty), a small number of generic or interchangeable characters (for example, "mechanic" or "comrade"), and a chorus that comments on ideas and actions being presented. In the teaching plays, Brecht overcomes both the institutional frame of the theatre, and the divide between actors and audience. This becomes clear in Brecht's famous definition of the *Lehrstücke* (teaching plays) as *"Stücke, die für die Darstellenden lehrhaft sind. Sie benötigen so kein Publikum" (plays that are instructive for the performer. They thus need no audience).*[7] Theatre, then, moves from being an artistic institution to be consumed by an audience to being a social situation determined by conscious acting and viewing. Seeing, previously considered a passive act of consumption, is conceived of as the first step toward acting.[8]

The *Lehrstücke* (teaching plays) constitute a corpus of work that is governed by intertextuality, for the whole of these works is constructed through repetitions, variations, and oppositions.[9] For example, the *Badener Lehrstück vom Einverständnis (Baden-Baden Lesson on Consent)* starts with the same poem that concludes the preceding *Der Flug der Lindberghs (Lindbergh's Flight)*, and *Die Maßnahme (The Measures Taken)* was intended to complement *Der Jasager. Der Neinsager (He Said Yes. He Said No)*. The teaching plays also repeat thematic elements, as quick plot summaries will illustrate.

In the *Badener Lehrstück (Baden-Baden Lesson)*, three mechanics and one pilot ask the masses and the chorus for help after a plane crash. The chorus shows that the technological sophistication of the pilot and the mechanics separates them from the collective. Exclusion from the collective means social death, but joining the collective requires relinquishing individuality, including any form of superiority that creates distinction. By doing that, death can be overcome and help is no longer needed.

Der Jasager. Der Neinsager (He Said Yes. He Said No) complex consists of three plays—a first and second version of *Der Jasager (He Said Yes)*, and *Der Neinsager (He Said No)*—all of them modeled after the Japanese Noh-play. All three plays have one basic fable—the son of a sick widow joins his teacher and some other students on an important and extremely difficult journey to the other side of high mountains. The boy cannot bear the hardship of this trip, and an old custom dictates that the collective kill any traveler too weak for this excursion. It further holds that the victim must accept his fate. The three plays present different solutions to the problem.

In *Die Maßnahme (The Measures Taken)*, four agitators report to the chorus on their successful participation in beginning the communist revolution in China. They also explain that they had to kill a young comrade in order to complete their work, and the chorus voices its approval. It then insists that the three surviving agitators reenact the situation in which they found themselves in order to demonstrate the failures of the young comrade that made it necessary to kill him.

In these plays, Brecht reinvents theatre by using the ancient component of the chorus on the one hand, while writing plays that can be staged anywhere and can thus escape the institution of "the theatre" on the other hand. Form, more that content, makes the teaching plays a spur-of-the-moment theatre, and that moment, determined by poverty in all its guises, permits the investigation of situations that have proven unsolvable by experience. These investigations, in which custom and teachings replace experience, create the barbarism of this specific Brechtian genre. However, this elemental human barbarism also points toward new paths of social change.

The teaching plays are indeed the result of Brecht's studies of Marxism, but, I would argue, that they are less a presentation of Marxist ideology than an exploration of the redistribution of poverty. The *Badener Lehrstück vom Einverständnis (The Baden-Baden Lesson on Consent)* teaches the acceptance of poverty:

> Wer aber den Wunsch hat, einverstanden zu sein, der hält bei der Armut. An die Dinge hält er sich nicht! Die Dinge können genommen werden und dann ist da kein Einverständnis. Auch an das Leben hält er sich nicht. Das Leben wird genommen werden und dann ist da kein Einverständnis. (3:38)[10]

[But whoever has the wish to be in consent, he holds to poverty. He does not hold onto things! The things can be taken, and then there is no consent. Also he does not hold onto life. Life will be taken, and then there is no consent.]

Here Brecht ties poverty to a fundamental aspect of his teaching plays—*Einverständnis* (consent), a principle that combines the impoverished condition with the intellectual and the ideological. *Einverständis* (consent) refers to accepting loss or withdrawal, but the final statement concedes the impossibility of a life accepting its own death. Thus, agreement arises in response to need; when poverty is removed, nothing is lost. Benjamin defines Brechtian theatre as "Entwicklung der Haltung, die Armut einem aufzwingt" (development of the attitude [disposition] which poverty forces upon him).[11] The teaching plays are exercises in developing this disposition, a disposition intended to overcome theatre as an institution. By applying the concept of poverty to theatre as an institution, Brecht determines theatre to be social experimentation.

In this context the big ideological questions that have haunted the teaching plays from the beginning—their relationship to Brecht's Stalinist commitment and their status as models of a pedagogy for future communist societies—move into the background. After years of criticism that denounced the teaching plays as ideologically biased, it has recently been noted that they are actually void of any concrete Marxist content.[12] As Brecht himself remarks, "Die Menge erwartet viel, die Klassiker sagten wenig" (10.1:528) (The crowd expects much, the classics said little). That, of course, does not eliminate brutality from the plays, but I would suggest that their brutality is rooted less in politics than in the poverty of experience and thus in the "prehistoric barbarism" that Benjamin describes. In his teaching plays, Brecht takes nothing that is based on experience for granted—neither Marxism, nor humanity. Ideological knowledge and human identity are not preexisting; they must be constructed in social situations, and the teaching plays provide these situations.[13] While Marxism is rarely mentioned, violence and sacrifice during moments of crisis are followed by processes of change. Revolution arises from change, creating situations in which people are completely devoid of experience. In its disregard for experience, change turns out to be barbaric. The teaching plays are exercises in acquiring the ability both to detect change and to discover what initiates it, a search that has nothing at its disposal but poverty.

Human presence is Brecht's answer to material (goods) and immaterial (experience and identity) poverty, and in this situation, human presence itself turns out to be barbaric. Although the teaching plays can be understood as theatrical pedagogy, their pedagogy lacks assurance—the only certainty offered in these plays is that we do not and will not get what we want or need. Thus, Brecht's most experimental work can be seen as a response to Benjamin's diagnosis of *Erfahrungsarmut* (poverty of experience):

> Erfahrungsarmut: das muß man nicht so verstehen, als ob die Menschen sich nach neuer Erfahrung sehnten. Nein, sie sehnen sich von Erfahrungen freizukommen, sie sehnen sich nach einer Umwelt, in der sie ihre Armut, die äußere und schließlich auch die innere, so rein und deutlich zur Geltung bringen können, daß etwas Anständiges dabei herauskommt.

> [Poverty of experience. This should not be understood to mean that people are yearning for new experience. No, they long to free themselves from experience; they long for a world in which they can make such pure and decided use of their poverty—their outer poverty, and ultimately also their inner poverty—that it will lead to something respectable.][14]

The teaching plays' impoverished form and content provide an environment in which poverty gains validity. The needs presented in the plays are never satisfied, but sometimes they are answered by the presence of the people in need. In the following, I will show how material and immaterial human poverty provide the raw material for the teaching plays. This occurs when the stage—the most basic theatrical element—is defined by the constellation of participants instead of a predefined space. This new social space then abandons coherent character—"bourgeois" character—for the examination of what is human.

Benjamin shows that the loss of experience brings about a loss of confidence in who we are, and Brecht's concept of barbarism provides an answer to this question. The teaching plays stage theatre as a forum for experience, but it is an experience lived by participants rather than inherited from previous generations: the first flight across the Atlantic in *Der Flug der Lindberghs (Lindbergh's Flight)*, the first transgression of a custom in *Der Neinsager (He Said No)*, and the first demonstration of revolutionary murder in *Die Maßnahme (The Measures Taken)*. For Brecht, initial experience is at first a barbaric experience that emerges out of a conflict which proves to be unsolvable by old conventions or received wisdom.

SOCIAL SPACE AND HUMAN STANDING

In his praise of the new barbarism, Benjamin discards *Innerlichkeit* (subjectivity) for the sake of what he calls *das Innere* (interiority). Brecht's teaching plays have often been attacked for their callousness and their disregard for subjectivity, but what has been overlooked in these plays is the creation of interiority as a replacement for subjectivity, a replacement that should profoundly influence our understanding of Brecht's concept of historical change:

> Die Beschreiber revolutionärer Vorgänge lassen oft jene inneren Widerstände verschwinden, die sich in den Massen gegen die Revolution halten oder neu erheben. Zeigend, wie das große allgemeine Interesse eine Bevölkerung mehr und mehr ergreift, indem die Masse sich ihres eigenen Interesses als Masse mehr und mehr bewußt wird, vernachlässigen die Beschreiber die echten kleineren Interessengegensätze, die immer noch lebendig sind oder neu zum Leben kommen. . . . [A]ber die innere Geschichte einer Revolution besteht gerade darin, daß das Proletariat, d.h. die Proleten sich dazu finden, als Klasse zu handeln. (23:36)

> [The describers of revolutionary events often let those inner resistances that persist or newly emerge in the masses against the revolution disappear. Showing how the great common interest more and more takes hold of a population in which the mass is becoming increasingly conscious of its own interest as mass, the describers neglect the real, smaller conflicts of interest that are still alive or newly coming alive. . . . [B]ut the inner history of a revolution consists exactly in the fact that the proletariat, that is to say the proletarians, find themselves acting as a class.]

Here, Brecht voices his frustration with conventional narratives of revolutions, a frustration that can be traced through his entire work. Brecht criticizes the homogeneity that historical narratives often assume (in this case, in their description of mass movements) but also often produce (as a consequence of their own genre). These descriptions presume a unifying experience that leads the masses to revolutionary uprising, an experience that Benjamin thought absent from the twentieth century. A narrative that describes a revolution from the perspective of political history can easily ignore the tensions within the "masses" that are produced by habit and by the drive to survive revolutionary upheaval. Brecht seeks to represent both the inner resistances to revolutionary change and the inner history of revolution. It is through this history that proletarians find themselves as a class.

But the problem Brecht poses is the same problem that today's cultural historians face: How can we know? The inner history of revolution goes unrecorded because it is not perceived as history while it happens. Because "die echten kleineren Interessengegensätze" (the real, smaller conflicts of interest) find no place in traditional narratives, Brecht uses his teaching plays to investigate the masses' resistance to the changing of established habits. This resistance takes place in actions and gestures that are too often thought small and insignificant. By confronting progressive theory with the apathy of habit that poses inner resistance, Brecht's teaching plays show how this confrontation affects individual and collective subjects. This helps explain resistance to revolutionary action and change among those who "should" support it, without resorting to tired and condescending notions of false consciousness.

Brecht explores this resistance to change on a microlevel in his concept of *gestus*, which constitutes a major element of the teaching plays. What Richard Schechner calls "restored behaviour" also works well as a definition of *gestus*.[15] Schechner describes restored behavior as "living behaviour treated as a film director treats a strip of film. These strips of behaviour can be re-arranged or reconstructed; they are independent of the causal systems (social, psychological, technological) that brought them into existence."[16] *Gestus*, as restored behavior, may signify history in detail as we have learned in *Furcht und Elend des Dritten Reiches (Fear and Misery of the Third Reich)*, where one can observe gestures of consent and support, and of dissent and resistance in unexpected moments. Restored behavior presents us with details from the past that are still able to motivate commitment or resistance to social change. By presenting situations that are void of experience, the teaching plays use *gestus* as restored behavior to present the learned habit. Although committed to social change, the plays, as we shall see, present the resistance to that change in much more detail because the traditional habit contains our past—something the new habit has yet to become. Thus, it becomes the lingering and scarcely decipherable trace of the experience destroyed in the war.

The teaching plays move "die echten kleineren Interessengegensätze" (the real, smaller conflicts of interest) that constitute the inner history of revolutions from the inner conflict of a single subject to a social conflict shared by the members of a group, and they perform this transition on stage. By presenting an extremely reduced fable in a limited public space, Brecht demonstrates the relativity of any given interest—ideologically and spatially. In *Der Jasager. Der Neinsager (He Said Yes. He Said No)*, for example, the boy convinces the others to break with tradition. Custom, habit, and manner determine speech and action in the play's brief scenes, which often consist of gestures and utterances that signify a single custom. The play relates the content of tradition (killing anybody who becomes too sick to continue during a journey across the mountains) to the courtesy that structures the relationships among the participants. Change can just as easily be stimulated by custom as inhibited by it.

In the teaching plays discussed here, the gestures that signify relations and traditions are positioned in a limited and socially constructed space. Brecht makes inner conflicts less a matter of psychological representation than of general social concern by using the placement of participants on stage to create a social space. In the *Badener Lehrstück (Baden-Baden Lesson)*, the stage emerges from the presence of the actors, *"in seinen Abmessungen der Anzahl der Mitspielenden entsprechenden Podium"* (3:27) *(podium corresponding in its dimensions to the number of players)*, a place where no space is wasted. Conflicts within small social units are signified in space when, for example, in *Der Jasager. Der Neinsager (He Said Yes. He Said No)* the performance space is divided into two rooms and a change of room accompanies every argument. At the height of the conflict, when students and teacher discuss killing the boy, the participants are positioned in room one or two according to their support for or opposition to the ritual killing. They signify a change of opinion by changing their physical location. Similarly, in *Die Maßnahme (The Measures Taken)* the stage is produced through an utterance when the "Kontrollchor" (Control Chorus) commands, "Tretet vor!" (3:75) (Step forward!). By having the group of four agitators step forward to a position in front of the chorus, Brecht presents a constellation that, from the start of the play, suggests a power structure that will eventually accept the death of the young comrade. The imbalance of power is reiterated in the stage directions for the smaller unit when the four agitators present the death of the comrade: *"Sie stellen sich drei gegen einen auf . . ."* (3:75) *(They arrange themselves three against one . . .)*. Here, the participants demonstrate their relation to one another through their spatial positioning.

The juxtaposition of *gestus* and space is essential to Brecht's concept of thought. In rejecting thought as a purely intellectual activity, Brecht defines it in terms of either practice or behavior. When Brecht searches for a definition of "eingreifendes Denken" (engaged thinking) through "solche Definitionen, die die Handhabung des definierten Feldes gestatten. Unter den determinierenden Faktoren tritt immer das Verhalten des Definierenden auf" (21:422) (such definitions that permit the handling of the defined field. Among the determining factors, the behavior of the

definer always appears), he maintains that such a definition is impossible
without active participants. The teaching plays take place in the absence
of a predefined space, and it is the mere presence of the participants that
defines the field in which the investigation will proceed. By providing this
social space, the teaching plays lay the groundwork for Brecht's complement to "eingreifendes Denken" (engaged thinking), a complement that
moves the teaching plays from theatrical to social action. Brecht describes
this as "Denken als *gesellschaftliches* Verhalten. Aussichtsreich nur, wenn es
um sich selbst und das Verhalten der Umwelt Bescheid weiß" (21:422)
(Thinking as *social* behavior. Full of promise only if it is informed about
itself and the behavior of the environment). To secure knowledge about
one's environment, one must limit that environment according to the
available means of perception.

In *Das Badener Lehrstück vom Einverständnis (The Baden-Baden Lesson
on Consent)*, Brecht presents an investigation of technological problem
solving within a social constellation determined solely by the physical presence of the participants. After a plane crash, the now-grounded airmen
approach the chorus for help. The chorus, in turn, takes account of the
spatial distance separating airborne flyers from the land-bound masses,
noting that this spatial and intellectual distance creates social ignorance:

> Zu der Zeit wo die Menschheit
> Anfing sich zu erkennen
> Haben wir Flugzeuge gemacht . . .
> Und sind durch die Luft geflogen. (3:27)

> [At the time when humanity
> Began to recognize itself
> We made aircraft . . .
> And flew through the air.]

The airmen consider flying to be their own technological achievement
rather than the culmination of a long, cooperative social process. Their
account of technological progress and human cognition, however, already
contains the seeds of self-criticism. While they as airmen have moved
ahead through technological achievement, they have also removed themselves from others. At a time when humanity begins to recognize itself,
their progress has two consequences: those left behind are removed from
technological progress, while the airmen are removed from social recognition. The chorus dismisses their account as a regression from the col-

lective understanding essential to social participation and human self-cognition. From the perspective of the collective, the airmen are "oben über uns" (up above us), "weit vor uns" (far ahead of us), and are using their ability to fly to escape from the social labor that human self-recognition entails rather than recognizing self-recognition as a social—and thus collective—accomplishment.

The play then raises the following question: How does intellectual progress relate to our understanding of what it means to be human? The chorus, in its evaluation of the accomplishment of the grounded airmen, relates their accomplishment to social confusions among human beings:

> Und es weiß seit langer Zeit
> Niemand mehr, was ein Mensch ist.
> Zum Beispiel: Während ihr flogt, kroch
> Ein euch Ähnliches vom Boden
> Nicht wie ein Mensch! (3:30)

> [And for a long time has known
> No one anymore, what a man is.
> For example: While you flew, crawled
> One like you from the ground
> Not like a man!]

Brecht presents the airmen's escape from social labor as symptomatic of the nonsimultaneity of progress: technological advancement meets human regression. In the play, self-recognition through the technological invention is presented as a matter of the past, as almost past, and this prehistory is confronted with a different kind of present that measures progress along social lines. Thus, when the leader of the chorus addresses the fallen mechanics with "Fliegt jetzt nicht mehr" (Fly now no more) and "Der niedere Boden / Ist für euch / Jetzt hoch genug" (3:28) (The low ground / Is for you / Now high enough), he warns the mechanics that their achievements will be measured according to a different standard and without any prefabricated concept of humanity. The play provides a negative answer to the question of what is human and then pushes the interrogation farther by putting the airmen in the position of crawling on the floor "nicht wie ein Mensch" (not like a man). Crouched on the floor, the mechanics are diminished in physical stature and importance during an inquiry in which they learn that all of their achievements and technological advances mean nothing to the questioning chorus. They reach their smallest size when they answer, "Wer seid ihr?" (Who are you?), with "Wir sind niemand" (We are no one) (3:40). Death is overcome with linguistic logic when "niemand" (no one) dies.

Brecht's attack on bourgeois psychological subjectivity offers an alternative concept of humanity, and this concept is both theatrical and social, which becomes clear by moving beyond the short list of agreed-upon teaching plays to other texts he wrote during the same period. The fragment *Aus Nichts wird Nichts (From Nothing Comes Nothing)* is a theatrical presentation of philosophical thought on human existence. In addition to various notes on theatre, history, and Marxism, the fragment contains the short sketch of a play. That sketch begins with a philosopher's surprise visit to a theatre where actors are preparing to perform "Eine amerikanische Tragödie" (10.1:692) (An American Tragedy). After a brief discussion with the philosopher, the actors change their program. They decide to perform something chosen especially for this philosopher, and he commends them for being indifferent to the content of their performance. What the actors want to perform is something from the daily life of the people, and when the philosopher hears this, he says they should perform the maxim "Aus nichts wird nichts" (from nothing comes nothing) because "da der Mensch nichts ist, kann er alles werden" (10.1:693) (since man is nothing, he can become everything). Immediately upon approaching their makeup tables, the actors demonstrate their potential to become everything. This contrasts with the thinker, who remains motionless in his chair while being carried around by the actors. The fable of the upcoming presentation grows out of the philosopher's theoretical maxim as it is then shaped by the actors' commitment to acting and simultaneous indifference to drama.

The actors end up performing the fable of Bogderkahn, who is nothing (he lacks food, housing, and work) until he is hired by two shepherds to protect their herds, which are threatened by robbers. Entering this social and economic realm, Bogderkahn acquires substance by earning three bread crusts a day and the right to live in a tent. Bogderkahn is a coward, and his fear keeps him from protecting the herds, but this only fuels his success. He never leaves the tent for fear of robbers, soldiers, and tigers. Paradoxically, by protecting himself in this way, he ascends from nothingness to shepherd to fur trader—a rise that culminates when he becomes a dictator who saves himself and others from a snow storm. At the climax of his rise, however, Bogderkahn stops relying on his survival instinct and turns instead to his intellect to perpetuate his career. The isolation that this entails renders him useless to others, and he recedes back into nothingness.

The opposition between acting and drama that Brecht sets up in this fragment destroys the stability of content and character (Bogderkahn lacks a fixed identity and constantly adapts himself to circumstance) by releasing both into a process of social interaction that produces "menschliche Geltung" (human validation). The philosopher in the theatre explains:

> Denkt euch, ihr spielt ein Spiel, in dem keiner die Maske kennt, die er aufhat. Wie soll er nun erkennen, wen er darstellt. Nur aus dem Verhalten der andern erkennt er, wer er ist. (10.1:716)

> [Just think, you are playing a game in which no one knows the mask that he has on. How should he recognize whom he performs. Only from the behavior of the others does he recognize who he is.]

Patrice Pavis points out that one conventional motivation for wearing masks is "the ability to observe others while being protected from observation oneself."[17] This definition rests on the assumption that those who wear the mask know its meaning and use it intentionally. In Brecht's concept of "menschliche Geltung" (human validation), the mask is neither chosen nor controlled by the wearer. Nor can the wearer directly perceive the mask; the wearer can only decipher the mask's meaning by interpreting the reactions of others. This maintains an arbitrariness that makes a coherent identity impossible. Brecht's concept of the mask invalidates individual subjectivity because in his concept of social space as inner circle, participants make mutual observation possible and social negotiation essential.

This is how Bogderkahn develops validity within the play: when others mistakenly credit him with killing the tigers and the robber found dead outside his tent, Bogderkahn accepts their belief that he is a great shepherd because he perceives himself retrospectively through the responses of others. He has no coherent identity to defend because, as Brecht suggests, what we think of as "identity" is *nichts* (nothing). Instead, "the subject" emerges into a role through interactive behavior and social signification. For Bogderkahn, the transformation of nothing into something depends on a market. As long as he meets demand, Bogderkahn rises to become "something." When he satisfies others' demands, their satisfaction makes him feel successful, leading him to become fearless and then negligent. Bogderkahn finally falls back into nothingness because he loses the social source of his human standing.

From the perspective of the philosopher for whom the actors perform, the process of human validation depends on masking, which the thinker considers the primary task of the performer: "Zunächst passen seine Bewegungen zu ihm, aber nicht zu der Maske. Er selber aber ist nicht. Bald seht ihr seine Bewegungen so werden, daß sie zu der Maske passen. So entsteht er" (10.1:716) (At first his movements suit him, but not the mask. But he himself is not. Soon you see his movements become so that they suit the mask. Thus, he emerges). Pavis writes that by denaturalizing the character, the mask introduces a foreign body into the spectator's sense of identification with the actor on stage.[18] By performing movements that fit the initially unknown mask, the Brechtian actor's behavior precedes her or his identification. The mask that triggers a reaction from those who see it represents the causality imposed on the subject by history. By changing her movements to accord with those demanded by the mask, the actor physically partici- pates in her human standing. By denying the wearer prior knowledge of the mask, Brecht disrupts the process of identification for the wearer herself. The psychological process of identification that is conventional for the bourgeois subject is replaced by a process of role-assumption within a social economy.

The gain and loss of human validation create Brecht's ever-changing social economies. These changes produce history and transform theory. From the perspective of social economy, we see how a theatrical fragment inserts itself into the middle of a philosophical sentence in order to demonstrate how the word *werden* (to become) between the two states of *Nichts* (nothing) can be experienced. Once released into process, *"Nichts"* (nothing) loses its identity and, in reference to Brecht's studies on dialec- tics, becomes its opposite, which is *Etwas* (something). The *"Etwas"* (something) is produced through acting, and the philosopher leaves the stage educated:

> Was ich weiß, ist, daß aus Staub Staub wird. Was ich aber gesehen habe, ist, daß dazwischen ein Körper ist, also höre ich den Staub zum Staub sprechen: Wer bist du? Und der Staub antwortet dem Staub: Etwas ist gewesen mit mir, vor ich Staub wurde. (10.1:705–06)
>
> [What I know is that from dust dust comes. But what I have seen is that a body is in between, thus I hear the dust speak to the dust: Who are you? And the dust answers the dust: Something has been with me before I became dust.]

The citation offers a retrospective view of an unspecified event, an event that produces nothing but dust as the most impoverished substance in the long run and entirely eliminates any prescribed meaning. We do not learn what happened before dust became dust. Likewise, the question "Wer bist du?" (Who are you?) remains unanswered. The statement "etwas ist gewesen mit mir" (something has been with me) merely reinforces the fact that the transition to and from the state of *Etwas* (something) is a social event, as the preposition *mit* (with) suggests. The short, open form of the teaching plays combines with the reduced fable to allow each maxim and event to be acted out in different ways. By presenting the insertion of the human body into knowledge, Brechtian theatre releases thought into circumstance and demonstrates the social modification of theory. Theoretical convictions in human life are conflictual, and knowledge is insecure and changing. Here, the concept of human validation becomes essential because it allows the redistribution of knowledge to be combined with a sharing of history.

In the framing narrative of *Aus Nichts wird Nichts (From Nothing Comes Nothing)*, the role of the consultant shifts. Whereas the Marxist-trained philosopher advises the actors in the beginning, in the end he compliments the actor playing Bogderkahn for presenting *Nichts* (nothing) not as a quantity, but as a quality: "Besonders gefiel mir, daß dein N i c h t s doch ein Mensch war, ein ganz bestimmtes Wesen mit Sonderzügen. Eine besondere einmalige Form des Nichts" (10.1:715) (It especially pleased me that your n o t h i n g was still a man, a quite specific being with special qualities. A particularly unique form of nothing). "Ein Mensch" (A man), as "eine besondere einmalige Form des Nichts" (a particularly unique form of nothing), is left unspecified. The thinker cannot describe the special qualities he sees on the stage. They can only be acted out by the collective in the process of human validation.

This uniquely theatrical form of nothingness signifies not only a distinction from others, but also a temporary condition, because the content of distinction is momentary and contingent. Brecht's notes on dialectics, which he wrote at roughly the same time as he composed this fragment, indicate that *Nichts* (nothing) and *Etwas* (something) should not be understood as opposites, but as qualities that signify changes in the process of human validation:

> Ist mein Denken so unsicher, vage und unvollständig, so ist es auch meine Existenz. Es stellt sich heraus, daß dieses »Ich-bin« nichts besonders Gleichbleibendes ist, das nur ein anderes kennt, nämlich das »Ich-bin-nicht«, sondern eine unaufhörliche Aufeinanderfolge von Mehroderwenigersein. (21:425)

[If my thinking is thus uncertain, vague and incomplete, so is my existence. It turns out that this "I-am" is nothing especially unchanging which knows only one other, namely that "I-am-not," but a neverending succession of being more or less.]

For Brecht, existence is not an essence. He replaces the existential question of "to be or not to be" with an economy of how to be either more or less in interaction with others. The self-affirmative "ich bin" (I am) becomes a social and mimetic "sein wie" (to be like) that can only be derived from the conduct of others. The teaching plays produce the necessary social space for participants to derive their actions from a social constellation and economy. In Brecht's teaching plays, experience is replaced by a mimetic activity in which the subjectivist injunction to "know thyself" is moved from the realm of psychology to that of acting and perception. As a result, no conclusions can be drawn from the play except for the original maxim "aus nichts wird nichts" (from nothing comes nothing), but that maxim has a more social meaning now than it did when it was first enunciated. Knowledge is just as dependent on human validation as is subjective agency. The poverty of experience that Benjamin diagnoses as a condition of the twentieth century, and which seems to be the raw material for this fragment, gains validity in Brecht's concept of the teaching plays.

EINVERSTÄNDNIS: CONSENT IN CRISIS

Brecht's teaching plays begin where *Aus Nichts wird Nichts (From Nothing Comes Nothing)* ends. They examine the challenge and the endurance of human standing. As theatrical experiments for a new society, the teaching plays seek human standing as it would exist according to social laws of supply and demand rather than as it does exist under market capitalism. These laws must be constantly reexamined, for, as we have seen, human standing remains unverified by experience—at least in the twentieth century. In addition to social confrontation, the teaching plays confront human standing with the theory, or *Lehre* (teaching; lesson), of Marxism, and it is the contradictions and violence of these confrontations that are performed on stage in the teaching plays.

Although the teaching plays have been repeatedly read as offering ideological instructions on how to achieve the goal of communism, Brecht actually brings pedagogy to a literal dead end when he describes the teaching plays as "Sterbelehre" (teaching of death), as learning by facing death. In the *Badener Lehrstück vom Einverständnis (Baden-Baden Lesson on Consent)*, Brecht presents the reeducation through which qualified individuals become members of a collective. When the victims of a plane crash ask the chorus for help and it demands in return, "Sagt uns, wer ihr seid" (3:28) (Tell us who you are), they cannot answer. The airmen have forgotten both their names and their faces in the process of technological achievement. Eventually, they arrive at the answer: "Wir wollen nicht sterben" (3:28) (We do not want to die). The death they fear is social rather than biological, as shown when the pilot, who refuses to become a member of the collective, must leave the stage because his face proves unrecognizable to the others. The mechanics learn this lesson: social recognition defies death, while social exclusion secures it. This is reinforced when the mechanics respond to pictures of dead bodies by saying, "Wir können nicht sterben" (We cannot die), and the chorus answers them, "Sterbt, aber lernt / Lernt, aber lernt nicht falsch" (3:37) (Die, but learn / Learn, but do not learn wrongly).

What, though, is "lernt falsch" (learn wrongly)? Wrong learning is asocial learning. Once this warning has been issued, the mechanics learn only by facing the chorus, which demands consent and social learning above all. As "der Grosse Chor" (the Great Chorus) in *Der Jasager. Der Neinsager (He Said Yes. He Said No)* asserts:

> Wichtig zu lernen vor allem ist Einverständnis
> Viele sagen ja, und doch ist da kein Einverständnis
> Viele werden nicht gefragt, und viele
> Sind einverstanden mit Falschem. Darum:
> Wichtig zu lernen vor allem ist Einverständnis. (3:49)
>
> [Important to learn above all is consent
> Many say yes, and yet there is no consent
> Many are not asked, and many
> Consent to something false. Therefore:
> Important to learn above all is consent.]

Einverständnis translates into English as both agreement and consent, but it also includes consensus, understanding, comprehension, appreciation, and sympathy. The passage above begins with a maxim followed by three different failures; the maxim is restated in the end. Brecht's teaching plays and fragments all demonstrate various failures of consent (and thus of comprehension). They play out false learning.

As the *Badener Lehrstück (Baden-Baden Lesson)* demonstrates, *Einverständnis* (consent) flows from active communication. Brecht does not demonstrate understanding or reasoning as individual intellectual achievements, but as the result of a collective effort to confront a common problem. *Einverständnis* (consent) emerges as an answer developed by participants, and "Ich bin einverstanden" (I consent; I agree; I am in agreement) becomes the rational confirmation of human standing. Each participant accepts the role assigned by the collective. Brecht writes, "»Ich« bin keine Person. . . . Ich entstehe in Form einer Antwort" (21:404) ("I" am not a person. . . . I emerge in the form of an answer). The question that one's existence answers can only be asked by others, and *Einverständnis* (consent) is the subject's acceptance of this collective decision, but the need for collective discipline also shows how contradictory *Einverständnis* (consent) can be. Brecht himself writes, "Einverstanden sein heißt auch immer nicht einverstanden sein" (21:357) (To be in agreement also always means not to be in agreement), reminding us that consent always contains dissent.

Whereas *Einverständnis* (consent) in the *Badener Lehrstück (Baden-Baden Lesson)* is presented as the successful conclusion of a teaching/learning process, Brecht examines how consent can produce resistance and disagreement in *Der Jasager. Der Neinsager (He Said Yes. He Said No)* and in *Die Maßnahme (The Measures Taken)*. *Die Maßnahme (The Measures Taken)* presents a conscious revocation of *Einverständnis* (consent), while *Der Jasager. Der Neinsager (He Said Yes. He Said No)* demonstrates the contingency of *Einverständnis* (consent) as situations change. Scholars have explored *Einverständnis* (consent) in terms of "consensus" as an indicator of agreement with ideological arguments or practices. Reading *Einverständnis* (consent) as a development of human standing, however, shifts the focus from the existence of agreement to the dynamics and implications of consent as social action. When read in this light, *Einverständnis* (consent) not only structures a particular teaching play, it serves as a major point of interreferentiality among all the plays examined here, though of course it plays a different role in different texts. The *Badener Lehrstück (Baden-Baden Lesson)* focuses on the changing position of the subject, unlike the *Der Jasager. Der Neinsager (He Said Yes. He Said No)* complex in which the sequence of the three plays explores changes in the boy's agreement.[19] In the first version of *Der Jasager (He Said Yes)*, the boy agrees to die in keeping with the old custom; his motivation is emotional. In the second version, he makes the same choice but bases his agreement on reason. The boy's reason for joining the research trip in the second version also differs from that of the first. In the second version, the teacher seeks medical advice in order to stop an epidemic that affects the entire town, and the boy asks to be killed rather than left behind when the three students prove unable to carry him. In *Der Neinsager (He Said No)*, the object of agreement changes. The boy and the students resolve to change the old custom, showing that each individual situation requires a renegotiation of agreement.[20]

In *Die Maßnahme (The Measures Taken)*, originally intended as a sequel to the *Der Jasager. Der Neinsager (He Said Yes. He Said No)* complex, Brecht again shifts the lesson of the agreement. Four Soviet agitators prepare a revolution in China. To do their subversive work, they must consent to the maxims of the Communist Party and to the erasure of their faces. The play then demonstrates how a young comrade retracts his consent by continually reverting to his subjective perception of the situations in which he finds himself. Ultimately, he revokes his *Einverständnis* (consent), creates an emergency, and is finally forced to agree to his execution. The comrade's consent elicits the chorus's assertion that he has consented not to his own value system, but to historical reality. The *Lehre* (lesson; teaching) that these teaching plays produce consists of *Einverständnis* (consent) as rational confirmation of the social production of experience.

The boy in *Der Jasager. Der Neinsager (He Said Yes. He Said No)* is praised by his mother and his teacher for his *Einverständnis* (consent) when they declare in one voice, "Viele sind einverstanden mit Falschem, aber er / Ist nicht einverstanden mit der Krankheit, sondern / Daß die Krankheit geheilt wird" (3:68) (Many consent to something false, but he / Does not consent to the sickness, but / That the sickness gets cured), thus declaring their agreement with the boy and with each other's perception of him. The consent here is already contradictory, containing Brecht's "nicht/sondern" (not/but) and signifying that consent follows from dissent. The boy's consent to curing the disease proves meaningless when his own situation changes and he himself falls ill, thus canceling the trip across the mountains and necessitating a return home. The lesson that the boy enunciates at the end of *Der Neinsager (He Said No)*—"in jeder neuen Lage neu nachzudenken" (3:71) (in every new situation to think anew)—confronts *Einverständnis* (consent) as a static entity and keeps it from developing into a rule or a law.

Every new situation requires a renegotiation of *Einverständnis* (consent), which can only take place in response to a reenactment of human standing. The social constellation of a group or unit changes with every new argument, and each argument is enunciated both in a clearly defined constellation of boy-teacher or mother-teacher and in the separate spaces of room one or two. What Brecht calls "Kräftefeld der widersprechenden Interessen" (21:512) (field of forces of contradictory interests) in his *Dreigroschenprozeß (Threepenny Trial)* is here clearly acted out by a literal change of positions, presented in slow motion, that mirrors the rational argument performed in the utterances that follow the pace of each body. Agreement, then, is the result of varying positions taken by different actors in a socially defined field (what Brecht calls *Interessenstellung* [position of interest]), and change is immediately signified within that field by the movement of the participants.

Asserting a position is demonstrated in *Der Jasager. Der Neinsager (He Said Yes. He Said No)* not only spatially, but also mentally and socially. From the beginning of the play, the boy violates established custom. First, he asks to join a journey from which children are traditionally excluded. Second, he falls ill and demands to be brought back to his mother rather than agreeing to be killed by his fellow travelers. The boy calls upon his intellect to formulate these innovative demands but only gains *Einverständnis* (consent) when his demands spur direct negotiation with his mother or his teacher. He can only change the custom once he is in the mountains—through additional human standing. While the boy, the teacher, and the students form a unit as travelers, the three students who seek to preserve the custom adopt a state of permanent human standing by staying together all of the time *"mit den Gesichtern gegeneinander"* (3:70) *(with faces toward each other)*, thus creating an inner circle by excluding the outside world. This positioning reassures them of each other's presence, and separates them from the outside world, thus intentionally limiting their comprehension by imposing a communal boundary on each individual imagination.

Upon observing the boy's inability to travel, the three students establish the social control that confronts the boy with his physical shortcomings. When the three students ask, "Bist du krank vom Steigen?" (Are you sick from climbing?), the boy answers:

Nein.
Ihr seht, ich stehe doch.
Würde ich mich nicht setzen
Wenn ich krank wäre?
Pause. Der Knabe setzt sich.
DIE DREI STUDENTEN. Wir wollen es dem Lehrer sagen. (3:70)

[No.
You see, I am still standing.
Would I not sit down
If I were sick?
Pause. The boy sits down.
THE THREE STUDENTS. We want to tell the teacher.]

The three students know more about the boy's condition than either the teacher or the boy himself. But the boy suggests the rationale that combines his logical thought with his physical gesture in a social context. He fails according to his own criterion, confirming to himself and everybody else that he is unable to continue the trip.

Brecht introduces this theatrical rationale only in *Der Neinsager (He Said No)*, the play in which the boy breaks with tradition by not consenting to his death. When the boy defends his "nein" (no) by insisting that his previous consent was mistaken, he argues, "Die Antwort, die ich gegeben habe, war falsch, aber eure Frage war falscher" (3:71) (The answer that I gave was wrong, but your question was more wrong). The boy roots his mistake in something more fundamental than individual error; it results from a flawed concept of *Einverständnis* (consent) in which one is asked to agree to something simply because it is traditional, but which is nevertheless wrong. His "nein" (no) creates the situation in which he, the teacher, and the students all encounter one another at the same time in order to discuss "overturning" the great custom.

In spite of all its traditional elements, the great custom promotes a direct encounter between everyone involved as the teacher explains to the boy:

Hör gut zu! Seit alters her besteht das Gesetz, daß der, welcher auf einer solchen Reise krank wurde, ins Tal hinabgeworfen werden muß. Er ist sofort tot. Aber der Brauch schreibt auch vor, daß man den, welcher krank wurde, befragt, ob man umkehren soll seinetwegen. Und der Brauch schreibt auch vor, daß der, welcher krank wurde, antwortet: Ihr sollt nicht umkehren. Wenn ich deine Stelle einnehmen könnte, wie gern würde ich sterben! (3:71)

[Listen well! Since ancient times there is the law that the one who becomes sick on such a journey must be thrown down into the valley. He is instantly dead. But the custom also prescribes that one ask the one who became sick whether one should turn back for his sake. And the custom also prescribes that the one who became sick answers: You should not turn back. If I could take your place, how gladly I would die!]

Here, we see the breakdown of representation in the face of death. The teacher cannot simultaneously assume the boy's position and maintain belief in the traditional rationale of the trip; thus, the conflict can be neither released into representation nor pacified by it. In his *Dreigroschenprozeß (Threepenny Trial)*, Brecht rejects representation as a political principle; in his concept of theatre, he rejects representation as a dramatic principle. Teaching in the face of death, then, refers to a teaching without representation, just as the social change that Brecht envisioned made representation superfluous. The teacher enunciates the law and issues directions on how it is to be acted out on both sides—that of the victim and of the enforcer. By demanding direct questions and answers, the custom invalidates personal representation, which demonstrates the cruelty of the power dynamics involved when law is translated into human action. This becomes obvious to all when they have to tell the boy directly that they are determined to kill him. By acting out the interrogation as required by the great custom, Brecht roots the subversion of tradition in the custom itself, for it is the effacement of individual identity in favor of role playing by everyone involved that reveals the brutality of the tradition to everyone. Only then is it rejected.

Although Brecht seeks to establish the social unit as the basis for all political change, the play demonstrates that applying progress to a social body can result in regressive politics. As a unit the three students are more intent on preserving the custom than are the authorities charged with enforcing it. The teacher mediates between the boy and the students by teaching them about conduct in public, and he accepts their collective decisions. After listening to the boy's argument that one should rethink convention in each new situation, the students find his suggestion reasonable, though not heroic. When the teacher warns the students that breaking the custom might bring them ridicule and shame, the students ask, "Ist es keine Schande, daß er für sich selber spricht?" (Is it no shame that he speaks for himself?). The teacher responds, "Nein, darin sehe ich keine Schande" (3:72) (No, I see no shame in that). By having the boy speak for himself, Brecht presents what he demands in the *Dreigroschenprozeß (Threepenny Trial)* as essential to any sociological experiment: The boy defends his self-interest in order to survive in a space of opposing interests. In so doing, the boy demonstrates the flaws of the old custom.

By speaking for himself and defending his own interest, the boy establishes his situation as new and unprecedented, and thus outside the purview of the old custom. The boy claims a new custom for himself: "Ich brauche vielmehr einen neuen großen Brauch, den wir sofort einführen

müssen, nämlich den Brauch, in jeder neuen Lage neu nachzudenken"
(3:71) (I need rather a new great custom that we must introduce immediately, namely the custom in every new situation to think anew). Though
physically weak, he becomes the center of the group when the three students brave laughter and humiliation to carry him back home. Aware that
their conviction is not shared by the public, they move "Entgegen dem
Gelächter, mit geschlossenen Augen" (3:72) (Against the laughter with
closed eyes), and they exclude themselves from the public, remaining separated from the crowd. The boy's rescue becomes a progressive act because
he egoistically demands the solidarity of the other students. He does not
ask to be left behind or brought back by only one of the others; he insists
that the whole group stay together, and the group performs the newly
founded custom through physical solidarity. They walk side by side,
forming a conspiratorial clique through which they demonstrate a unity
of reason and habit. The cruel procedure of seeking consent in direct confrontation in *Der Jasager. Der Neinsager (He Said Yes. He Said No)* can produce progress out of a traditional custom, indicating that *Einverständnis*
(consent) can be a social vehicle for the renewal of human standing.

SUBJECT BOUND/THOUGHT UNBOUND

> Given that the body must react and adapt to all the demands made by the
> mind, and to those demands only, it is first of all necessary to train the actor's
> mind to construct demands.
> —Franco Ruffini, "Stanislavski's System"

Brecht's teaching plays employ a mode of comprehension that is "lehrhaft
für die Darstellenden" (instructive for the performers), and they are
intended for a redistributive theatre defined as a space and situation in
which any participant may become an actor. Within this space, thought,
which remains inert so long as it is trapped within an individual mind, is
released into social interaction and thus permitted to come to life. The
need to free thought through social interaction constitutes a core principle for training Brechtian actors. Therein lies the *Lehre* (lesson; teaching)
of Brecht's teaching plays: intellectual growth through physical action and
social interaction. Brecht himself extends this theatrical principle to a historical dimension that is also based on consent:

Das Gefühl, vom Anlaß getrennt, keineswegs mehr das empfundene
Einverständnis mit der betreffenden Wirklichkeitsphase, nimmt eine

Eigenentwicklung, und ohne weiteren Stoff zu benötigen, wächst ins
Ungemessene, einzig von der Phantasie genährt. So werden die Gefühle
zu geflissentlichen Mißverständnissen, sind nicht von der Einigung mit
der Wirklichkeit erzeugt, sondern erzeugen Veruneinigung mit ihr.
Richtig ist es, sogleich dem Gefühl die bemessene Haltung zu stellen,
das gegebene und zu findende Wort, die es weitergebende Geste und es
so, im Zusammengehen mit der sich doch ändernden Wirklichkeit, in
seine Abfolgen zu verwandeln: welche Maßnahmen eine Kunst sind wie
die Musik und ebenso lehrbar. (21:406)

[The feeling, separated from the cause, in no way anymore the felt (conscious) consent to the relevant phase of reality, takes a development of
its own and, without needing further material, grows into the unmea-
sured, nourished solely by the imagination. Feelings thus become intentional misunderstandings, are not produced from the agreement with
reality, but produce disagreement with it. It is right to present at once
the feeling with the measured disposition, the given and to-be-found
word, the gesture that carries it farther and thus, accompanied by the
reality yet changing itself, to transform it into its successions: which
measures are an art like music and just as teachable.]

This direct critique of bourgeois subjectivity is formulated out of the
poetics of the teaching plays. Brecht also directly attacks subjectivist ethics
that have been seen since Lessing as an emotional response independent
of the outside world, which defines self-reference or identification. Here,
Brecht's concept of the teaching plays is at its most disturbing: after all,
emotional self-reference allows the individual to stay clean by seeing her-
or himself as superior to real life, which is never "as it should be." To separate one's emotions from the event that initially evoked them is to maintain individual integrity. Brecht's concept of revolution attacks integrity
because, as an internalized and essentialized condition, it cannot be contained in the spatial and temporal limitations that are essential for Brecht's
concepts of action and perception. Individual understanding is misunderstanding because it ignores the "no" of others that constitutes reality.
The refusal of *Einverständnis* (consent) separates emotional commitment
from its initial situation, thus creating misunderstanding. By translating
each thought and emotion into a gesture, Brecht uses the body to limit
thought to the here and now.

Die Maßnahme (The Measures Taken) demonstrates the confusion of
the here and now when the young agitator falls into *Veruneinigung* (disunity; disagreement) with the rest of the collective and with "reality"
itself, thereby endangering the revolution, and is killed. From the begin-

ning of the play, the young comrade represents an emotional commitment to the revolution when he proclaims, "Mein Herz schlägt für die
Revolution. Der Anblick des Unrechts trieb mich in die Reihen der
Kämpfer. Ich bin für die Freiheit. Ich glaube an die Menschheit" (3:75)
(My heart beats for the revolution. The sight of injustice drove me into
the ranks of the fighters. I am for freedom. I believe in humanity). Moral
and emotional integrity, rather than historical necessity, fuels his commitment to communism. He expresses his attachment to communism in
the present tense but uses the past tense to describe the initial experience
that triggered those feelings. By the end of the play, we learn that it is the
comrade's "Empörung über das Unrecht" (indignation over injustice) that
makes him reveal the subversive activity of the collective. This leads to the
Maßnahme (measure).

Brechtian *Einverständnis* (consent; agreement) has less to do with consensus than with perception and negotiated understandings of reality in
the moment of its occurrence. *Einverständnis* (consent; agreement) in that
moment is *verstehen* (to understand), the comprehension of reality and the
commitment to change it by acting as part of this reality. Agreement, on
the other hand, primarily refers to the perception of reality and the commitment to act as part of this reality without attempting to change it. This
is the merciless lesson that Brecht once summarized as such:

> Wir aber raten euch: seid
> Einverstanden. Denn so geschieht es
> Wie ihr hier saht, und nicht anders
> Flüchtet nicht. (10.1:498)

> [But we advise you: be
> In consent. Because it happens thus
> As you saw here, and not differently
> Do not flee.]

Staying is Brecht's imperative for any revolutionary participation. *Einverständnis* (consent) is close to Nietzsche's famous "Ja" (yes); it mirrors
Nietzsche's acceptance of the world as it is.[21] To leave an intolerable situation, whether physically or by allowing thought and emotions to alter
the experience by making it *anders* (different), undercuts any revolutionary possibility. The imperative to stay is made in the plural in German, suggesting that staying not only refers to a space or place, but also
to a social setting that consists of others. The imperative to stay in this

public sphere guarantees that events will be socially verified. Verification, then, is another form of *Einverständnis* (consent) because the communal judgment that something happened "nicht anders" (not differently) is bought through consensus. In *Die Maßnahme (The Measures Taken)*, the three agitators choose to stay at the scene of the crime, which is the crime of exploitation. To stay they must pretend to support exploitation and maintain their masks by participating in it. The young comrade cannot accept this. He distances himself from the horror he encounters in order to save his individual integrity by honoring his earlier emotional response to injustice.

The young comrade's refusal to consent causes his *Veruneinigung* (disunity; disagreement) with the agitators and creates the crisis. The agitators' decision to kill the young comrade does not result from his mistakes, but from his intentional abandonment of the collective. Revolutionary activity in Brecht rests on being and remaining part of the collective that is committed to the revolution precisely because collectivity opens the social space in which perception and understanding can take place. The collective thus provides the foundation for the simultaneous interchange between thought and action that alone can transform society. By radically limiting the number of people comprising the collective, the space in which they interact, and the time in which they encounter the problems of revolution, the teaching plays confront all participants—actors and observers—with experimental situations that allow them to work through the barriers to true understanding, to *Einverständnis* (consent).

The fundamental split between the young comrade and the three agitators is not ideological, but social. The three agitators draw their rationale from the collective, while the young comrade employs his own value system. This becomes obvious when, during their first encounter, the young comrade asks for goods and technology to promote the revolution, while the agitators transfer material problems into social ones: "Wir hatten kein Brot für den Hungrigen, sondern nur Wissen für den Unwissenden, darum sprachen wir von dem Urgrund des Elends, merzten das Elend nicht aus, sondern sprachen von der Ausmerzung des Urgrunds" (3:79) (We had no bread for the hungry, but only knowledge for the unknowing, therefore we spoke of the source of the misery, did not eradicate the misery, but spoke of the eradication of the source). The agitators' response to despair is basically a teaching play within *Die Maßnahme (The Measures Taken)* that examines the question of what to do when poverty makes charity impossible. The agitators recognize that this poverty can only be addressed through disciplined collective action. The young comrade cannot resist helping the coolies fight their exploitation, but this compassionate action fails on two separate counts: it neglects to engage the coolies in a productive teaching situation because it allows the comrade to place himself above them, and it endangers the collective by provoking suspicion from the coolies' superiors.

Political action must be rooted in social reality, a point Brecht presents when the young comrade and the agitators discuss the workings of the Communist Party and ask, "Wer aber ist die Partei?" (But who is the Party?). The young comrade still thinks of the Party as a public institution, but the three agitators define party as a strictly social entity:

> Wir sind sie.
> Du und ich und ihr—wir alle.
> In deinem Anzug steckt sie, Genosse, und denkt in deinem Kopf . . .
>   (3:119)

> [We are.
> You and I and all of you—all of us.
> It sticks in your suit, comrade, and thinks in your head . . .]

In the play the Communist Party is not the representative organ of communists or communist ideology, but the result of social unity based both on human standing that is achieved by accepting and fulfilling a role assigned by others, and on *Einverständnis* (consent), or the collective agreement to and understanding of a given situation. The party does not represent a utopian model of administrative control and mindless activism, but a social constellation that changes with each interaction among its members.

> Zeige uns den Weg, den wir gehen sollen, und wir
> Werden ihn gehen wie du, aber
> Gehe nicht ohne uns den richtigen Weg
> Ohne uns ist er
> Der falscheste.
> Trenne dich nicht von uns! (3:119–20)

> [Show us the way that we should go, and we
> Will follow it like you, but
> Do not go the right way without us
> Without us it is
> The falsest.
> Do not separate yourself from us!]

The problem here is not that the young comrade is mistaken, but that he is about to leave the collective to pursue his insight individually. In leaving he withdraws from the collective commitment and transforms what should be a collective political act into an individual moral decision. The comrade's moral integrity is intertwined with his perception of the historical situation: "Mit meinen zwei Augen sehe ich, daß das Elend nicht warten kann" (3:120) (With my two eyes, I see that the misery cannot wait). The overwhelming misery of the coolies fuels his desire for immediate relief even at the cost of genuine improvement: "denn der Mensch, der lebendige, brüllt, und sein Elend zerreißt alle Dämme der Lehre. Darum mache ich jetzt die Aktion, jetzt und sofort; denn ich brülle und zerreiße die Dämme der Lehre" (3:119) (. . . because the man, the living one, bellows, and his misery bursts all dams of the teaching. Therefore, I do the action now, now and at once; because I bellow and I burst the dams of the teaching). The comrade seeks satisfaction based on his individual notion of moral integrity, an integrity that ignores the obstacles that would transform his rebellion into a disaster for the collective.

The young comrade revokes his *Einverständnis* (consent) and follows his individual perception of the situation. Like the boy in *Der Jasager. Der Neinsager (He Said Yes. He Said No)* who breaks with tradition by arguing rationally for his personal survival, the young comrade breaks ranks with the collective. The young comrade does so, however, without consultation and in response to the social misery around him. A chain of failures results from his impatience: he disrupts interaction between others in order to avoid pain when, for example, he prevents a coolie from slipping, or when he prevents the arrest of a striker. By striving to establish his own integrity and compassion, he keeps the exploitive system from revealing its worst horrors and thus provoking social revolution.

To promote change in the absence of agreement about the need for change, the young comrade relies on himself alone to represent those in misery: "Im Anblick des Kampfes verwerfe ich alles, was gestern noch galt, kündige alles Einverständnis mit allen, tue das allein Menschliche. Hier ist eine Aktion. Ich stelle mich an ihre Spitze" (3:93) (In sight of the struggle, I reject everything that was still valid yesterday, cancel all consent with everyone, do that which is alone human. Here is an action. I place myself at its head). The comrade ideologically represents the unemployed as he perceives their interests through the lens of his own compassion. The three agitators, in contrast, read the situation differently: "Die Wege zur Revolution zeigen sich. Unsere Verantwortung wird größer" (3:90) (The ways to the revolution reveal themselves. Our responsibility becomes greater). What the comrade perceives as intolerable misery that must be stopped immediately, the three agitators recognize as a component of revolution. The comrade creates a historical flaw by disrupting the social interaction that produces an understanding of the social crisis and thus leads to political progress.

For Brecht, the decoding of the present as history—especially when revolution emerges—is the opposite of the emotional commitment that motivates the young comrade. Participating in a revolution requires staying united with the condition that eventually leads to revolution—something that requires patience and endurance in the face of suffering. Patience and endurance are closely tied to fundamental concepts of Brechtian theatre: delay and disruption. Disruption can signify a single moment as historical and a single gesture as an action in History. Disruption creates a moment that can combine action with intellectual reflection.

Die Maßnahme (The Measures Taken) is a presentation of past events that grows out of delay and disruption. When the chorus voices its *Einverständnis* (consent) with the three agitators, they interrupt its congratulations with "Halt, wir müssen etwas sagen" (3:75) (Stop, we must say something). That initiates the agitators' recounting of the story and thus the play itself. The presentation in *Die Maßnahme (The Measures Taken)* begins when the three agitators follow the chorus's order to "Stellt dar, wie es geschah" (3:75) (Perform as it occurred). The interrogation asks for a demonstration of the "how" rather than a performance of the "what" because both the fable and the outcome are already known.

In the process of the play, the dialogic structure is explicitly interrupted when the chorus demands the presentation of the *Maßnahme* (measure), and the agitators opt for delay, saying "Wartet ab!" (3:95) (Wait!). By interrupting the chorus and delaying the narrative, the play provides the time and space for *gestus* to unfold. Brecht's concept of *gestus* is explained most clearly in his essay "Über reimlose Lyrik mit unregelmäßigen Rhythmen" (On Rhymeless Verse with Irregular Rhythms) in which he both justifies a concept of poetry that he developed while thinking constantly about the theatre and invents "gestisches Sprechen" (gestic speaking), which he describes as "die Sprache sollte ganz dem Gestus der sprechenden Person folgen" (22.1:359) (the language should entirely follow the *gestus* of the person speaking). The teaching plays assume a lyrical form without rhyme, and the dialogue in *Die Maßnahme (The Measures Taken)* adheres tightly to this form."" Brecht uses gestic language to open a different historical perspective that he describes as "die Darstellung gewisser Interferenzen, ungleichmäßiger Entwicklungen menschlicher Schicksale, des Hin-und-Her historischer Vorgänge, der »Zufälligkeiten«"

(22.2:1015) (the representation of certain interferences, disproportionate developments of human destinies, of the back and forth of historical events, of "coincidences"). *Gestus* is thus the signifier of contradictions in history: progress, regress, and the contingency between these two. The teaching plays provide a playing field upon which we can trace such historical changes in a small group of participants. Brecht seeks to limit our observation to the realm of our participation. The subject thus has to be bound to the collective—that is the first revolutionary step. Action and interaction are what make individual thought a common property. But thought and desire tied to the here and now create the delay of progress that causes the young comrade to break with the collective.

Delay and duration also help produce the brutality of the *Lehrstücke* (teaching plays). Brecht describes the tension between subjective time and duration, and the needs of the subject in his *Lehrgedicht (Teaching Poem)*:

> Wärme ists, was du brauchst, und Brot und schnell
> brauchst du's von allen Lehren der Welt nur die,
> wie du schnell bekommst, was
> dir mangelt.
> Und jetzt erfährst du als erstes:
> Verbanne zuerst die Schnelligkeit
> ganz aus dem Kopf!
> Wo die Not am größten ist, ist die Hilfe am fernsten.
> Ebenso kalt wie der Wind ist die Lehre ihm zu entgehen.
> (15:155)

> [It's warmth that you need, and bread and quickly
> you need it of all the lessons of the world only this,
> how you quickly get what
> you lack.
> And now you experience first of all:
> Banish foremost the velocity
> completely from the head!
> Where the need is greatest, the help is farthest.
> Just as cold as the wind is the teaching to escape it.]

Against the immediacy of physical needs stands instruction, which draws its knowledge from historical time. The brutality of this difference in time marks the experience that destroys the validity of ideology. This poem and the *Lehrstücke* (teaching plays) demonstrate the incompatibility of physical needs and an ideological project. For instance, when the mechanics in the *Badener Lehrstück (Baden-Baden Lesson)* declare at the moment of their death, "Wir haben nicht viel Zeit" (We do not have much time), the chorus responds "Habt ihr wenig Zeit / Habt ihr Zeit genug" (3:37) (If you have little time / You have time enough). The chorus speaks for the time of the historic process against subjective time.

A proper understanding of time is also what the comrade in *Die Maß- nahme (The Measures Taken)* lacks, for his betrayal of the revolution grows out of impatience. The comrade holds on to the principle of subjective time, believing that the end of his life is the end of the world: "Mit meinen zwei Augen sehe ich, daß das Elend nicht warten kann. Wie leicht, wenn wir nichts tun, verlaufen sie sich und gehen heim. Darum widersetze ich mich eurem Beschluß zu warten" (3:91) (With my two eyes, I see that the misery cannot wait. How easily, if we do nothing, they go astray and go home. Therefore, I disobey your resolve to wait). But subjective time stands in con- trast to the historical process once a clear historical telos is defined. The three agitators respond to the *Widersetzung* (disobedience) of the young comrade:

> Deine Revolution hört auf, wenn du aufhörst.
> Wenn du aufgehört hast
> Geht unsere Revolution weiter. (3:92)

> [Your revolution ceases when you cease.
> When you have ceased
> Our revolution goes on.]

Here, the three agitators explain their refusal to join the comrade's attempt to precipitate an early revolution, and they introduce a distinction between two revolutions—that of the comrade ("deine Revolution" [your revolu- tion]), and that of the party ("unsere Revolution" [our revolution])—a dis- tinction that prefigures the death sentence pronounced on the comrade. The comrade loses his *Haltung* (disposition) when he says, "ich . . . kündige alles Einverständnis mit allen, tue das allein Menschliche" (3:93) (I . . . cancel all consent with everyone, do that which is alone humane). With "das allein Menschliche" (that which is alone humane), he defends his identity as a comrade, which he feels should be equal to his identity as a human being when poised against the teleology of the revolutionary project. Upon ceasing to agree with the agitators, the comrade loses the *Haltung* (disposition) that granted him participation in the revolutionary process. With this loss, he fails to learn the lesson because *Haltung* (disposition) signifies duration: "Die

Haltung hält länger als die Handlungsweise: sie widersteht den Notwendigkeiten" (3:120) (The disposition lasts longer than the behavior: it resists the necessities). *Sterbelehre* (teaching of death) removes what Althusser calls "despotic time," or time without duration, from the revolutionary process.[23] Subjective time is no longer valid; *Haltung* (disposition) imprints duration onto the subject:

> Wenn ich mit dir rede
> Kalt und allgemein
> Mit den trockensten Wörtern
> Ohne dich anzublicken
> (Ich erkenne dich scheinbar nicht
> In deiner besonderen Artung und Schwierigkeit)
>
> So rede ich doch nur
> Wie die Wirklichkeit selber
> (Die nüchterne, durch deine besondere Artung unbestechliche
> Deiner Schwierigkeit überdrüssige)
> Die du mir nicht zu erkennen scheinst. (11:165)

> [When I talk with you
> Coldly and generally
> With the driest words
> Without looking at you
> (I seemingly do not recognize you
> In your particular nature and difficulty)
>
> So I thus only talk
> Like the reality itself
> (Sober, through your particular nature incorruptible
> Weary of your difficulty)
> That you seem to me not to recognize.]

This poem comments on the *Lehrstücke* (teaching plays) in several ways. The teaching plays' callousness results from a notion of subjectivity that dismisses individuality as idealist and fictional. Here again, subjectivity is released into intersubjectivity—note the dialogic structure of the poem. But this form of intersubjectivity, in the poem as well as in the *Lehrstücke* (teaching plays), is not a means to produce subjectivity: it rejects any form of subjective identification—the major force of bourgeois drama—and leaves the opposite as the other. The reality of this non-subjectivity must be constructed and made legible in the teaching plays.

Social literacy depends on human interaction, on being needed or being called upon and responding to this demand. Once subjective interpretations and wish fulfillments are disrupted, members of the social unit can decipher history—"die Wege zur Revolution zeigen sich" (the ways to the revolution show themselves):

> Die entscheidenden Vorgänge zwischen den Menschen, . . . finden in riesigen Kollektiven statt und sind vom Blickpunkt eines einzelnen Menschen aus nicht mehr darzustellen. Der einzelne Mensch unterliegt einer äußerst verwickelten Kausalität und kann Meister seines Schicksals nur als Mitglied eines riesigen und notgedrungen in sich selbst widerspruchsvollen Kollektivs werden. *Er registriert nur schwache, dämmrige Eindrücke von der Kausalität, die über ihn verhängt ist.* (23:41)

> [The decisive events between men, . . . take place in giant collectives and are from the point of view of an individual man no longer representable. The individual man succumbs to an extremely tangled causality and can become master of his fate only as a member of a giant and necessarily self-contradictory collective. *He registers only weak, dim impressions of the causality that is imposed upon him.*]

In this passage, Brecht outlines a crisis of modern theatre: its inability to represent the decision-making process among people in modern mass societies. According to Brecht, this inability is rooted in subjective perception, which registers only a dim impression of the causality that determines the life of individuals in mass societies. Individual perception cannot recognize the forces shaping an individual's life. This pessimism seems almost Kafkaesque insofar as the causalities that govern life become inexplicable and incomprehensible. The statement appears to contradict the optimism often associated with the power of cognition advocated by Brecht's epic theatre, but only if one ignores the difference between individual and social cognition. The individual turns out to be unequipped to comprehend her position within the huge collective of people. How, then, can the solitary and the social negotiate revolutionary thought? This is one of the driving questions of Brechtian theatre.

DEFACEMENT AND DEATH

Der Gestus der kommunistischen Trauer um einen Kommunisten ist ein ganz besonderer Gestus (22.1:331).

[The *gestus* of communist mourning over a communist is a very particular *gestus.*]

Discussions of the teaching plays, whether aesthetic or ideological, ultimately turn to the scenes in *Die Maßnahme (The Measures Taken)* when the
measure is taken and the young revolutionary submits to his own execution.
That this scene has become the focus of the entire teaching play discussion
is partially justified, for *Die Maßnahme (The Measures Taken)* indeed brings
to culmination important elements in the preceding teaching plays. For
example, the play begins by presenting the repetition of a specific historical
event, as in *Der Ozeanflug (The Flight over the Ocean)*. Further, the chorus
disciplines the performance and gives voice to ideology, as in both *Der
Ozeanflug (The Flight over the Ocean)* and the *Badener Lehrstück (Baden-
Baden Lesson)*. Unlike these two works, however, *Die Maßnahme (The Measures Taken)* is not concerned with survival (at least not at first glance), but
with the act of killing, as in *Der Jasager. Der Neinsager (He Said Yes. He Said
No)*. The brutality of the killing is emphasized in both plays through the
demand of *Einverständnis* (consent), an imperative that makes the barbarism of the act highly conscious, public, and consensual.

In *Die Maßnahme (The Measures Taken)*, death results from the confusion between human standing and *Einverständnis* (consent), a confusion that coincides with the "Verwirrung der Lehre" (confusion of the
teaching) that makes the measures taken a necessity. The confusion occurs
during the unmasking of the comrade, and it is worth remembering that
his killing is not intended as punishment. Instead, death is the imposition
of another disguise designed to throw off those who have targeted the
comrade and the collective following the tearing off of the mask. Brecht
also explores the cruelty inherent in unveiling the face as a disruption of
human standing, which complicates the question of *Einverständnis* (consent). Here, *Die Maßnahme (The Measures Taken)* extends the examination of modern subjectivity present in the other teaching plays by prob-
lematizing the theatrical and social implications of the face. Critical
anthropology and performance theory describe the face as caught on the
border between an essentializing fetish of physiognomic interpretation
(window to the soul) and a functional notion of masking that permits a
critical investigation of human standing.[24] The killing takes place in an
emergency that results from the young comrade's decision to destroy his
mask and make himself identifiable.

By removing the mask, the comrade seeks to reverse the *Auslöschung*
(erasure) that was the initial revolutionary act which united him and the
three agitators in one collective. *Auslöschung* (erasure) includes erasure,
giving up one's name, and masking the face, which then becomes masked
as one of the "leere Blätter, auf welche die Revolution ihre Anweisung

schreibt" (3:78) (empty pages on which the revolution writes its instruc-tion). This famous citation has been read as evidence of Brecht's Stalinist commitment. But if we remember Brecht's concept of the mask as a sig-nifier of human standing, where knowledge can only be deciphered by interpreting the behavior of others, it becomes clear that the revolution-ary instructions of the mask must be performed before they can be read. Each person who accepts the revolution's instructions can decode them only by observing the behavior of others toward her- or himself. Likewise, each person is responsible for behaving toward wearers of other masks in ways that permit them to decode the instructions written thereupon.

But the masks do not serve as sheets of paper for revolutionary instruction alone; they also hide the revolutionaries, introducing what Pavis calls a "foreign body" into society. The masked revolutionaries become Chinese "geboren von chinesischen Müttern, gelber Haut, sprechend in Schlaf und Fieber chinesich" (3:104) (born of Chinese mothers, yellow skin, speaking in sleep and fever Chinese). The masking shapes the revolutionaries' lives, enjoining them to accept the economic and political status quo. The numerous mistakes of the young comrade evolve out of this situation: from his initial argument that he cannot stay true to his disguise because he cannot keep himself from responding to Chinese injustice as a revolutionary from Moscow rather than as a coolie. He continues to make this mistake until the very end when he tears off his mask to reveal his true—that is, individual—passionate disagreement with existing social conditions. Revolution's instructions must contain some agreement with the world as it is as a precondition to the revolu-tionary change ahead.

In revoking *Einverständnis* (consent) when he tears off the mask that guides his interaction with the revolutionary collective, the comrade also revokes human standing:

> Ich sah zuviel.
> Darum trete ich vor sie hin
> Als der, der ich bin, und sage, was ist.
> *Er nimmt die Maske ab.*
> Wir sind gekommen, euch zu helfen
> Wir kommen aus Moskau.
> *Er zerreißt die Maske.* (3:93)

> [I saw too much.
> Therefore, I step before them

As the one who I am and say what is.
He takes the mask off.
We have come to help you
We come from Moscow.
He tears up the mask.]

The comrade seeks to reveal the man behind his mask. He intentionally separates from the collective to express his ultimate commitment to the Chinese people. What he achieves instead is isolation from them. The poor perceive him as an enemy because he deprives them of their sleep to explain to them their deprivation. Instead of creating solidarity with those he subjects to compassion, the comrade ends up isolated from and misunderstood by them. He thus deprives himself of the cultural solidarity that sustains the revolutionary project.

With the young comrade's unmasking, Brecht problematizes the status of the face as a guarantor of the social contract. The face can be recognized only when opposed by another face, as Emanuel Levinas has shown.[25] The young comrade unmasks in order to reveal his true face to the oppressed, but he ends up isolated and unrecognized by them. Only the determined act of the collective recognizes the young comrade's transformation, which, as we shall see, has nothing to do with recognizing his identity.

Und wir sahen hin, und in der Dämmerung
Sahen wir sein nacktes Gesicht
Menschlich, offen und arglos. Er hatte
Die Maske zerrissen. (3:93)

[And we looked, and in the twilight
We saw his naked face
Human, open and guileless. He had
Torn up the mask.]

What horrifies the other members of the collective is the unexpected nakedness of the face, a nakedness that cannot be veiled again. The destroyed mask cannot be replaced because it consisted of the genealogy of the revolutionary collective.

When Brecht applies nakedness and exposure to the face as the most public part of the body, it becomes what anthropologist Michael Taussig calls the face—a "public secret." Taussig perceives the face as a fetish in constant transit between the face as window to the soul and the face as mask: "Either of these functions—mask, or window to the soul—is a wonder; together they make an orgy of disproportion compounded by the fact that the face never exists alone; fated in its very being to be only when faced by another face."[26] In *Die Maßnahme (The Measures Taken)*, Brecht moves the question of face-as-fetish inside the collective, where the face is employed not as marker of identity, but rather as a cultural disguise and a tool for political education.

The face-as-fetish is the basis for any public situation, and in this situation "the face is the evidence that makes evidence possible."[27] Evidence, Brecht's paranoia that can be traced throughout his work from the early *Lesebuch für Städtebewohner (A Reader for Those Who Live in Cities)* on, is the enemy of subversion. The mask, as disguise and boundary, also veils the genealogy of the young comrade. Before the agitators ask the comrade for his *Einverständnis* (consent) to his own execution, they encounter an unexpected effect of the teaching: "Freilich das Gesicht, das unter der Maske hervorkam, war ein anderes, als das wir mit der Maske verdeckt hatten, und das Gesicht, das der Kalk verlöschen wird, anders, als das Gesicht, das uns einst an der Grenze begrüßte" (3:124) (Indeed, the face that emerged from under the mask was a different one from the one that we had covered up with the mask, and the face that the lime will wipe out different from the face that once greeted us at the border). The removal of the mask not only reveals the comrade's vulnerable face, it also brings up the memory of the face the mask once covered, a memory so vague that its validity can only be confirmed through the recognition of further changes in the face. Here, Brecht anticipates Taussig's descriptions of state-sponsored unmaskings of political opponents: "Hence unmasking leads . . . to a certain refacement, but hardly the face we once knew. Something new has emerged. A mystery has been reinvigorated, not dissipated, and this new face has the properties of an allegorical emblem, complete with its recent history of death and shock, which gives it this strange property of 'opening out.'"[28] Because the comrade's face cannot be unambiguously identified by those who know him, it becomes an emblem within a revolutionary allegory that remains, as we shall see, strictly negative.

Brecht presents the revolution as an allegory that leaves us in the dark not only about the participants, whom we know only as anonymous members of a chorus and as masked Russian revolutionaries who are simultaneously Chinese, but also about the revolution itself, for the description of the measures taken stop the narrative description of the revolution. Furthermore, we do not learn anything about the theory that the revolutionaries are supposed to teach. Scholars have noticed the almost complete absence of Marxist content in the teaching plays; *Die Maßnahme (The Measures Taken)* only refers to the "Lehre der Klassiker" (teaching of the classics) and the "ABC des Kommunismus" (ABCs of communism). One might conclude that Brecht leaves even the theory (Marxism) and history (the revolution) in disguise in order to avoid producing evidence.

But in draining participants, theory, and history of their individual content, Brecht creates an intimate interrelation among the three. When the comrade abandons the collective and destroys his mask, he simultaneously erases the revolution's theoretical writings. Whereas the collective demonstrates patience toward theory because theory is designed less to help in any single situation than to provide general revolutionary methods "welche das Elend in seiner Gänze erfassen" (3:118) (which grasp the misery in its totality), the comrade wishes not to comprehend misery, but to stop it in any manifestation. His shortcut between theory and practice follows the same path as the shortcut between the Chinese workers and himself—identification:

> Dann sind die Klassiker Dreck, und ich zerreiße sie; denn der Mensch, der lebendige, brüllt, und sein Elend zerreißt alle Dämme der Lehre. Darum mache ich jetzt die Aktion, jetzt und sofort; denn ich brülle und ich zerreiße die Dämme der Lehre. *Er zerreißt die Schriften.* (3:119)

> [Then the classics are rubbish, and I tear them up; because the man, the living one, bellows, and his misery bursts all dams of the teaching. Therefore, I do the action now, now and at once; because I bellow and I burst the dams of the teaching. *He tears up the writings.*]

The "Dämme der Lehre" (dams of the teaching), another imposed limitation well known from Brecht's teaching plays—from the limitation of space to the limitations of language and expression—can be read as another form of disguise. The allegorical constellation of humans, history, and theory prevents revolutionary potential from spinning out of balance due to an overload of theoretical information. The only assurance we gain from Brecht's *Lehrstücke* (teaching plays) are that these very "Dämme der Lehre" (dams of the teaching) will impose limits that will guarantee unity—the unity between participants, the unity between thought and action, the unity between self-perception and perception through others, and the unity of space and time. The mask ensures survival in illegality and shields the person who wears it both from the hostile status quo and from the contradictions between her or his own desires and the teaching. By destroying his disguise, the young comrade abandons the collective labor in order to achieve unity between himself, his convictions, and the historical situation around him. He seeks to become a conventionally "whole" person, and that desire must prove fatal—either to him or to the revolution.

Brecht's and Taussig's observations about refacement may be partially explained through traditions in the theatre that create a double effect of masking, an effect similar to Brecht's concept of human standing, which demands that "the face under the mask must act. Further, if one wants the mask to live, the face must take on the same expression as the mask."[29] Here, *Die Maßnahme (The Measures Taken)* pushes Brecht's concept of human standing further by invoking the physical and social transformation generated by wearing the mask. The subversive work begins when the faces of the revolutionaries are erased through the famous *Auslöschung* (erasure), an act dedicated to a single imperative: "Ihr dürft nicht gesehen werden" (3:104) (You may not be seen). Erasing their former identities leaves the revolutionaries without names or genealogies as "leere Blätter, auf welche die Revolution ihre Anweisung schreibt" (3:104) (empty pages on which the revolution writes its instruction). Note that it is not Marxist ideologues, but the revolution as an entity in itself that writes the instructions. Likewise, the revolutionaries are not transformed into mindless ideologues, but into Chinese workers by assuming a disguise that encompasses faces, language, and history:

DER LEITER DES PARTEIHAUSES *gibt ihnen Masken, sie setzen sie auf*: Dann seid ihr von dieser Stunde an nicht mehr Niemand, sondern von dieser Stunde an und wahrscheinlich bis zu eurem Verschwinden unbekannte Arbeiter, Kämpfer, Chinesen, geboren von chinesischen Müttern, gelber Haut, sprechend in Schlaf und Fieber chinesisch. (3:104)

[THE LEADER OF THE PARTY HOUSE *gives them masks, they put them on*: Then from this hour on you are no longer no one, but from this hour on and probably until your disappearance unknown workers, fighters, Chinese, born of Chinese mothers, yellow skin, speaking in sleep and fever Chinese.]

What the revolution's instructions demand is not that the agitators submit to a specific ideology, but that they become subsumed into the suppressed class of a different culture. The instructions cannot be read from the mask itself because they remain unknown until the revolutionaries participate in the lives and the social struggle of those their masks represent.

Besides becoming members of the suppressed group they seek to liberate, the revolutionaries must also remain members of the collective. *Die Maßnahme (The Measures Taken)* stays true to Brecht's concept of human standing in that the mask cannot be deciphered by the one who wears it, thus the wearer remains dependent on those who can read it. In *Die Maßnahme (The Measures Taken)*, the revolutionary instruction is the disguise, and revolutionary activity consists of participating in the lives of those who should be revolutionized. From this perspective, the young comrade does not opt out of the horror of ideology, but out of the horrors of oppressed lives. Brecht's concept of revolution combines the social and the theatrical in the maxim that to live in misery is to live in perfect disguise, a Brechtian lesson introduced in the final song in *Die Dreigroschenoper (The Threepenny Opera)*.

With the emphasis on the face in social situations, Brecht's teaching plays make an unexpected and precocious contribution to the discourse on mass media. Benjamin points out that one major element of the teaching plays, the *gestus*, is drawn from the visual techniques of film. Benjamin also cautions us, in midst of his celebration of film as a revolutionary art form, that film promotes the revival of physiognomy. The realist element promoted through technological enhancements such as the close-up reintroduces the prehistoric force of mimesis into the twentieth century. Facial close-ups allow readings of the face as an expression of the inner soul that then involves the audience in mimetic and identificatory activities. In *Die Maßnahme (The Measures Taken)*, Brecht leaves this reading of the face in the negative. The agitators resist a physiognomic reading of the young comrade's face. The comrade's masking and unmasking enable the agitators to recognize alteration and difference, but they do not offer a conclusive reading of his face.[30] From this perspective, human standing can be understood as an exercise in opposition to physiognomy. When history turns out to be the genealogy of the body, when thought becomes visible through disposition, and when social relations are less intentional than mimetic, however, we might need a practice that challenges the certainty of our readings.

The public announcement that initiates *Die Maßnahme (The Measures Taken)* is an announcement of death. Death, according to Benjamin, lends authority to narrative: "Der Tod ist die Sanktion von allem, was der Erzähler berichten kann. Vom Tode hat er seine Autorität geliehen. Mit anderen Worten: es ist die Naturgeschichte, auf welche seine Geschichten zurückverweisen" (Death is the sanction for everything that the storyteller can tell. He has borrowed his authority from death. In other words, his stories refer back to natural history).[31] Mentioning their comrade's death provides the authority necessary to stop the chorus, and reenacting the killing transforms the members of the chorus from *Urteilende* (judgers) into *Lernende* (learners) by demonstrating to them that they are aware of the fact but ignorant of the experience. Demonstrating the death disrupts the coherence of the historical narrative and permits the insertion of natural history that promotes learning in the play.

In *Die Maßnahme (The Measures Taken)*, Brecht inserts natural history into history. The young comrade's face, as one of the "leere Blätter, auf welche die Revolution ihre Anweisung schreibt" (empty pages on which the revolution writes its instruction) recurs in the annals of history as a scarred insertion that Brecht describes in a poem thus:

> Unrecht ist menschlich
> Menschlicher aber
> Kampf gegen Unrecht!
> Macht aber doch halt auch hier
> Vor dem Menschen, laßt ihn
> Unversehrt, den Getöteten
> Belehrt nichts mehr!
> Schabe nicht, Messer, ab
> Die Schrift mit der Unreinheit
> Du behältst
> Einzig ein leeres Blatt sonst
> Mit Narben bedeckt! (10.1:400)

> [Injustice is human
> But more human
> Fight against injustice!
> Do but also stop here
> Before the man, leave him
> Unharmed, the one killed
> Is taught by nothing anymore!
> Do not scrape off, knife,
> The writing with the impurity
> You retain
> Only an empty page otherwise
> Covered with scars!]

Here, *Menschlichkeit* (humanity) is juxtaposed to ideological teaching that can write its instructions only on the living body. The sheet that replaces subjectivity remains empty once a person is killed. What fills the sheet instead are scars that remain from the injured body. But the stanza that ends with the warning not to kill gives way to the following contradiction:

> Solch ein reinliches Blatt
> Narbenbedeckt, laßt uns
> Einfügen endlich dem Bericht von
> Der Menschheit! (10.1:400)

> [Such a clean page
> Scar-covered, let us
> Insert finally in the account of
> Humanity!]

The warning in the first stanza is followed by acceptance in the second. Successful teaching depends on consent, a consent repeatedly violated in the *Lehrstücke* (teaching plays) and reestablished only through death. But the sheet covered with scars also stands against baseless optimism and expectation. In *Die Maßnahme (The Measures Taken)*, the four agitators interrupt the report of the successful revolution to insert the execution of the comrade as the inescapable contradiction to ideological consent. Death and disappearance are performed by the four agitators, each of whom plays the comrade's role in turn, keeping the dead comrade constantly present as an unstable void.

Remembering, according to Walter Benjamin, has to do with death. The demonstration of the killing of the comrade and the destruction of his body are a re-presentation of the past. Brecht's theatrical technique of the *Wieder-holung* (bringing back) of death constructs a form of remembering. Benjamin distinguishes memory as *Gedächtnis* from remembering as *Erinnerung*, defining memory as conservative and remembering as destructive. Benjamin draws this definition from Marcel Proust's notion of *memoire involontaire* (involuntary memory), the notion upon which Adorno bases his concept of *Erfahrung* (experience) as "unwillkürliche Erinnerung" (involuntary remembering). Remembering is thus the construction of something new that remains outside the subject's control. In Brecht's theatre this occurs, for example, when Kragler is brought into the scene in *Trommeln in der Nacht (Drums in the Night)* by the citation of his name, and in *Die Maßnahme (The Measures Taken)* it happens when the past event becomes something new that emerges out of the play of the four agitators.

Brecht locates *Erfahrung* (experience), which results from the construction of an unpredictable history, in the space created by *Abstand* (distance), by the distance between *Historisierenden* (historicizer) and *His-
torisierter* (historicized), by the distance between actor and character, and
by *gestus* as the distance between signifier and signified. Brecht's theatre
inserts the past into the presentation of the present, and *Abstand* (distance) provides the space in which this insertion can take place.

Brecht's theatre also inserts the past into the present, and in doing so
it signifies the painful aspects of history. The insertion of revolutionary
barbarism into the historical account suggests a reading of the teaching
plays as works of mourning. Brecht writes, "Worüber ein Mensch in
Trauer verfällt und in was für eine Trauer, das zeigt seine Größe. Die
Trauer auf eine große Stufe zu heben, sie zu einer gesellschaftlichen nüt-
zlichen Sache zu machen, ist eine künstlerische Aufgabe" (21:403) (What
a man sinks into mourning about and into what kind of mourning, that
shows his greatness. To raise mourning to a high level, to make it a socially
useful thing, is an artistic task). The reduced form and the impoverished
content of the plays highlight the *gestus* as an elementary theatrical element. In the quotation above, Brecht introduces the *gestus* of mourning,
a gestus that he leaves unspecified, yet still privileges over others. According to what we know about *gestus*—it shows one person in relation to others and signifies thought as social—we can formulate a preliminary
understanding of Brecht's concept of mourning. Here again, Brecht inte-
grates the gestus into his concept of human standing when a person's
greatness is determined by the object of her or his mourning and by how
this mourning is carried out. To make the act of mourning useful for society is left to the arts. We may then conclude that Brecht considers the acting out of mourning to be a theatrical endeavor.

5

Brecht's Archaeology of Knowledge

We are rewriting all the history books about the ancient world because of the new political order in our own time.

—Fredrik T. Hiebert[1]

What enables us to rewrite history is not the changes in the past, but in the present. Walter Benjamin has taught us that every moment in the present quotes the past anew and, in so doing, creates a spectrum of diverse fragments of the past instead of a continuous chronology.[2] As recent discoveries in archaeology show, the fall of communism not only rewrites recent history, but also ancient history, a rewrite that might reveal different genealogies of civilization by uncovering the existence of people and cultures where previously "there was thought to be just space and emptiness."[3] History, then, depends on the time and place from which it emerges, a situation that suggests the simultaneous existence of a variety of histories that survive less as coherent narratives than as unfamiliar archaeological findings, findings that might suggest the prehistorical status of our own present.

"Archaeology" might be a productive term to describe Brecht's concepts of history and thought. Given Brecht's suspicion of canonized historical narratives, history as knowledge is confronted by the history enacted in a defined space in his works. History, then, is not the consistent product of chronology, but takes place as a social and theatrical event. The same is true for Brecht's concept of thought—any idea is prehistorical before being released into *Einverständnis* (consent), where it is confronted with rejection (the "nein" [no] of others). Comprehending thought becomes a social activity, and as such, it is as unpredictable as the historical process itself. Brecht's approach to history, which is predominantly theatrical in its reenactment of the past, also considers the past to be unpredictable and dependent on the present of performance.

In addition to extreme historical change, Brecht also considers the regression of history into nature or prehistory. He observed the transformation of history into nature in the moment when "progress" ignorantly celebrated its greatest triumphs in the form of World War I and the introduction of industrialized warfare: "Der gigantische Bau der Gesellschaft / . . . sinkt zurück in barbarische Vorzeit" (15:155) (The gigantic construct of society / . . . sinks back into barbaric prehistory).[4] Progress coexists with prehistoric barbarism, and Brecht's concept of revolution includes historical progress and regress. Brecht equates intellectual progress with social ignorance. As a result, we fall back into a barbaric state when our intellect does not comprehend the historical situation around us and our actions are unable to sustain us. Progress is a *fortschreiten* (to progress, to stride forward), a moving ahead from others that creates a disjunction between people or between the intellect and the body.

"Daß die Menschen leben müssen—nur dieser Umstand macht sie vernünftig" (21:568) (That men must live—only this fact makes them reasonable). This Brechtian insight combines barbaric prehistory with progressive thought, and Brecht's concept of revolution contains both. Brecht's early and teaching plays show that he is less interested in coherent narratives of past events or political progress than in various forms of adaptation to and survival of historical change. In the theatrical fragments and philosophical aphorisms examined in this chapter, Brecht develops a concept of revolution that goes far beyond the Marxist understanding of the word and includes the word's entire etymological complexity from the revolving changes in nature to ultimate social and political transformation.

No text from Brecht demonstrates the enormous possibilities and contradictions of this undertaking more than the *Fatzer* fragment. Written intermittently between 1926 and 1930 but never completed, *Fatzer* functions as a bridge between Brecht's early plays, especially *Trommeln in der Nacht (Drums in the Night)*, his teaching plays, and the philosophical reflections of the *Geschichten vom Herrn Keuner (Stories of Mr. Keuner)* and the *Buch der Wendungen (Book of Changes)*. Existential questions such as how to survive a war—whether by participation and transformation (as in *Trommeln (Drums)*, or by desertion and resistance (as in *Fatzer*)—are examined in teaching-play style while positioned in elaborate contexts (dialogues, songs, theoretical reflections) that are missing in the classic teaching plays. Heiner Müller, who created a stage version of the vast *Fatzer* material, calls the fragment a "Jahrhunderttext" (text of the century) in terms of poetic quality and textual density.[5] Müller convincingly applies the fragment's qualities to the historical range of experiences in Brecht's life, which extends from his first shocking experience of the fast-paced big city after World War I to the anticipation of a revolution in Germany to his final disillusionment in the face of rising German fascism. One might add that *Fatzer* incorporates much of the history of the twentieth century by starting out with World War I, anticipating fascism, and reflecting on industrialization from a postindustrial perspective. In sum, these events offer a pessimistic perspective on revolutionary change.

THE GENEALOGY OF TERROR

Der Prozeß, in dem Leben abstirbt, ist nicht der Zeitpunkt der Katastrophe. Leben kann Tod sein und noch eine Weile weitermachen.

[The process by which life expires is not the moment of the catastrophe. Life can be death and still carry on awhile.]

—Oskar Negt and Alexander Kluge

If there is any single emotion that has discredited revolution in Western culture, it is terror, which as *terreur* has dominated the memory of the French Revolution. Since then, terror has been used as the predominant standard of measure for the legitimization of revolutions and, especially, communist statehoods. Communists responded by pointing to established "bourgeois" terrors visited upon the working class: hunger, deprivation, and the internalization of power. Communist revolutions, in turn, have been discredited—even by those who applaud overthrowing property rights and class structures—for their destruction of entire cultures. Revolutionaries' demand for permanent cultural change extends terror beyond the moment of revolution and into the process of state formation. As a result, Stalinism and Maoism have always been identified with the perpetuation of terror.

Terror can be defined as the prolonging of fear for those who are subjected to it and the permanence of the threat for those who engage in it. The psychoanalytic assumption that terror is, in the end, fueled by our death drive has been enriched by Oskar Negt and Alexander Kluge, who apply Freud's principle of deferred action to the history of events in their book *Geschichte und Eigensinn (History and Obstinacy)*.[6] The terror of change becomes a signifier for the terrors of tradition, where death is carried over into historical experience. Revolution, which is conventionally considered to be fueled by awareness and will power, turns out to be a passage from civilization to nature. This could be considered a prehistoric moment—a moment Brecht examines in the *Fatzer* fragment.

In *Fatzer*, Brecht presents this historical zone as a prehistoric moment of political change—the original sin of revolution. As in *Trommeln in der Nacht (Drums in the Night)*, Brecht uses a familiar historical event to demonstrate this prehistory—here, the "aller Moral entblößten Zeit des ersten Weltkrieges" (10.1:469) (time, bereft of all morals, of the First World War)—in order to explore an unfamiliar and untold history of desertion and survival. The fragment's fable presents four men—Fatzer, Koch (later Keuner), Büsching, and Kaumann (later Leeb)—who desert from the German army during World War I and end up in the city of Mühlheim an der Ruhr, where they remain in hiding while struggling to secure the barest necessities such as water, food, and shelter. As the four men experience increasing deprivation and desperation, and finally resort to murder, the play investigates "die blutigen Spuren einer Art neuen Moral" (10.1:469) (the bloody traces of a kind of new morality) that can only be deciphered from the bloody traces they leave behind. Fatzer, Koch, Kaumann, and Büsching decide to stay together first as friends and later as a collective in order to ensure their own survival and promote a general uprising that, in their estimation, can alone end the war. Johann Fatzer, who convinces his friends to desert, ensures their downfall by preaching solidarity while practicing egoism. He promises discipline but instead sleeps with Therese Kaumann, his friend's wife; he promises adequate food but cuts off access to the food supply by fighting with a group of townspeople. In turn, his friends save themselves by pretending that they do not know Fatzer when he is about to be arrested. In the end, Koch, Kaumann, Büsching, and Therese reach the verdict that Fatzer must be killed for putting his own interests before those of the collective.

After four years of work, Brecht termed Fatzer *unaufführbar* (unperformable) and left it as a fragment (10.2:1118).[7] Brecht's reasons for considering the play unfit for the stage may lie in the extraordinary richness of the text: like the teaching plays, *Fatzer* examines collective discipline and death as disguises, but it pursues those explorations in a setting that includes immediate material contingencies that the teaching plays avoid such as subsistence, sexuality, and naked violence. Brecht subsumes these three topics under the comprehensive notion of *Furchtzentrum* (fear center) as a permanent disturbance, a disturbance that makes a smooth conclusion of the play as unlikely as smooth conclusions to people's lives. Besides incorporating elements of the early plays and the *Lehrstücke* (teaching plays), *Fatzer* also enacts the lessons of Brecht's most chilling poetry from the *Lesebuch für Städtebewohner (A Reader for Those Who Live in Cities)* in which he offers lines such as "Verwisch die Spuren" (Erase the traces) and "Du darfst nicht gewesen sein" (You are not permitted to have been) as intonations on how to retain anonymity. These poems' concern for loss and survival is loosely connected to the teaching plays—in fact, Brecht suggests these connections himself[8]—but in *Fatzer* these survival lessons gain more importance because here emergency and terror extend throughout the entire fragment.

In *Fatzer*, Brecht traces terror through a number of different settings. He begins with the concrete historical event of World War I, then moves to the fight against hunger and the use of organized terror to ensure discipline within the collective. This discipline ultimately ensures Fatzer's death sentence. Terror is shown to have been a product of World War I that turned its participants into different human beings, a process described by Fatzer, Büsching, and Koch simultaneously as:

> Schlachtschiffe, Flugzeuge und Kanonen
> Sind gegen uns gerichtet
> Die Mine und das Gelbkreuzgas
> Zu unserer Vernichtung, daß wir
> Vertilgt werden vom Erdboden
> Alles läuft gegen uns, arbeitet und
> Hält nicht an
> Unsere Mutter ist ein Tank und
> Kann uns nicht schützen
> Wir müssen
> Kaputtgehen (10.1:453)

> [Battleship, aircraft and cannon
> Are leveled against us
> The mine and the mustard gas
> For our annihilation, so that we
> Will be wiped off the face of the earth
> Everything runs against us, works and

> Does not stop
> Our mother is a tank and
> Cannot protect us
> We must
> Break down]

World War I's horrors serve as the point of departure for Fatzer, Koch, Büsching, and Kaumann, who conclude, as Walter Benjamin put it, that "der ›Ausnahmezustand‹, in dem wir leben, die Regel ist" (the "state of emergency" in which we live is not the exception but the rule) and that a commitment to survival constitutes preparing a revolution.[9] Moreover, they find themselves in a historical situation in which everything from enemy gas and land mines to their own weaponry works systematically toward their destruction. Fatzer recognizes from the start that the threat posed by the war is unstoppable for the time being. The men are reborn—already brutalized—in the midst of death through the tank as the quintessential war machine that nevertheless proves ill-equipped to protect them from destruction. The men represent a new twentieth-century species, a species created by the first fully industrialized warfare in human history, which was an experience that made all past experience meaningless. Reborn through a tank that renders them helpless, they come to represent the first "new" men with nothing at their disposal but their own fear of death and a primordial urge to survive.

Fatzer convinces his three friends to leave the terror of front-line combat "zu entgehen der Vernichtung" (10.1:453) (to escape the annihilation), an attempt that leads to another regime of terror that ultimately betrays them all. By deserting the war, the men find themselves in a crisis situation reminiscent of that in *Die Maßnahme (The Measures Taken)* (the so-called "äußerste Verfolgung" (extreme persecution) that culminates in the killing of the young comrade). In *Die Maßnahme (The Measures Taken)*, the chorus voices the revolutionary telos that both justifies the killing and then proceeds in an organized manner except for the disturbances created by the young comrade. In contrast, the rebellion in *Fatzer* has no political rationale and emerges entirely from the will to survive. Justification comes after the fact when the chorus and anti-chorus comment on what they observe of the collective. The two choruses voice opposite interpretations of the immediate action, thus creating a dialectical argument without ever reaching consensus or *Aufhebung* (abrogation).[10] The political lesson, then, relies entirely on human action, a cruel prospect when one is confronted by a man-made catastrophe from which escape is impossible because "überall / Ist der Mensch" (10.1:452) (every-where / Is man). The fragment ends with Koch's recognition of the neces-sity of the war, but this should not be read as an endorsement of the war as a step toward political progress. It is, instead, an acknowledgment of the human reality that Koch and his friends have found inescapable.

This recognition of the universal presence of humanity stands together with that of the universal need for subsistence: "Obdach und Wasser und Fleisch" (10.1:440) (Shelter and water and meat). The acqui-sition of these goods is complicated both by the circumstances in which the four men find themselves and by the historical situation, which proves incomprehensible. Fatzer outlines this incomprehensibility in three speeches: "Über die Abhängigkeit des Menschen von der Natur" (On the Dependence of Man Upon Nature) discusses constant human change, biological and social (10.1:399); "Über die Unbeurteilbarkeit men-schlicher Handlungen" (On the Unjudgeability of Human Actions) inval-idates individual causality in the face of perpetual changes in people and situations (10.1:438); and the "Rede vom Massemensch" (Speech on the Mass Man) replaces individual causality with mechanical determinism (10.1:465–66). The undiminished need for subsistence, then, meets the absence of meaning, and this prehistoric condition creates terror.

What is referred to as the "Unbeurteilbarkeit menschlicher Handlun-gen" (unjudgeability of human actions) reveals itself through a conflict between Fatzer and Koch/Keuner that centers on disparity and identity. Fatzer continually disappoints his comrades and the chorus by insisting on the disparity between word and deed. The chorus warns:

> Wen ihr beim Wort nähmet, der
> Ist's, der euch enttäuscht! (10.1:440)
>
> [Whom you would take at his word, he
> It is, who disappoints you!]

This warning is offered specifically to the collective but also more gener-ally to anyone inclined to take others at their word, and it presents duplic-ity and gullibility as two aspects of the same problem. To take someone at her or his word assumes continuity of character, and the *Fatzer* fragment questions that continuity. Fatzer uses the rebirth of the men, who emerge like babies from a mother-tank, to show that all people are constantly recreated, for situations are "die Mütter der Menschen" (10.1:462) (the mothers of men). In contrast to the chorus, Koch demands that a man stay true to his word, thus instituting the state of terror over Fatzer. Whereas Fatzer holds on to the "Unbeurteilbarkeit des Menschen" (unjudgeability of man), Koch insists on *Beurteilbarkeit* (judgeability), which in the end leads to the *Urteil* (judgment) that Fatzer must die.

The verdict against Fatzer evolves from the "Furchtzentrum des Stückes" (fear center of the play) that Brecht describes as the destruction of unity: "Während der Hunger sie anfällt, geht das Dach über ihren Köpfen weg, verläßt sie ihr bester Kamerad und spaltet sie der Sexus" (10.1:428) (While hunger attacks them, the roof over their heads absconds, their best comrade deserts them and *sexus* divides them). Hunger, homelessness, social isolation, and sexual desire indeed create the center of the play; for anarchy, solidarity, ideology, and terror evolve out of this cluster of problems. Any attempt by the four men to solve a problem rooted in one of these areas is subverted by unresolved tensions rooted in one of the other areas. Fatzer divides the group by committing what, in their situation, is considered a *Sexverbrechen* (sex crime) with Therese Kaumann. The sexual act is presented differently in the various versions of the fragment, ranging from consensual intercourse (when Therese demands sexual satisfaction) to rape (in which case, Therese takes part in the verdict against Fatzer). The organized terror can then be understood as a direct response to the fear caused by sex and the social division that this fear creates rather than as a simple response to sexual violence.

The destruction of unity leads to irresolution, anarchy, and brutality until the four men form "eine Art Sowjet" (10.1:428) (a kind of Soviet), thus changing from a group of friends into a collective. In this unprecedented situation, the collective must engage in the prehistoric task of securing subsistence (Fatzer's task) and developing a sociopolitical superstructure (Koch's task). Fatzer's failure to provide food strengthens Koch's project by allowing Koch to use problems with hunger and sex "bewußt (zynisch) für die Revolutionierung" (10.1:428) (consciously [cynically] for revolutionizing). Under Koch's leadership the fear center becomes a system that creates a revolutionary logic to discipline rather than liberate the members of the collective.

The battle over discipline is complicated by a dilemma of perception. The actions of Fatzer and his friends signify the traces of a new morality, but they are not yet conscious of this morality, nor can they control its meaning. Thus, each member of the collective plays a highly arbitrary role, and as we shall see later, only terror can impose a new order for the collective. Throughout the play, Fatzer is presented as the one man who makes survival impossible, but Brecht also demonstrates that Fatzer's behavior is a problem of perception: "[D]ie andern schlagen ihn tot, weil er ihnen ein Egoist ist, der in Wirklichkeit doch Kollektivist ist . . ." (10.1:471) ([T]he others kill him because to them he is an egoist, who is in reality a collectivist after all . . .). Both perceptions are to some extent accurate, for Fatzer's collectivism grows out of the enormity of his egoism: "Sie merken seinen Egoismus nicht, solang er sich auf viere erstreckt" (10.1:464) (They do not notice his egoism as long as it extends to four). The distinction between egoism and collectivism is, then, one of degree rather than of kind. This is congruent with Brecht's notion of socialism in which the conventional contradiction between *Gemeinnutz* (common interest) and *Eigennutz* (self-interest) is irrelevant because *"Eigennutz ist Gemeinnutz"* (22:58) (self-interest is common interest). Brecht assumes a correspondence between what is good for one and what is good for all.

Discipline is established through ideology and the installment of majoritarian decision making. What ends in terror begins with ideology and majority rule, and the fragment's various phases demonstrate where ideologies and majorities are flexible and where they are not. In recurring discussions the collective negotiates the right to property, the freedom of the woman, and Fatzer's death sentence. While the votes on women's freedom and Fatzer's sentence change as different interests gain priority in different parts of the text, both the condemnation of and the need for private property remain constant. Kaumann owns the apartment that provides the collective's only refuge, and his status as owner remains unquestioned regardless of what is said about the abstract problem of property. This alters the perception of sexuality and ultimately determines other decisions. In fact, it is Kaumann—husband and proprietor—who exacerbates the terror by threatening to throw them all out into the streets, thus creating the condition for the verdict against Fatzer.

Kaumann's invocation of the prerogatives of ownership appears at first to solidify an alliance among the other three, leading Koch and Büsching to declare their intent to join Fatzer and leave the apartment. When, however, "Es regnet" (It rains) and "Sie hören den Regen" (10.1:434) (They hear the rain), the need for shelter triumphs. The rain dissolves all solidarity with Fatzer, a fact that goes unremarked in the play. Brecht emphasizes the barrier to solidarity by presenting rain as a threat to survival and showing how that threat erases an ideological commitment made only moments before. Like Fatzer, everyone in the collective proves to be *unbeurteilbar* (unjudgeable) and the product of the given situation.

Fatzer's insistence on *Unbeurteilbarkeit* (unjudgeability), combined with the *Bedrängnis* (dire straits) in food and housing, fosters Koch's urge to create a new morality based on judgment and reliability. The advice to question others before taking them at their word is reversed by Koch, who seeks to develop a sincerity that will transform any *Beurteilung* (judgment) into a *Verurteilung* (conviction): "so heiß essen, wie gekocht wird" (10.1:461) (to eat as hot as it gets cooked). Fatzer's persecution begins when he is arrested by his former friends, who tie him up with ropes and inform him, "Damit du nicht herumgehen kannst wie ein anderer Mensch / Binden wir dich" (10.1:490) (So that you cannot walk around like any other man / We bind you). Fatzer bound explicitly recalls "Prometheus gefesselt" (10.1:432) (Prometheus bound). The traces of a new morality also emerge when we learn that the collective redefines punishment as help. The imperative that the chorus voices—"Flüchtet nicht!" (10.1:498) (Do not flee!)—is carried out by the collective when they bind Fatzer with a rope, which makes escape impossible. "Einen Strick um den Leib / Mußt du haben, damit du klug bist" (10.1:490) (A rope around the body / You must have so that you are smart) demonstrates one of the key lessons that Brecht sought to investigate in the teaching plays: individual intelligence cannot substitute for collective intelligence.

By transforming the fight for survival and the pursuit of pleasure into revolutionary concepts, Koch creates his own asceticism out of the collective's situation and abstracts this situation to form a universal revolutionary goal. Fatzer responds to the *Furchtzentrum* (fear center) by selfishly pursuing satisfaction, but Koch responds to the threats of hunger, isolation, and sexual desire by developing an ideological system in which he "beginnt also alle auftauchenden Schwierigkeiten . . . bewußt (zynisch) für die Revolutionierung zu verwenden" (10.1:428) (thus begins to use all emerging difficulties . . . consciously (cynically) for revolutionizing). Koch stays true to all elements of asceticism that Nietzsche describes as the "drei grossen Prunkworte des asketischen Ideals" (three great catchwords of the ascetic ideal), which are "Armuth, Demuth, Keuschheit" (poverty, humility, chastity).[11] In Fatzer's case this would mean the sharing of the meat, the submission to the rule of the collective, and sexual abstinence, but he fails each test, thus encouraging Koch's sense of moral superiority. The conflict between Fatzer and Koch ends in terror, but it starts as a conflict between Fatzer's drive to satisfy himself and Koch's commitment to self-denial and asceticism.

According to Nietzsche, asceticism is not an escape from life, but a force of life against the "K r a n k h a f t i g k e i t im bisherigen Typus des Menschen, zum Mindesten des zahm gemachten Menschen" (sickliness of the type of man who has lived up to now, at least of the tamed man).[12] It is a wrestling with death. Brecht's understanding of asceticism matches Nietzsche's, as is especially clear when Brecht reflects about the teaching of sexual love: "Unrichtig handeln, die dem Lernenden das Geschlechtliche als natürlich hinstellen, als sauber, harmlos und verständlich. Recht aber haben, die es ihm als unnatürlich beweisen, also als schmutzig, gefährlich und unverständlich" (10.1:527) (Those act wrongly who present sexuality to the learner as natural, as clean, harmless and understandable. But those are right who prove it to him to be unnatural, thus to be dirty, dangerous and incomprehensible). According to Brecht, teaching that sexuality is dangerous and filthy is the essence of teaching terror and thus a lesson in knowing how to be scared, which is also the ultimate lesson of the teaching plays. Brecht agrees with Freud that the sexual experience is frustrating and terrifying. The frustration (that is, the impossibility of complete satisfaction) is due to deference, while the terror results from the anal phase of human development. The anal phase places sex in a realm that is characterized by deference and which has proven to be irreconcilable with our aesthetic culture.[13] It is thus both deference and terror that create what Freud calls the egoistic drive that provides us with identity and culture through sublimation. For Freud, civilization results from the "unausgleichbare Differenz" (irreconcilable difference) between the egoistic and the sexual drives.[14] By leaving the latter unsatisfied, asceticism—and here Freud agrees with Nietzsche—keeps sexual desire alive; it is thus a life-confirming force. Thus, Koch's terror results from the same drive that Freud considers essential for both sexuality and culture, which is the same drive that Nietzsche holds essential for culture and morality. The wrestling between life and death, then, is represented through Fatzer's conflict with Koch when the latter imposes celibacy, which elicits in Fatzer the desire to disobey. Koch's ascetic commitment to revolutionary change creates the terror.

Fatzer examines asceticism not only as a state of mind, but also as a historical force essential for revolutionary movements in history. Nietzsche considers asceticism to be "der fleischgewordene Wunsch nach einem Anders-sein, Anderswo-sein," (the incarnate wish for being otherwise, being elsewhere), and it is only the power of this desire that keeps the ascetic where he or she is, fighting to alter the status quo.[15] The terror grows out of the conflict between Fatzer's refusal to adapt to historical change when he refuses to be "wie ein Rad" (like a wheel) and Koch's obsession with creating a revolutionary condition, a condition that he can bring into existence in his mind but not in the world. Fatzer's failure and Koch's condemnation of it create a dynamic of terror sufficient to produce a new morality when Koch demands that Fatzer's execution be carried out in a moral way, that is "in Demut" (in humility) rather than in pride. This reinscribes Christian theology on Koch's secular revolutionary morality. With *Fatzer*, Brecht creates a Nietzschean genealogy of morals that stretches from the securing of memory through punishment to a concept of history that traces uncivilized prehistory in any historical and political event. Koch cannot accept this uncivilized state and desires to live differently. The frustration rooted in this desire leads him to condemn Fatzer for embodying an escape from the world that Koch seeks to change.

By transferring Fatzer's difference into ideology, Koch seeks to establish an essential identity located between thought and deed, and between himself and the world—an identity that results in a murder, which he announces with the following words:

> s' wird nicht so heiß gegessen, wie gekocht wird
> Drum wollen wir jetzt einmal, sagen wir zum Spaß
> So heiß essen, wie gekocht wird (10.1:461)

> [it doesn't get eaten as hot as it gets cooked
> That's why we now want for once, for fun let's say
> To eat as hot as it gets cooked]

Fatzer's failure to provide the promised food leads "Koch" (Cook) to make *kochen* (to cook) the guiding principle of terror against him. In so doing he eliminates the difference between word and deed and the temporal distance between the two. Here, as elsewhere, ideology replaces matter. Fatzer, who considers himself and others *unbeurteilbar* (unjudgeable), becomes, according to Koch's ideology, the total enemy, the outcast: "Die Moralischen halten Gericht ab über einen Aussätzigen" (10.1:471) (The moral ones sit in judgment on an outcast). This anticipates Fatzer's final fate and endorses his claim to be beyond judgment because splitting the collective into a group of those who are "moral" and a single outcast disqualifies any verdict.

Koch's desire to eliminate difference becomes the guiding principle when the collective is about to carry out the verdict. Koch gives strict orders not to do "zwei Dinge, sondern / Eines. Nicht leben und töten, sondern / Nur töten" (10.1:450) (two things / but One. Not to live and kill, but / Only to kill). The advice not to live, but to kill and to kill exclusively is congruent with the situation of the collective at that point because Koch is the only one who knows that their situation is hopeless and that everyone's destruction has become inevitable. In administering the verdict, Koch applies meaning to the group's inevitable destruction by transforming Fatzer's life and death into a lesson. The collective engages in the ritualized murder of Fatzer to produce meaning by creating the memory of a revolution that never materialized. The three "moral" members of the collective proclaim:

> Uns kennt man nicht
> Aber den
> Soll man kennen.
> Ihn wollen wir umbringen, aber
> Seinen Namen lassen wir. Denn so
> Soll er sein von jetzt ab. (10.1:494)

> [One does not know us
> But him
> One should know.
> We want to kill him, but
> We leave his name. Because so
> He should be from now on.]

The revolutionary collective is unknown because it consists of men who have to remain in hiding. Fatzer, one of whose crimes was stepping out of hiding, has left the other three, and in turn they seek to establish his memory by eliminating his physical existence. Nietzsche argues that punishment is the fundamental stimulus to memory, and Brecht builds on this insight when the fragment presents Fatzer's execution in such terms. Fatzer, also introduced as "das schöne Tier" (the beautiful animal), has become "krank und schlecht" (sick and bad) through egoism and sex. Both qualities account for what Brecht calls "dialektische Tragik" (dialectical tragedy): "indem er sie verlockt, ihn zu vernichten, vernichtet er sie" (10.1:468) (as he tempts them to destroy him, he destroys them). Fatzer seduces the collective to asceticism and morality. Koch's revolutionary asceticism assigns a moralistic meaning to Fatzer the animal. The final verdict against Fatzer is then phrased in ascetic terms when Koch says: "Seid nicht hochfahrend, Brüder / Sondern demütig und schlagt es tot / Nicht hochfahrend, sondern: unmenschlich!" (10.1:450) (Do not be

proud, brothers / But humble and kill it / Not proud, but: inhuman!).
Koch orders his comrades to kill out of humility rather than moral superiority, which makes the murder a sacrifice.

MEMORY AND MORALITY

Nietzsche taught us that the creation of memory is a barbaric task: "vielle-
icht ist sogar nichts furchtbarer und unheimlicher an der ganzen
Vorgeschichte des Menschen, als seine M n e m o t e c h n i k" (perhaps
there is nothing more terrible and strange in man's pre-history than his
technique of mnemonics).[16] According to Nietzsche, memory is the fruit of
conscience and responsibility, both engraved on humanity through a long
history of unspeakable punishments. Similarly, Brecht presents memory
and forgetfulness as conflicting interests that he personifies through Koch
as the terrorist of memory and Fatzer as the forgetful animal. In addition,
the conflict between memory and forgetting is closely intertwined with
the revolutionary goals of all four men. This approach to the past as contemporary politics recalls Benjamin's concept of revolution as a concept of
remembering. Benjamin draws on Nietzsche, Freud, and Marx to outline
an approach that moves between catastrophe and revolution; in this tension, memory and remembering acquire political functions:

> »Die Funktion des Gedächtnisses« (sc. der Verfasser identifiziert die
> Sphäre des »Vergessens« und des »unbewußten Gedächtnisses«) »ist der,
> Eindrücke zu konservieren; die Erinnerung zielt auf ihre Zersetzung. Das
> Gedächtnis ist im wesentlichen konservativ, die Erinnerung destruktiv.«

> ["The function of memory" (sc. the author identifies the sphere of "for-
> getting" and of "unconscious memory") "is to conserve impressions;
> remembering aims at their replacement. Memory is essentially conserv-
> ative, remembering destructive."][17]

Benjamin's distinction between memory and remembering follows
Freud's belief that conscious memory represents the subject's intentional
creation of her or his own past.[18] The first step of analysis is to destroy this
conscious past and to enter the repressed, forgotten past. Remembering is
thus the destruction of the subject's willfully created narrative. What
Freud applies to memory, Nietzsche applies to morality as the history of
our conscience in his *Genealogie der Moral (On the Genealogy of Morality)*,
which seeks to explore "das Urkundliche, das Wirklich-Feststellbare, das

Wirklich-Dagewesene" (that which can be documented, which can actually be confirmed and has actually existed).[19] *Fatzer* engages in the necessary, destructive work of tracing the genealogy of the bloody remnants of twentieth-century morality and takes the first step toward a psychoanalysis of post–World War I German culture.

The fragment does this by combining history with ideology to examine memory as a willfully created narrative. Although *Fatzer* is sprinkled with references to Marx and Lenin, the exchanges between the four men remain largely unaffected by these theories. What we witness are relentless attempts to make sense of a present time experienced as unprecedented rather than an effort to remember the past. Instead of creating a specific political goal, the group develops its ideological maxims to ensure the discipline essential to survival, a discipline that Fatzer continues to resist. The men contextualize their impending demise in historical and existential (rather than political) terms by predicting that their enemy will only be destroyed "lang nach unserm Tod" (10.1:460) (long after our death). Koch the ideologue seeks to apply historical-revolutionary meaning to Fatzer's failures by establishing an example:

> Die Hälfte dieser Menschheit lebt
> Einzig vom löchrigen Gedächtnis der andern Hälfte
> Alle diese Nächte
> Schlaf ich nicht mehr aus Furcht, es könnte
> Etwas im Sand verlaufen und vergessen werden
> Dieweil es einer darauf anlegt, daß
> Grad dies im Sand verläuft und
> Vergessen wird (10.1:461)

> [Half of humanity lives
> Solely from the hole-filled memory of the other half
> All these nights
> I sleep no more for fear, there could be
> something in the sand lost and forgotten
> As long as someone intends that
> Precisely this in the sand be lost and
> Forgotten]

Koch applies the economy of exploitation—people living off of other people—to the economy of memory. He tries to protect his memories by avoiding sleep and the dreams that serve as repositories for the destructive

activity of remembering. For Koch, memory is tied to interests and forgetting, and he fears that forgetting will aid his enemy, Fatzer, who lives
through amnesia.

The terrors of memory are accompanied by the terror of an emerging
morality, a morality that is incomprehensible in the moment of its production. This brings to mind Nietzsche's *Genealogie der Moral (On the
Genealogy of Morality)* as the search for "das ungeheure, ferne und so ver-
steckte Land der Moral—der wirklich dagewesenen, wirklich gelebten
Moral . . ." (the vast, distant and hidden land of morality—of morality as
it really existed and was really lived . . .),[20] and one could say that in
Fatzer, Brecht creates a barbaric prehistory of the twentieth century by
presenting Koch's willful creation of memory and further preservation of
it through punishment. Koch, the terrorist of memory, comes across as its
very creator who also seeks to control its working through time. Nietzsche
distinguishes between morality as an immaterial value system and the
production of morality through human conflict. What begins as a game
of domination develops over time into a moral system designed to manifest as universal morality the power of the one who dominates. Morality
is nowhere in sight when Brecht points to the "blutigen Spuren einer Art
neuen Moral" (10.1:469) (bloody traces of a kind of new morality). Tracing the brutality of power plays, however, reveals the disparity between
morality lived and morality idealized.[21]

Nietzsche locates memory in space when he talks about the hidden
country of morality. Brecht does the same when he introduces the
"Ruhrort Fatzer" (Ruhrplace Fatzer) as the site of Fatzer's third and worst
failure. When Fatzer risks discovery by walking openly through
Mühlheim, he gives Koch a pretext for invoking terror. Brecht enshrines
this place, memorializing the birthplace of terror and the morality it seeks
to create by naming it "Ruhrort Fatzer" (Ruhrplace Fatzer):

> *Ruhrort Fatzer*:
> Einzuprägen wäre noch die Gegend:
> > Dies finstere Viereck zwischen Kränen und Eisenhütten
> > Durch die dieser Johann Fatzer
> > Seine letzten Tage herumging
> > Aufhaltend das Rad (10.1:463)

> [*Ruhrplace Fatzer*:
> The area still ought to be imprinted:
> > This dark square between cranes and ironworks

Through which this Johann Fatzer
Wandered his last days
Delaying the wheel]

"Ruhrort Fatzer" (Ruhrplace Fatzer) is an undistinguished industrial land-scape. Fatzer's walk, arising from his indifference, represents a counter-revolutionary act, but it is not directed against the revolution because there is none. It is, instead, his refusal to submit to history. By defining revolution as an inevitable component of history, and not solely as radi-cal political and social change, Brecht uses the term *revolution* in all its etymological complexity ranging from revolving solar systems to recur-rences in nature to the promise of radical social change.[22] The revolution that the group anticipates derives its meaning from the etymological root of the word *revolving*. The circular movement of history ensures the occurrence of revolution not through a political telos, but merely as inevitable change in time. Thus, Fatzer's greatest crime is already inscribed in "Ruhrort Fatzer" (Ruhrplace Fatzer)—he impedes the wheel of time and becomes an obstacle to the historical process. After Fatzer's final fail-ure—his walk through Mühlheim—the group realizes that its destruction is inevitable.

With "Ruhrort Fatzer" (Ruhrplace Fatzer), Brecht creates a memory space similar to that suggested by Cicero in his Simonides story in which the poet Simonides survives the collapse of a festival hall where he had recited a poem. He is the only survivor, and the victims are completely defaced. In order to proceed with the funeral ceremony, the victims must be identified, and Simonides rises to the challenge by recalling the seating order of the banquet, which was determined by each guest's position in society. Anselm Haverkamp shows that the spatial memory which makes the identification of the dinner guests possible substitutes for the mem-ory of people. In order to memorize, we depend on the "order of things" in a defined space.[23] By naming a place after a person and defining that place as space, Brecht establishes his own mnemonic device. With "Ruhrort Fatzer" (Ruhrplace Fatzer), Brecht establishes the memory of Fatzer as a place, which he describes as geometrical space defined by cranes and ironworks. In this constellation, Fatzer is remembered as a name detached from the person who bore it. This anticipates Fatzer's eventual execution with its contradictory attempts to erase him as a man and to enshrine his name as a warning.

Brecht problematizes space in a way that extends to the realm of his-torical representation. While the setting of *Fatzer* is concretely historical—

a place named "Mühlheim an der Ruhr" during World War I—the place grows anonymous during the course of events.[24] Brecht throws us into disarray just as he did in *Trommeln in der Nacht (Drums in the Night)*, where the only revolutionary movement consists of moving around Berlin only to fail in finding the place where "revolution" actually takes place. In *Fatzer*, Mühlheim becomes a spectrum of spaces that range across public and private spheres. The characters orient themselves—especially in situations concerning their food supply—by determining who is following whom and why. As a result, spatial orientation results from social orientation just as it did in *Trommeln in der Nacht (Drums in the Night)* and in the *Lesebuch für Städtebewohner (A Reader for Those Who Live in Cities)*. Mühlheim during World War I becomes predominantly a site of survival on the most elementary level: four men depend on one another in a hostile environment. Social dependency in an unprecedented situation suggests the prehistoric barbarism that Benjamin diagnoses as the German condition after World War I.[25] This detachment from humanity is amplified by the barrenness of Mühlheim. While the brutal battles for survival in *Trommeln in der Nacht (Drums in the Night)* and *Im Dickicht der Städte (In the Jungle of Cities)* take place in impoverished but lively environments, Mühlheim seems to be deserted, without industries or a working class. Mühlheim was, after all, a major site of coal mining and steel production, and its emptiness in *Fatzer* suggests a postindustrial landscape where subsistence might require a return to prehistoric barbarism.[26] In Heiner Müller's words, *Fatzer* provides a "Blick auf den Nullpunkt des Jahrhunderts" (glimpse of the zero point of the century).[27] The fragment lends itself to historical reflection, which might lead us to insert natural history into history, resulting in a montage that, although it represents only a brief period of time and action, allows reflection on the entire twentieth century.

BODY IN TIME: *HALTUNG*

Human prehistory inscribes itself on the history of the body so that its traces remain permanently embedded in the historical record, although this only becomes clear when the human body is recognized as historical rather than natural. According to Foucault's reading of Nietzsche, "The body manifests the stigmata of past experience and also gives rise to desires, failings, and errors."[28] Desires, failings, and errors are the tools that Fatzer uses to betray the revolution. Brecht knows very well that the human body is a counterrevolutionary force: "der Mensch ist zu haltbar, er geht zu schwer kaputt" (2:224) (man is too durable, he breaks down with too much difficulty). Durability resists those alterations that seem necessary for revolutionary change. In his concept of revolution, Brecht seeks to transform *Haltbarkeit* (durability) into *Haltung*, the conscious disposition that adapts to change. *Haltung* (disposition) includes the historical concept of *enthalten* (to contain) that we know from Brecht's genealogy of history in which the proletarian eventually subsumes both the bourgeois and the aristocrat. Brecht seeks to transform the egoistic durability of the human body into revolutionary endurance. *Haltung* (disposition), then, becomes the lasting adaptation to historical change.

In *Fatzer*, Brecht presents a concept of history that takes to heart one of Benjamin's theses on history, which posits that the future will not be homogeneous, empty time, but time filled with the meaningful consequences of the past as catastrophy.[29] Brecht's fragment presents a prehistory that is not a history of events, but of the production of conditions from which the future is to be built, and this future reveals itself through the human body. In his "Rede vom Massemensch" (Speech on the Mass Man), Fatzer articulates the transition from past to future:

> Wie früher Geister kamen aus Vergangenheit
> So jetzt aus Zukunft, ebenso
> Klagend beschwörend und ungreifbar
> Einzig bestehend aus Stoff deines eigenen Geists
> Seiner Furcht zuvorderst. Denn immer Furcht
> Zeigt an, was kommt, direkt vom Aug
> Geht ein Strang zu Furcht. (10.1:465)

> [Just as ghosts previously came from the past
> So now from the future, equally
> Complaining imploring and intangible
> Solely consisting of the stuff of your own mind
> Right at the front of its fear. Because fear always
> Points out what is coming, directly from the eye
> Goes a line to fear.]

Ghosts are presented as coming into the present from a subject's future rather than from her or his past, and the injuries of the future are as indelibly imprinted in the mind as are the injuries of the past. "Ich studier sie. / So wie sie / Ist die Zukunft / Die sehr schlecht ist," (I study it. / Just as it /

Is the future / That is very bad) says Fatzer (10.1:464), anticipating the
destruction that the four men sought to escape in the past. Here, Brecht
agrees with Benjamin's rejection of the future as empty, homogenous time.[30]
But Brecht, unlike Benjamin, has no messianic perspective; for Brecht, the
"good old" gives way to the "bad new." According to Benjamin, the connection between past and future is *Wunsch* (wish; desire), which moves
ahead of time, and the earlier a wish is enunciated, the more probable is its
fulfillment. The wish articulated brings the future into the present through
the energy of its drive.[31] It might be hard to imagine that ghosts from a
future announced through fear are the result of our own desires, as Brecht
claims, but we need only to recall Freud's *Jenseits des Lustprinzips (Beyond
the Pleasure Principle)* to be reminded that the death drive is an integral part
of our pleasure structure.[32] We may conclude that Brecht's ghosts from the
future help to structure the present through their driving energy.

   If it is fear that shows us what the future will bring, we must learn to
accept fear as a signifier. What we may then expect from the future is what
we already know from the present: "das Schicksal des Menschen ist der
Mensch" (18:71) (the destiny of man is man). What we then see in our
present and future is the same—other people. When Brecht writes that
fear signifies the change ahead because "immer Furcht / Zeigt an, was
kommt, direkt vom Aug / Geht ein Strang zu Furcht" (10.1:465) (fear
always / Points out what is coming, directly from the eye / Goes a line to
fear), and that fear results from visual perception, he argues that our fear
mirrors the fear we have observed in others. Brecht locates the perception
of the future in mass society and through observation as a replacement for
subjective experience. The individual members of a mass society detect the
future by reading the faces of others. This theatrical and social act can
replace the subjective experience, which was lost to the twentieth century
due to World War I. The "Massemensch" (mass man) is "mechanisch /
Einzig durch Bewegung zeigt er sich" (10.1:466) (mechanical / Solely
through movement, he shows himself). Mutual observance of one
another's physical movements in mass society is thus the material from
which Brecht draws human cognition, something that has long been recognized in his theatrical concept of *gestus* (the corporeal signifier of relations among people). Mass society provides evidence for what Brecht considers to be a transhistorical truth: that any progress—whether intellectual,
economical, or technological—rests on relations among people.

   If this truth is transhistorical, however, it can only become a socially
useful truth when it can be perceived. Brecht believes that theatre makes
this possible because it allows people to practice the required art of per-

ception. Because Brecht thinks the human body understands and adapts to the future before the conscious mind comprehends it, he insists that the body prerecords the future for those who can read it. It can only be read, however, in social settings in which multiple bodies interact. The stage provides a limited and controlled space for the observation of such interaction, and Brecht develops his concept of *gestus* to describe the ways in which bodies signify these transhistorical truths.

If reading people's movements and gestures through the concept of *gestus* reveals aspects of the future, one might ask if our body language also contains aspects of the past. In the "Fatzerkommentar" (Fatzer Commentary), Brecht asks whether Fatzer's walk through Mühlheim could be understood not only as a fictional, but also as a general historical fact. A transfer from fiction to historical facticity can take place if the public believes that the walk occurred. If a sufficient number of people believe that they witnessed Fatzer's walk, then it happened. Brecht provides the following explanation:

> Außer den Taten der Menschen, die wirklich getan wurden, gibt es solche, die hätten getan werden können. Diese letzteren Taten sind ebenso abhängig von den Zeiten wie jene ersteren und es gibt von ihnen ebenso eine Geschichte, die ihre Zusammenhänge über viele Zeiten hinweg zeigt, wie von jenen. Gewisse Bilder, die die Menschen sich von sich selber machen, sind gewissen Zeiten eigentümlich, in denen eben diese Gesten von ihnen aneinander beobachtet werden, weil gerade diese Gesten von Wichtigkeit sind. Also erkennen die Menschen an gewissen Merkmalen die wahrhaftigsten Bilder ihres Lebens, an den Zusammenstellungen von Figuren in bestimmten Haltungen, welche die wahrhaftigen Interessen der Menschen dieser Zeit zeigen. (10.1:516)

> [Besides the acts of men that were really performed, there are such that could have been performed. These latter acts are just as dependent on the times as the former, and there is likewise a history of them that shows its correlations over long periods of time, as there is of the others. Certain pictures that men make of themselves for themselves belong to certain times in which precisely these gestures of theirs are observed in one another because exactly these gestures are of importance. Thus, men recognize the truest pictures of their life by certain features, in the arrangements of figures in certain dispositions, which signify the true interests of the men of this time.]

Brecht conceives of acting and perception as elements with which to build a binding public sphere and uses them to extend his concept of history.

His history of possibility is derived neither from Marx's revolutionary telos, nor from Benjamin's messianic perspective, but from the observation of people's unconscious performance of gestures. Theatre, then, can provide a space where the observation of gestures can be rehearsed for a continuous negotiation of the historical process.

The history of possibility, then, sheds new light on Brecht's concept of *gestus*. As a theatrical concept, *gestus* unites language and the body; as Jameson has shown, it is also a theatrical technique that alienates intellectual thought.[33] In *Fatzer*, Brecht alienates subjective thought by insisting that one should adapt to the historical situation in which one finds oneself even though it might appear meaningless. This process does not unfold according to our intentions, and Brecht considers the subject incapable of understanding the historical process. "Die Begnügung mit der Geste" (10.1:469) (Contentment with the gesture), then, seems to be the subject's fitting adaptation to the historical process. In fact, the subject's actions often produce unintended outcomes; struggling for democracy may well lead to dictatorship, as Brecht saw at the end of the Weimar Republic. The unpredictability of history, then, is the antagonist of subjective imagination. This makes the meaningless gesture the true but limited signifier of the historical condition of our lives.

The signification of living conditions also affects Brecht's concept of ideology. In fact, one could claim that Brecht himself derived his political orientation from the observation of people's gestures in troubling times. In his 1938 essay "Über reimlose Lyrik mit unregelmäßigen Rhythmen" (On Rhymeless Verse with Irregular Rhythms), Brecht describes how he develops his concept of *gestus* from the observation of city life during the Weimar Republic: "Mein politisches Wissen war damals beschämend gering; jedoch war ich mir großer Unstimmigkeiten im gesellschaftlichen Leben der Menschen bewußt, und ich hielt es nicht für meine Aufgabe, all die Disharmonien und Interferenzen, die ich stark empfand, formal zu neutralisieren" (22.1:359) (My political knowledge was at that time shamefully negligible; however, I was conscious of great inconsistencies in the social life of the people, and I did not consider it to be my task to neutralize formally all the disharmonies and interferences that I strongly felt). Having not yet turned to Marxist analysis, Brecht observes social contradictions from the point of view of language and disposition rather than that of social structure, and observation rooted in language continues to influence his theatre more than Marxist ideology when he describes his theatre as an experiment: "die Vorgänge zwischen den Menschen als widerspruchsvolle, kampfdurchtobte, gewalttätige zu zeigen" (22.1:359) (to show the affairs between men as full of contradictions, conflict-ravaged, violent). To do so, Brecht develops *gestus* as the corporeal signifier of his theatre. When Brecht describes what he observed during hunger demonstrations in Weimar-Era Berlin by noting that "die Sprache soll ganz dem Gestus der sprechenden Person folgen" (22.1:359) (the language should entirely follow the *gestus* of the person speaking), we can conclude that this coordination of speech and movement foreshadows a revolutionary attitude in the demonstrating masses. That attitude was not sufficient, however, to prevent the rise of fascism in Germany. What the history of possibility in *Fatzer* shows us instead is that with the concept of *gestus*, we are able to read contradictory gestures as other history and, as *Trommeln in der Nacht (Drums in the Night)* demonstrates, also as other ideology.[34]

Brecht's wide-ranging concept of *gestus* extends from the estrangement of ideology to the signification of history and can sometimes seem to verge on a nearly universal signifier, but in fact it works within strict limitations. Just as Brecht's Galilei describes his scientific experiments as an exercise in limitation—"Es ist nicht das Ziel der Wissenschaft, der unendlichen Weisheit eine Tür zu öffnen, sondern eine Grenze zu setzen dem unendlichen Irrtum" (5:68) (It is not the goal of science to open a door to infinite wisdom, but to set a limit on infinite error)—so also Brecht seeks with *gestus*, the quintessential element of his theatrical experiments, to limit the potentially unlimited error inherent in the perception of human life and history. To read *gestus*, one must understand the contradictions that work against the creation of coherent meaning and train one's perception instead on that which can be accurately perceived: human action.

Gestus is a temporal signifier because of its mimetic quality and its physical limitations:

> Die Gesten der Menschen
> Sind entweder allzu erklärlich
>   (jetziger Zustand)
> Oder unerklärlich
>   (einstiger Zustand)
> Sie können nur nachgeahmt werden. (10.1:525)

> [The gestures of men
> Are either all-too explicable
>   (present condition)

> Or inexplicable
>   (erstwhile condition)
> They can only be imitated.]

Any relation to the past or the future depends on people observing whomever is physically present. Gestures defy verbal explanation, and the body engages in mimetic action that, in Brecht's theatre, replaces intellectual comprehension. Any understanding, then, remains located in the present tense and in the interpersonal or social realm.

By combining image and *gestus*, Brecht's history of possibility offers a social version of Benjamin's "Dialektik im Stillstand" (Dialectics at a Standstill) as developed in "Über den Begriff der Geschichte" (On the Concept of History), which Brecht called "klar und entwirrend" (clear and disentangling) at the time it was written. Benjamin's concept of historical materialism privileges the present moment, the moment when the historian quotes the past.[35] To make sense of the fragment from the past that he or she cites, the historian must interpret the present as much as the past, for it is only from the perspective of the former that he or she can write history.[36] "Denn es ist ein unwiederbringliches Bild der Vergangenheit, das mit jeder Gegenwart zu verschwinden droht, die sich nicht als in ihm gemeint erkannte" (For it is an irretrievable image of the past which threatens to disappear in any present that does not recognize itself as intended in that image).[37] The image, like a dream, appears once and is then lost forever. Because our conscious understanding cannot instantaneously comprehend this image, we must rely on mimesis to grasp that image.[38] "Dialektik im Stillstand" (Dialectics at a Standstill) is the moment of citation as "revolutionäre(n) Chance im Kampfe für die unterdrückte Vergangenheit" (revolutionary chance in the fight for the oppressed past).[39] To grasp this oppressed past, Benjamin engages in the hermeneutics of the artwork, whereas Brecht engages in the hermeneutics of people.

Historical mimesis can be described as the maintenance of *gestus* over long periods of time, and when such a *gestus* is maintained, a person's *Haltung* (disposition) is created. *Haltung* (disposition) combines Brecht's theatrical aesthetics with his understanding of history. Etymologically related to *halten* (to hold; to maintain; to last), the diverse meanings of *Haltung* (disposition) range from *halten* as prevailing and persisting, to *enthalten* as containing historical change (in *Trommeln in der Nacht [Drums in the Night]* and *Im Dickicht der Städte [In the Jungle of Cities]*), to *aushalten* as enduring the difference between theory and practice as it is presented in the teaching plays, the *Geschichten vom Herrn Keuner (Stories of Mr. Keuner)*, and the *Buch der Wendungen (Book of Changes)*.

Haltung (disposition), or the lack of it, also constitutes the conflict in *Fatzer*. Both Fatzer and Koch lack the endurance that *Haltung* (disposition) demands: Fatzer rebels against the seemingly meaningless discipline when he refuses to adapt like a wheel to the historical process, and Koch lacks patience with the group's situation and thus tries to transform every need into part of a consistent ideology that imposes moral imperatives on the collective. Koch's effort to erase the difference between ideology and life results in terror. *Haltung* (disposition), as the adaptation to time and circumstance, allows us to decipher historical change through a reading of each other's gestures. Lessons such as "Wo die Not am größten ist, ist die Hilfe am fernsten" (15:155) (Where the need is greatest, the help is farthest) and "Die Wege zur Revolution zeigen sich" (3:90) (The ways to the revolution reveal themselves) are reminders that if we intend to promote historical and political change, we must first fight the urge for "deeper" readings of people's intentions. We should instead direct our attention to the mechanics of everyday life, where meaningless routine secures survival at the cost of the suppression of individuality.

Thought in Time: *Lehre*

Me-ti sagte: Wenn man Bronze-oder Eisenstücke im Schutt findet, fragt man: was waren das in alter Zeit für Werkzeuge? Wozu dienten sie? Aus den Waffen schließt man auf Kämpfe; aus den Verzierungen auf Handel. Man ersieht Verlegenheiten und Möglichkeiten aller Art.
Warum macht man es mit den Gedanken aus alten Zeiten nicht auch so?
(18:94)

[Me-ti said: When one finds bronze or iron pieces in the rubble, one asks: what kind of tools were these in ancient times? What purposes did they serve? From the weapons, one settles on combat; from the ornaments, on trade. One sees all kinds of difficulties and possibilities.
Why does one not also do it with the thoughts from ancient times?]

Prehistory offers an appealing perspective for Brecht's concepts of history and theatre because the evidence of a lost civilization that emerges from the rubble provokes astonishment. We approach the evidence by asking children's questions like "what" and "how," and in order to answer these questions, we carefully examine the fragmented evidence and go from there. This method comes remarkably close to Benjamin's concept of historical materialism, which is based on the interpretation of the past through a chaos of fragments. The archaeological perspective is so intriguing because the temporal gulf separating the distant past from us heightens our awareness of the present as a distinct perspective. The old seems to be unknown, and by becoming subject to discovery, it turns into the new. To produce strangeness and astonishment is exactly what Brecht sought to do in his epic theatre, which, as Benjamin has shown, is specifically designed to present long historical developments.[40] To find old thoughts in the rubble and, by finding them, make them new is a fitting task for the theatre.

In 1930, Brecht broke off his work on *Fatzer* as well as on all of his other experimental fragments and teaching plays. Heiner Müller once noted that Brecht never had any illusions about the potential and persistence of German fascism.[41] He went into exile knowing that it meant losing the living theatre that had provided the foundation for his experiments. After 1933, Brecht's reflections grew much more streamlined and finally emerged as the consistent concept of epic theatre that accompanies his canonized epic plays. Before that process became dominant, Brecht began *Buch der Wendungen (Book of Changes)*, his most philosophical work. The *Buch der Wendungen (Book of Changes)* grows partly out of the *Geschichten vom Herrn Keuner (Stories of Mr. Keuner)*, which Brecht started as a series of supplemental commentaries for *Fatzer*, and partly out of "der Denkende" (the thinker), who advises the actors in *Aus Nichts wird Nichts (From Nothing Comes Nothing)*. Brecht also considered adding a Keuner figure to both *Die Maßnahme (The Measures Taken)* and the fragment *Der böse Baal der asoziale (The Evil Baal, the Asocial)*. *Me-ti: Buch der Wendungen (Me-ti: Book of Changes)* is thus thematically intertwined with the fragments and the teaching plays, and one can read the short aphorisms as summary reflections on historical change and theoretical thought as they appear when traced through long periods of time.

Hindsight allows one to keep track of both natural history and human progress, and it makes the retrospective viewpoint a critical element of estrangement in Brecht's theatrical work. A retrospective can question the concept of progress as the engine of revolutionary thought by tracing progress over much longer periods of time than we usually consider when discussing revolutions. How does progress occur and when does it become regress? The interchangeablility of progress and regress is a recurrent issue in Brecht's representations of great historical themes in works such as *Leben des Galilei (The Life of Galileo)* or *Mutter Courage (Mother Courage)*. Even in his reflections on acting, Brecht takes long duration in time and history into account. He always admired Chinese and Japanese acting traditions for their ability to preserve a single gesture over centuries because such stability helps to signify change. Brecht writes about the Chinese actor:

> Und er hatte seine Neuerung aus dem Alten zu entwickeln. So kommt in die Stetigkeit, die das Kennzeichen einer wirklichen Kunst (wie einer Wissenschaft) ist, das natürliche Moment des Aufruhrs, der deutlich sichtbare, beurteilbare, verantwortliche Akt des Bruchs mit dem Alten. (22.1:128)

> [And he had to develop his innovation out of the old. Thus comes in the constancy, which is the hallmark of a real art (just as of a science), the natural moment of revolt, the clearly visible, judgeable, responsible act of the break with the old.]

To master and eventually overcome the old, we must live through it and let ourselves be mastered by it. These lessons in patience are fundamental to Brecht's theatre and represent a thematic continuity from Brecht's early plays to the teaching plays to his philosophical aphorisms.

History is both duration and change: to live it, we need *Haltung* (disposition); to comprehend it, we need dialectics. In his notes on dialectics, Brecht criticizes the teleological perspective that ties dialectics to progress; and the *Buch der Wendungen (Book of Changes)*, the *Geschichten vom Herrn Keuner (Stories of Mr. Keuner)*, the fragments, and the teaching plays can all be read as a complex critique of progress. For Brecht, the reading of history as inherently progressive is a symptom of impatience and wishful thinking: "Dieser Begriff Fortschritt hat große Annehmlichkeiten politischer Art, aber für den Begriff Dialektik hat er nachteilige Folgen gehabt" (21:519) (This term progress has great amenities of a political sort, but for the term dialectics it has had detrimental consequences). A notion of progress can comfort us in the midst of present mishaps by providing us with a telos that promises a better future, but this promise is purchased through the exclusion of life from thought. Beginning with his early plays, Brecht uses dialectics to present changes in human life:[42] "Dialektik ist . . . etwas, was die Natur hat (immer gehabt hat)" (21:519) (Dialectics is . . . something that nature has [has always had]). In his theoretical texts, however, he relates dialectics much more to the lasting recurrences of natural history than to political progress. Brecht's notion of dialectics includes life and thought equally, which introduces regress to the idea of progress and patience to thought. Me-ti once observes, "das Denken löst sich leicht los. Das ist eine Eigenschaft

des Denkens" (18:88) (thinking easily detaches itself. That is a characteristic of thinking). Thought disconnected from its origin, the thinker,
takes on its own dynamic, which might at first appear to be progressive
by moving ahead from social life like the airmen in the *Badener Lehrstück
vom Einverständnis (The Baden-Baden Lesson on Consent)*. The more we
feel a need for progress, the more we submit to thought. This causes the
downfall of Jae in the fragment *Jae Fleischhacker in Chikago* when he
seeks to get rid of his body in order to rise more easily: "'s ist tollkühn,
zu steigen. Eine / Hand ist dabei nichts, ich hau sie ab und / Lache,
brauch sie nicht mehr und / Kämpfe / mit meinem Kopf weiter"
(10.1:294) (it's foolhardy to climb. A / Hand thereby is nothing, I cut it
off and / Laugh, don't need it anymore and / Fight / on with my head).
Jae seeks to speed up his ascending social mobility by eliminating the
meat-hacker body that only hinders him because his hand "Stinkt doch
nach Schmutz der Tief" (10.1:304) (Stinks still like the filth of the
depths). Leaving his body behind, Jae begins his ascent from butcher to
capitalist and ends up slaughtering people for profit. Jae's progress is
bought at the cost of the regress and destruction of others. Progress and
regress are parts of the same economy, and the application of dialectics
to social life can show that.

The back and forth of dialectics not only informs Brecht's approach to
thought, but also his approaches to time and history. *Gestus* serves as a signifier of the motion of history, of the "Hin und Her historischer Vorgänge"
(22.2:1015) (Back and Forth of historical events). Disconnected thought
can create progress and coherent meaning out of the past, a process that
Brecht finds suspicious. Brecht's criticism of the application of meaning to
history brings Foucault to mind, for Brecht also sees history as the fight for
domination rather than as a narrative of rational development: "Die
»Notwendigkeit« des gegebenen geschichtlichen Prozesses ist eine Vorstel-
lung, die von der Mutmaßung lebt, für jedes geschichtliche Ereignis müsse
es zureichende Gründe geben. . . . In Wirklichkeit gab es aber wider-
sprechende Tendenzen, die streitbar entschieden wurden, das ist viel
weniger" (21:523) (The "necessity" of the given historical process is an idea
that lives from the conjecture, for every historical event there would have
to be sufficient reasons. . . . But in reality there were contradictory ten-
dencies that were decided belligerently, that is much less). Accepting this
"much less" in history and philosophy is ultimately more essential to
Brecht's theatre than is the representation of ideology and political change.
For Brecht, dialectics offers a way to trace constant change in life and
thought rather than a philosophical path to progress.

Progress, for Brecht, has a negative connotation as the *fortschreiten* (to stride forward; to advance; to progress; to pass; to proceed) from others; it implies moving ahead and thus destroying unity even when it is well-intentioned: "Bei allen Gedanken muß man also die Menschen suchen, zu denen hin und von denen her sie gehen . . ." (18:71) (With all thoughts, then, one must seek the people to whom and from whom they go . . .). Theatre, then, can provide a site for tracing ideas back to their progenitors and to those affected by them. Tracing ideas back and forth forms the basic structure of Brecht's theatre, especially in the teaching plays. In *Der Jasager. Der Neinsager (He Said Yes. He Said No),* for example, any modification of an idea occurs in an argument performed spatially through a change of position. The fragment *Der Brückenbauer (The Bridge Builder),* which Brecht wrote at the same time as the teaching plays, examines how knowledge is to be distributed. A bridge builder is commissioned by the townspeople to superintend the town's bridge, a task that he performs with dedication to the benefit of the entire town. After two years on the job, the bridge builder informs the town that repair work is needed or else the bridge will collapse during the coming spring flood. Because people bidding for the job fail to compromise, the town decides to forgo the repairs. The bridge builder persists in trying to improve the bridge by himself, and the people chase him out of town as a threat to their unity. The conflict follows the same pattern as in each teaching play: intellectual progress conflicts with social unity.

The fragment differs, however, in that it is not an ideological, but a technological lesson that is the subject of debate. The conflict between the bridge builder and the town is reminiscent of the one between science and the church in *Leben des Galilei (The Life of Galileo).* The townspeople understand the problem but are unwilling to risk their unity by deciding among the different interests that are at stake. The bridge builder responds by separating himself from the people and assuming the role of lecturer, an elevated position that is not sanctioned by the general public. From this elevated position, he attempts both to educate the people in technology and to condemn corruption. During his speech the townspeople exclude the bridge builder while negotiating a solution among themselves. They consider hierarchies and interests within the town— forces that the bridge builder defines as corruption—rather than the condition of the bridge. Instead of accepting the town's decision, the bridge builder becomes a doomed social worker much like the young comrade in *Die Maßnahme (The Measures Taken).*

The townspeople maintain unity not only among each other, but also between thought and action. They discuss their immediate actions rather than the bridge builder's problem, deliberating "über die Uneinigkeit, über die Folgen der Uneinigkeit, über den Eigennutz, über das Nichtsehenwollen des Eigennutzes, über den Wert der Brücke, über den Wert der Menschen, über das Blindsein, über das Wissen und über das Reden" (10.1:678) (about disunity, about the consequences of disunity, about self-interest, about the deliberate blindness of self-interest, about the value of the bridge, about the value of men, about being blind, about knowledge, and about speaking). In short, the townspeople do not talk about the bridge at all, but only about its value, which determines their interests. From here they draw their conclusion: they decide that the snow will not thaw, that the water will not rise, and that the bridge is strong enough to withstand any flood. In short, they decide that the bridge builder is unwise. The townspeople then give the sign "daß die Tafeln mit den Berechnungen des Brückenbauers zertrümmert würden, und wiesen den Brückenbauer aus der Stadt" (10.1:678) (that the tables with the calculations of the bridge builder would be destroyed, and expelled the bridge builder from the city). The townspeople give in entirely to their immediate interests and prejudices instead of maintaining a morality that pretends to serve a greater good or tradition.

"Aber der Brückenbauer begriff sie nicht" (10.1:678) (But the bridge builder did not comprehend them) becomes the refrain that introduces everything the bridge builder does. Disconnected from the "everybody else," he loses his social comprehension and relies increasingly upon sterile reason. He lectures the townspeople about "Schneeschmelze, über die Folgen der Schneeschmelze, über die Schwäche der Brücke. Über die Vernunft, über die Bestechung, über den Eigennutz, und über die Brückenbaukunst" (10.1:677) (melting snow, about the consequences of melting snow, about the weaknesses of the bridge. About reason, about corruption, about self-interest, and about the art of bridge building). His unceasing attempts to teach what is of no interest and to criticize those in the majority leads to his physical as well as social exclusion because such attempts represent his effort to elevate himself to a superior position based on immaterial systems of reason and virtue. But reason must adapt to the environment from which it emerges. Reason "muß verkrüppelt sein. Es muß eine regulierbare, jeweils mehr oder weniger mechanisch vergrößer- oder verkleinerbare Vernunft sein. Sie muß weit und schnell laufen können, aber zurückpfeifbar sein" (22.1:334) (must be crippled. It must be a regulatable, in each case more or less mechanically increasable or decreasable reason. It must be able to run far and fast, but be able to be whistled back). By describing it in mechanical terms, Brecht presents reason as something to be handled physically. *Begreifen* means "to grasp" as understanding not only with our heads, but also with our hands; it means comprehending the world as it is. According to Brecht, reason has to be both adaptable and corruptible, and it always needs to be subject to the people. *Der Brückenbauer (The Bridge Builder)* is a parable that traces ideas to and from "the people," one of the primary tasks of the theatre. Brecht's demand in the *Dreigroschenprozeß (Threepenny Trial)* that everyone should absolutely represent her or his own interests is put into practice by the townspeople. However, we never learn what the interests of the bridge builder are because he strives to represent the interests of everyone through insights not shared by anyone.

The contradiction between knowledge and consent cannot be solved the instant that it occurs; instead, it unfolds over time in unexpected ways that modify the distribution of power. The fragment *Der böse Baal der asoziale (The Evil Baal, the Asocial)* can be read as an archaeological rediscovery of *Baal*—one that rewrites it in the form of a teaching play that comments on the original text. A retrospective on Baal's exploitation of all people and things includes the following advice from the actress who plays his girlfriend:

> Ich habe dargestellt eine Frau, welche einem Mann verfällt und dienstbar wird. Ich hätte sollen nicht dienstbar sein. Wenn ich aber verfallen wäre, hätte ich sollen die Lehre vergraben, wissend, daß ich Böses tue und krank bin. Dieses hätte ich sodann vergessen sollen vollständig und völlig verfallen und keinen Gedanken denkend an die Lehre und das übrige, bis meine Zeit gekommen wäre, wo ich wieder vergessen hätte meinen Verfall vollständig. (10.1:670)

> [I represented a woman who submits to a man and becomes subservient. I should not have been subservient. But if I had been submissive, I should have buried the teaching knowing that I do evil and am sick. This I should have then forgotten completely, and completely submissive and thinking no thought on the teaching and the rest, until my time had come in which I would have again forgotten my submission completely.]

For Brecht, teaching as a theatrical event means representing failure. The teaching plays are especially devoted to representing lessons that are not learned. Brecht describes this failure as *verfallen* (submission to subservience), which brings to mind the young comrade in *Die Maßnahme*

(The Measures Taken) who fails to observe the lesson given by the agitators—"verfalle aber nicht dem Mitleid" (3:80) (but do not submit to compassion)—and gives in to compassion. Anyone who cannot follow the teaching should simply forget it, as Baal's girlfriend states, rather than refute it as the young comrade tries to do. The antidote to *verfallen* (submission to subservience) is *Haltung* (disposition), which enables us to engage actively in *Lehre* (teaching), what I would call Brecht's concept of archaeology. Socially meaningless ideas should thus be kept out of the social sphere: "Auch soll der Denkende in dämmriger Kammer essen mit dem Gesicht zur Wand" (10.1:518) (The thinker should also eat in a gloomy chamber with his face to the wall). This advice for a thinker whose time has not yet come insists that the environment should remain unaffected by intellectual insight.

The forgetting of *Lehre* (teaching) that Brecht suggests brings together his concepts of theory, practice, forgetting, and remembering, which are all expressed through his concept of *gestus*. In the "Fatzerkommentar" (Fatzer Commentary), one finds instructions on how to deal with *Lehre* (teaching), which is described as something that may be held in contempt if one is strong enough to live by it but should be respected if one cannot live by it. But the "Fatzerkommentar" (Fatzer Commentary) appears to give the opposite advice when explaining why teaching should be honored: "Daß es nicht in Vergessenheit gerät und die wahren Richtlinien, / denen Gewalt angetan wurde, unverändert geblieben sind, wenn / die Gewalt eingegangen ist" (10.1:529) (So that it does not sink into oblivion and the true guidelines, / to which violence was done, have remained unchanged, when / the violence has perished). Violence might prevail over teaching, but only for a limited time, and teaching can then be reintroduced because it remains unchanged. This permanence of *Lehre* (teaching) seems to contradict everything that we take for granted in Brecht's work with its devotion to historical change.

To illuminate this apparent contradiction, we might recall Brecht's concept of *Wiederholung* (repetition; reiteration), less in the sense of "repetition," although this meaning is implied, and more in the sense of a *Wieder-holung* as a "bringing back," a return. Whereas repetition leads to memorization, bringing back or digging up the lesson that has once been buried fits Brecht's concept of archaeology. Bringing back long forgotten thoughts allows them to be considered anew. When a pupil laments to Me-ti that his teaching is not new, for it has been taught by others before him, Me-ti responds, "Ich lehre es, weil es alt ist, das heißt, weil es vergessen werden und als nur für vergangene Zeiten gültig betrachtet werden könnte. Gibt es nicht ungeheuer viele, für die es ganz neu ist?" (18:96) (I teach it because it is old, that is, because it could be forgotten and viewed as valid only for past times. Are there not terribly many for whom it is quite new?). The teaching of the old is thus perceived as new by those who never had access to it. *Wieder-holung* (bringing back) thus has a different function than repetition: it is knowledge brought back for the sake of redistribution.

To overcome the divide between the teaching remembered and the teaching forgotten, *Lehre* (teaching) must become part of *Haltung* (disposition). "Haltung hält länger als die Handlungsweise: sie widersteht den Notwendigkeiten" (18:34) (Disposition lasts longer than behavior: it resists the necessities) refers to the preservation of thought through time as a constant part of social interaction. *Haltung* (Disposition) lasts longer than the conditions that produce it, preserving thought through time and remaining a constant part of social interaction. *Haltung* (Disposition) thus becomes a major element of Brecht's concept of *Lehre* (teaching), not as expression, but as demonstration: "WER LEHRT, IST NICHT DER BESTE. Einer nützt. Er lehrt den andern. Nicht daß sie so sind wie er, sondern daß sie anders sind als sie selber—das nützt ihnen" (18:34) (THE ONE WHO TEACHES IS NOT THE BEST. One is useful. He teaches the others. Not so that they are as he is, but so that they are different from themselves—that is useful to them). *Lehre* (teaching) is not the teaching of a specific theory or practice. Instead, it puts the learner into the position of being different and asks her or him to act from this distinct position. *Haltung* (Disposition), then, is the external demonstration of usefulness and mimetic learning in the *Wieder-holung* (bringing back) of *Lehre* (teaching) through time. In this interaction, knowledge can be redistributed, and history can be shared.

Lehre (teaching), as a theatrical task, involves learning what is already known, and the place for this kind of learning is the theatre:

> Wenn du reden kannst, dann
> Lerne das Reden / wenn du
> Nicht reden kannst, dann lerne
> Das Schweigen. (10.1:521)

> [If you can talk, then
> Learn to talk / if you
> Cannot talk, then learn
> To be silent.]

We rehearse what we know, and through this we establish an order of
what we traditionally keep separated—"Bewegungen, Gedanken, Wünsche" (movements, thoughts, desires)—in order to comprehend the
divide between *Haltung* (disposition) and *Anschauung* (outlook). By acting out what we know, we develop *gestus* as the restored behavior that is
the physical archaeology of knowledge. Knowledge thus becomes a social
labor that keeps the *Ungleichzeitigkeit* (unsimultaneousness) of progress
present at all times. It is the line of failures—from Fatzer to the bridge
builder to Baal's girlfriend and ultimately to the young comrade in *Die
Maßnahme (The Measures Taken)*—that is necessary for Brecht's *Lehre*
(teaching). These failures reconnect *Urteil* (judgment) to *Erfahrung* (experience). Brecht's concept of *Lehre* (teaching) is designed to comprehend
revolution and to recognize that revolution includes failure. Archaeology
as "Vergrabung der Lehre" (burial of the teaching) secures the survival of
a lesson that is doomed to be ignored at the moment of its occurrence.
What lasts forever are "die chinesischen Bauernhütten aus Stroh, die können immer wieder aufgebaut werden" (18:158) (the Chinese farmers'
straw huts, they can always be rebuilt again). Building straw huts can be
read as the original act of civilization—as long as one recognizes that
Brecht sees this original act recurring throughout our history.

Notes

CHAPTER 1. BRECHT AND THEORY

1. John Fuegi, *Brecht & Company: Sex, Politics, and the Making of the Modern Drama* (New York: Grove Press, 1994).

2. Fredric Jameson, *Brecht and Method* (London: Verso, 1998), 178.

3. Theodor W. Adorno, "Engagement," in *Noten zur Literatur* (Frankfurt a.m.: Suhrkamp, 1974), 409–30.

4. Helmut Fahrenbach, *Brecht zur Einführung* (Hamburg: Junius, 1986), 98–103.

5. Theodor W. Adorno, *Ästhetische Theorie* (Frankfurt a.m.: Suhrkamp, 1970), 360. English translation from Theodor W. Adorno, *Aesthetic Theory*, ed. Gretel Adorno and Rolf Tiedemann, trans. Robert Hullot-Kentor (Minneapolis: University of Minnesota Press, 1997), 242.

6. Adorno, "Engagement," 419–21.

7. Theodor W. Adorno, "Erpreßte Versöhnung," in *Noten zur Literatur* (Frankfurt a.m.: Suhrkamp, 1974), 260. English translation from Theodor W. Adorno, "*Extorted Reconciliation: On Georg Lukács' Realism in Our Time*," in *Notes to Literature*, vol.1, ed. Rolf Tiedemann, trans. Shierry Weber Nicholsen (New York: Columbia University Press, 1991), 224.

8. Adorno, *Ästhetische Theorie*, 187. English translation from Adorno, *Aesthetic Theory*, 123.

9. Adorno, "Engagement," 426. English translation from Theodor W. Adorno, "Commitment," in *Notes to Literature*, vol. 2, ed. Rolf Tiedemann, trans. Shierry Weber Nicholsen (New York: Columbia University Press, 1992), 90.

10. Adorno, *Ästhetische Theorie*, 366. English translation from Adorno, *Aesthetic Theory*, 123.

11. Heiner Müller, "Ich wünsche mir Brecht in der Peep-Show: Heiner Müller im Gespräch mit Frank Raddatz," in *Gesammelte Irrtümer 2* (Frankfurt a.m.: Verlag der Autoren, 1990), 118. English translation by Chris Long.

12. Georg Lukács, "Es geht um den Realismus," in *Die Expressionismusdebatte: Materialien zu einer marxistischen Realismuskonzeption*, ed. Hans-Jürgen Schmitt (Frankfurt a.m.: Suhrkamp, 1973), 192–230.

13. Theodor W. Adorno, "Balzac-Lektüre," in *Noten zur Literatur* (Frankfurt a.m.: Suhrkamp, 1974), 148. English translation from, Theodor W. Adorno, "Reading Balzac," in *Notes to Literature*, vol. 1, ed. Rolf Tiedemann, trans. Shierry Weber Nicholsen (New York: Columbia University Press, 1991), 128.

14. Lukács, "Es geht um den Realismus," 197. English translation from Georg Lukács, "Realism in the Balance," in *Aesthetics and Politics*, trans. Rodney Livingstone (London: NLB, 1977), 32.

15. Lukács, "Es geht um den Realismus," 205. English translation from Lukács, "Realism in the Balance," 39.

16. Terry Eagleton, *The Ideology of the Aesthetic* (Oxford: Blackwell, 1990), 325.

17. Reinhart Koselleck, "›Erfahrungsraum‹ und ›Erwartungshorizont‹—zwei historische Kategorien," in *Vergangene Zukunft: Zur Semantik geschichtlicher Zeiten* (Frankfurt a.m.: Suhrkamp, 1989), 349–75.

18. Max Horkheimer and Theodor W. Adorno, "Dialektik der Aufklärung," in Max Horkheimer, ›Dialektik der Aufklärung‹ und Schriften 1940–1950, ed. Gunzelin Schmid Noerr, vol. 5 of *Gesammelte Schriften* (Frankfurt a.m.: Fischer, 1987), 74. English translation from Max Horkheimer and Theodor W. Adorno, *Dialectic of Enlightenment*, ed. Gunzelin Schmid Noerr, trans. Edmund Jephcott (Stanford: Stanford University Press, 2002), 40.

19. Koselleck, "›Erfahrungsraum‹ und ›Erwartungshorizont‹," 363. English translation from Reinhart Koselleck, "'Space of Experience' and 'Horizon of Expectation': Two Historical Categories," in *Futures Past*, trans. Keith Tribe (Cambridge: The MIT Press, 1985), 278.

20. Lukács, "Es geht um den Realismus," 201–205. English translation from Lukács, "Realism in the Balance," 39.

21. As it is described in Horkheimer's and Adorno's *Dialektik der Aufklärung (Dialectic of Enlightenment)*, the fragments are an elaboration of the two presuppositions: "schon der Mythos ist Aufklärung" (Myth is already enlightenment) and "Aufklärung schlägt in Mythologie zurück" (enlightenment reverts to mythology). Horkheimer and Adorno, "Dialektik der Aufklärung," 21. English translation from Horkheimer and Adorno, *Dialectic of Enlightenment*, xvi.

22. Horkheimer and Adorno, "Dialektik der Aufklärung," 112. English translation from Horkheimer and Adorno, *Dialectic of Enlightenment*, 70.

23. Horkheimer and Adorno, "Dialektik der Aufklärung," 218–19. English translation from Horkheimer and Adorno, *Dialectic of Enlightenment*, 155.

24. Susan Buck-Morss, *The Origin of Negative Dialectics: Theodor W. Adorno, Walter Benjamin, and the Frankfurt Institute* (New York: Free Press, 1977), 59.

25. Jameson, *Brecht and Method*, 8–9.

26. Adorno, "Erpreßte Versöhnung," 262. English translation from Adorno, *"Extorted Reconciliation,"* 225.

27. Adorno, "Balzac-Lektüre," 147. English translation from Adorno, "Reading Balzac," 128.

28. Peter Zadeck, about what he has learned from Brecht. Peter Zadeck, interview with Olivier Ortolani, "Liberating Chaos: A Conversation with Peter Zadeck," trans. Ilka Saal, *Grand Street* 69 (1999): 68.

29. Bertolt Brecht, "Die Expressionismusdebatte," in *Die Expressionismusdebatte: Materialien zu einer marxistischen Realismuskonzeption,* ed. Hans-Jürgen Schmitt (Frankfurt a.M.: Suhrkamp, 1973), 303. English translation by Chris Long.

30. Rainer Nägele, "Reading Benjamin," in *Benjamin's Ground: New Readings of Walter Benjamin,* ed. Rainer Nägele (Detroit: Wayne State University Press, 1988), 17.

31. About the philosophy of history and subject formation in drama, see Astrid Oesmann, "*Nathan der Weise:* Suffering Lessing's *Erziehung,*" *The Germanic Review* 74:2 (1999): 131–45.

32. Horkheimer and Adorno, "Dialektik der Aufklärung," 255. English translation from Horkheimer and Adorno, *Dialectic of Enlightenment,* 186.

33. Adorno, "Erpreßte Versöhnung," 258. English translation from Adorno, *"Extorted Reconciliation,"* 222.

34. Adorno, *Ästhetische Theorie,* 365. English translation from Adorno, *Aesthetic Theory,* 246.

35. Adorno, *Ästhetische Theorie,* 364–65. English translation from Adorno, *Aesthetic Theory,* 246.

36. Adorno, *Ästhetische Theorie,* 194. English translation from Adorno, *Aesthetic Theory,* 128.

37. Hohendahl, in *Prismatic Thought,* also remarks on Adorno's distinct notion of Marxism—distinct, as Hohendahl points out, because Adorno replaces the concept of base and superstructure with the concept of nature and labor. Peter Uwe Hohendahl, *Prismatic Thought: Theodor W. Adorno* (Lincoln: University of Nebraska Press, 1995), 213.

38. All parenthetical citations of Bertolt Brecht appear as (vol.:page) and refer to Bertolt Brecht, *Werke: Große kommentierte Berliner und Frankfurter Ausgabe,* ed. Werner Hecht, Jan Knopf, Werner Mittenzwei, and Klaus-Detlef Müller, 30 vols. (Frankfurt a.M.: Suhrkamp, 1989–2000).

39. Adorno, *Ästhetische Theorie,* 272. English translation from Adorno, *Aesthetic Theory,* 182.

40. Adorno, *Ästhetische Theorie,* 272. English translation from Adorno, *Aesthetic Theory,* 183.

41. Adorno, *Ästhetische Theorie,* 133. English translation from Adorno, *Aesthetic Theory,* 86.

42. Theodor W. Adorno, *Negative Dialektik* (Frankfurt a.M.: Suhrkamp, 1966), 167–68. English translation from Theodor W. Adorno, *Negative Dialectics,* trans. E. B. Ashton (New York: The Seabury Press, 1973), 165.

43. Adorno, *Negative Dialektik,* 165. English translation from Adorno, *Negative Dialectics,* 163.

44. Adorno, *Negative Dialektik,* 165. English translation from Adorno, *Negative Dialectics,* 163.

45. Theodor W. Adorno, "Rede über Lyrik und Gesellschaft," in *Noten zur Literatur* (Frankfurt a.M.: Suhrkamp, 1974), 56. English translation from Theodor W. Adorno, "On Lyric Poetry and Society," in *Notes to Literature*, vol. 1, ed. Rolf Tiedemann, trans. Shierry Weber Nicholsen (New York: Columbia University Press, 1991), 43.

46. Theodor W. Adorno, "Parataxis," in *Noten zur Literatur* (Frankfurt a.M.: Suhrkamp, 1981), 475. English translation from Theodor W. Adorno, "Parataxis," in *Notes to Literature*, vol. 2, ed. Rolf Tiedemann, trans. Shierry Weber Nicholsen (New York: Columbia University Press, 1992), 135.

47. Adorno, "Parataxis," in *Noten zur Literatur*, 477. English translation from Adorno, "Parataxis," in *Notes to Literature*, 137.

48. Adorno, "Parataxis," in *Noten zur Literatur*, 475. English translation from Adorno, "Parataxis," in *Notes to Literature*, 135.

49. Adorno, "Parataxis," in *Noten zur Literatur*, 479. English translation from Adorno, "Parataxis," in *Notes to Literature*, 138.

50. Adorno, *Ästhetische Theorie*, 387. English translation from Adorno, *Aesthetic Theory*, 261.

51. Susan Buck-Morss, *The Dialectics of Seeing: Walter Benjamin and the Arcades Project* (Cambridge: The MIT Press, 1989), 68.

52. Theodor W. Adorno, "Die Idee der Naturgeschichte," in *Philosophische Frühschriften*, vol. 1 of *Gesammelte Schriften*, ed. Rolf Tiedemann (Frankfurt a.M.: Suhrkamp, 1973), 354–55. English translation by Chris Long.

53. Georg Lukács, *Theorie des Romans: Ein geschichtsphilosophischer Versuch über die Formen der großen Epik* (Darmstadt and Neuwied: Luchterhand, 1971), 32. English translation from Georg Lukács, *The Theory of the Novel*, trans. Anna Bostock (Cambridge, Mass.: The MIT Press, 1971), 41.

54. Buck-Morss, *The Dialectics of Seeing*, 68.

55. Ibid., 160

56. Walter Benjamin, "Ursprung des deutschen Trauerspiels," in *Gesammelte Schriften*, vol. I.1, ed. Rolf Tiedemann and Hermann Schweppenhäuser (Frankfurt a.M.: Suhrkamp, 1980), 353. English translation from Walter Benjamin, *The Origin of German Tragic Drama*, trans. John Osborne (London: Verso, 1998), 177.

57. Adorno, "Die Idee der Naturgeschichte," 357–58. English translation by Chris Long.

58. Theodor W. Adorno, "Charakteristik Walter Benjamins," in *Über Walter Benjamin*, ed. Rolf Tiedemann (Frankfurt a.M.: Suhrkamp, 1970), 17. This essay also appeared in Theodor W. Adorno, "Charakteristik Walter Benjamins," in *Prismen: Kulturkritik und Gesellschaft* (Frankfurt a.M.: Suhrkamp, 1955), 283–301, here 289. English translation from Theodor W. Adorno, "A Portrait of Walter Benjamin," in *Prisms*, trans. Samuel Weber and Shierry Weber (Cambridge: The MIT Press, 1981), 233.

59. Richard Wolin, *Walter Benjamin: An Aesthetic of Redemption* (New York: Columbia University Press, 1982), 231.

60. Walter Benjamin, "Über einige Motive bei Baudelaire," in *Gesammelte Schriften*, vol. I.2, ed. Rolf Tiedemann and Hermann Schweppenhäuser (Frankfurt a.M.: Suhrkamp, 1980), 646. English translation from Walter Benjamin, "On Some Motifs in Baudelaire," in *Selected Writings*, vol. 4, ed. Howard Eiland and Michael W. Jennings, trans. Harry Zohn (Cambridge, Mass.: The Belknap Press, 2003), 338.

61. Rainer Nägele, "Augenblicke: Eingriffe. Brechts Ästhetik der Wahrnehmung," *Brecht Yearbook* 17 (1992): 29–51.

62. Marc Silberman, *German Cinema: Texts and Contexts* (Detroit: Wayne State University Press, 1995), 202.

63. Walter Benjamin, "Theater und Rundfunk," in *Gesammelte Schriften*, vol. II.2, ed. Rolf Tiedemann and Hermann Schweppenhäuser (Frankfurt a.M.: Suhrkamp, 1980), 775. Walter Benjamin, "Theater and Radio," in *Selected Writings*, vol. 2, ed. Michael W. Jennings, Howard Eiland, and Gary Smith, trans. Rodney Livingstone (Cambridge, Mass.: The Belknap Press, 1999), 584.

64. Helmut Lethen, *Verhaltenslehren der Kälte: Lebensversuche zwischen den Kriegen* (Frankfurt a.M.: Suhrkamp, 1994).

65. Benjamin, "Über einige Motive bei Baudelaire," 615. English translation from Benjamin, "On Some Motifs in Baudelaire," 319.

66. Bettine Menke, "Das Nach-Leben im Zitat. Benjamins Gedächtnis der Texte," in *Gedächtniskunst: Raum-Bild-Schrift: Studien zur Mnemotechnik*, ed. Anseln Haverkamp and Renate Lachmann (Frankfurt a.M.: Suhrkamp, 1991) 74–110, here 84–85.

67. Adorno, "Die Idee der Naturgeschichte," 357. English translation by Chris Long.

68. Theodor W. Adorno, "Rückblickend auf den Surrealismus," in *Noten zur Literatur* (Frankfurt a.M.: Suhrkamp, 1981), 105. English translation from Theodor W. Adorno, "Looking Back on Surrealism," in *Notes to Literature*, vol. 1, ed. Rolf Tiedemann, trans. Shierry Weber Nicholsen (New York: Columbia University Press, 1991), 89.

69. Max Ernst, *Die Erfindung der Natur: Max Ernst, Paul Klee, Wols und das strukturale Universum*, ed. Karin Orchard and Jörg Zimmermann (Freiburg/Breisgau: Rombach, 1994), 9. English translation by Chris Long.

70. Michael Taussig, *Mimesis and Alterity: A Particular History of the Senses* (New York and London: Routledge, 1993). Hayden White, *Figural Realism: Studies in the Mimesis Effect* (Baltimore: The Johns Hopkins University Press, 1999).

71. Horkheimer and Adorno, "Dialektik der Aufklärung," 210. English translation from Horkheimer and Adorno, *Dialectic of Enlightenment*, 148.

72. Horkheimer and Adorno, "Dialektik der Aufklärung," 81. English translation from Horkheimer and Adorno, *Dialectic of Enlightenment*, 44.

73. Theodor W. Adorno, "Zu Subjekt und Objekt," in *Philosophie und Gesellschaft: Fünf Essays*, ed. Rolf Tiedemann (Stuttgart: Reclam, 1984), 76. English translation from Theodor W. Adorno, "Subject and Object," in *The Essential Frankfurt School Reader*, ed. Andrew Arato and Eike Gebhart, (New York: Urizen Books, 1978), 499.

74. Buck-Morss, *The Dialectics of Seeing*, 264.

75. Walter Benjamin, "Über das mimetische Vermögen," in *Gesammelte Schriften*, vol. II.1, ed. Rolf Tiedemann and Hermann Schweppenhäuser, (Frankfurt a.M.: Suhrkamp, 1980), 210. English translation from Walter Benjamin, "On the Mimetic Faculty," in *Selected Writings*, vol. 2, ed. Michael W. Jennings, Howard Eiland, and Gary Smith, trans. Edmund Jephcott (Cambridge, Mass.: The Belknap Press, 1999), 720.

76. Buck-Morss, *The Dialectics of Seeing*, 70.

77. Walter Benjamin, "Das Kunstwerk im Zeitalter seiner technischen Reproduzierbarkeit," in *Gesammelte Schriften*, vol. I.2, ed. Rolf Tiedemann and Hermann Schweppenhäuser, (Frankfurt a.M.: Suhrkamp, 1980), 488. English translation from Walter Benjamin, "The Work of Art in the Age of Its Technological Reproducibility," in *Selected Writings*, vol. 4, ed. Howard Eiland and Michael W. Jennings, trans. Harry Zohn and Edmund Jephcott (Cambridge, Mass.: The Belknap Press, 2003), 260.

78. Benjamin, "Das Kunstwerk," 500. English translation from Benjamin, "The Work of Art," 266.

79. Benjamin, "Das Kunstwerk," 500. English translation from Benjamin, "The Work of Art," 266.

80. Buck-Morss, *The Dialectics of Seeing*, 267.

81. Walter Benjamin, "Lehre vom Ähnlichen," in *Gesammelte Schriften*, vol. II.1, ed. Rolf Tiedemann and Hermann Schweppenhäuser (Frankfurt a.M.: Suhrkamp, 1980), 210. English translation from Walter Benjamin, "Doctrine of the Similar," in *Selected Writings*, vol. 2, ed. Michael W. Jennings, Howard Eiland, and Gary Smith, trans. Michael Jennings (Cambridge, Mass.: The Belknap Press, 1999), 698.

82. Taussig, *Mimesis and Alterity*, 46.

83. The term *sensuous knowledge* is from Michael Taussig.

84. Horkheimer and Adorno, "Dialektik der Aufklärung," 210. English translation from Horkheimer and Adorno, *Dialectic of Enlightenment*, 148.

85. Horkheimer and Adorno, "Dialektik der Aufklärung," 210. English translation from Horkheimer and Adorno, *Dialectic of Enlightenment*, 148.

86. Horkheimer and Adorno, "Dialektik der Aufklärung," 210. English translation from Horkheimer and Adorno, *Dialectic of Enlightenment*, 148.

87. Taussig, *Mimesis and Alterity*, 46.

88. Ibid., 45.

CHAPTER 2. PREHISTORIES

1. Brecht links his concept of epic theatre inseparably to history. This historical perspective also ties Brecht to Marx, though, as Hans Mayer has convincingly shown, it does so more in terms of historical materialism than in terms of revolutionary teleology. Hans Mayer, "Brecht und die Tradition," in *Brecht* (Frankfurt a.M.: Suhrkamp, 1996), 97–241. But, as Reinhold Grimm has argued, Brecht's historical materialist perspective on the past was complicated by an epistemological skepticism reminiscent of Nietzsche. Reinhold

Grimm, *Brecht und Nietzsche oder Geständnisse eines Dichters: Fünf Essays und ein Bruchstück* (Frankfurt a.M.: Suhrkamp 1979).

2. Hans-Thies Lehmann and Helmut Lethen place Brecht in a continuum along with Marx, Nietzsche, and Freud, by pointing out that each of them seeks to undermine any idealist notion of the subject and thus the basis of coherent historical representation.

3. The point about betrayal is made by Jan Knopf, *Brecht Handbuch: Theater* (Stuttgart: Metzler, 1980), 23; Della Pollock comes to the same conclusion in her essay "The Play as Novel: Reappropriating Brecht's 'Drums in the Night,'" *Quarterly Journal of Speech* 74 (1988): 296–309; Peter Brooker sees Kragler as an unheroic and cynical character in Peter Brooker, *Bertolt Brecht: Dialectics, Poetry, Politics* (London: Croom Helm, 1988), 29.

On the problem of the representation of history in this play, see Antony Tatlow, "Geschichte und Literaturgeschichte: Brecht's *Trommeln in der Nacht*," in *Akten des VII. Internationalen Germanisten-Kongresses, Göttingen 1985: Kontroversen, alte und neue XI: Historische und aktuelle Konzepte der Literaturgeschichtsschreibung; zwei Königskinder: Zum Verhältnis von Literatur und Literaturwissenschaft*, vol. 11, ed. Albrecht Schöne, Wilhelm Vosskamp, and Eberhard Lämmert (Tübingen: Niemeyer, 1986), 105–10.

4. In her study on Brecht and postmodernism, for example, Elizabeth Wright offers postmodern readings of Brecht's early plays, especially *Baal* and *Im Dickicht der Städte (In the Jungle of Cities)*. Elizabeth Wright, *Postmodern Brecht: A Re-Presentation* (London and New York: Routledge, 1989).

5. About the teaching plays as a comprehensive pedagogical concept, see Reiner Steinweg, *Das Lehrstück: Brechts Theorie einer politisch-ästhetischen Erziehung* (Stuttgart: Metzler, 1972); and Reiner Steinweg, ed., *Auf Anregung Bertolt Brechts: Lehrstücke mit Schülern, Arbeitern, Theaterleuten* (Frankfurt a.M.: Suhrkamp, 1978). While I rely on Steinweg, I disagree with his claim that the teaching plays are based on a consistent theory of pedagogy. The plays' theatricality undermines any consistency. While Nägele, Bathrick, and Huyssen appreciate the teaching plays as a radically new form of theatre and offer fundamentally new readings, they all treat them in isolation from the rest of Brecht's work in order to recover their aesthetic power. Rainer Nägele, "Brecht's Theater of Cruelty," in *Reading After Freud: Essays on Goethe, Hölderlin, Habermas, Nietzsche, Celan, and Freud* (New York: Columbia University Press, 1987), 111–34. David Bathrick and Andreas Huyssen, "Producing Revolution: Heiner Müller's *Mauser* as Learning Play," in Andreas Huyssen, *After the Great Divide: Modernism, Mass Culture, Postmodernism* (Bloomington: Indiana University Press, 1986), 82–93.

6. Bertolt Brecht, "Meine Arbeit für das Theater," in *Brechts ›Trommeln in der Nacht‹*, ed. Wolfgang M. Schwiedrzik (Frankfurt a.M.: Suhrkamp, 1990), 155. English translation by Chris Long.

7. Except where otherwise noted, all parenthetical citations of Bertolt Brecht appear as (vol.:page) and refer to Bertolt Brecht, *Werke: Große kommentierte Berliner und Frankfurter Ausgabe*, ed. Werner Hecht, Jan Knopf, Werner Mittenzwei, and Klaus-Detlef Muller, 30 vols. (Frankfurt a.M.: Suhrkamp, 1989 2000).

8. Hans-Thies Lehmann shows that Brecht's work, especially his concept of epic theatre, is part of the dramatic tradition because of Brecht's insistence on the fable. He compares this "traditional" aspect of epic theatre to Brecht's radically new approach in the

teaching plays. Hans-Thies Lehmann, "Schlaglichter auf den anderen Brecht," *The Brecht Yearbook* 17 (1992): 1–12. Nägele points out that Brecht's early plays, *Im Dickicht der Städte (In the Jungle of Cities)* and *Mann ist Mann (Man Equals Man)* already "reject the basis of traditional bourgeois drama: motivation." Nägele, *Reading After Freud*, 132.

9. Max Horkheimer and Theodor W. Adorno, "Dialektik der Aufklärung," in Max Horkheimer, ›*Dialektik der Aufklärung*‹ *und Schriften 1940–1950*, ed. Gunzelin Schmid Noerr, vol. 5 of *Gesammelte Schriften* (Frankfurt a.m.: Fischer, 1987), 112. English translation from Max Horkheimer and Theodor W. Adorno, *Dialectic of Enlightenment*, ed. Gunzelin Schmid Noerr, trans. Edmund Jephcott (Stanford: Stanford University Press, 2002), 70.

10. Horkheimer and Adorno, "Dialektik der Aufklärung," 266. Michel Foucault, *Discipline and Punish: The Birth of the Prison*, trans. Alan Sheridan (New York: Vintage, 1979), especially Part Three, 135–70.

11. The play's epic component has even been read as a Bakhtinian novel: see Pollock, "The Play as Novel," 296–309.

12. For an examination of *gestus*, see Hans-Martin Ritter, *Das gestische Prinzip bei Bertolt Brecht* (Köln: Prometh Verlag, 1986), 33. This book offers new insights on *gestus* in relation to fable and realism. For an investigation of *gestus*, especially in Brecht's early plays, see Reinhold Grimm, "Brecht's Anfänge," in *Brecht und Nietzsche oder Geständnisse eines Dichters: Fünf Essays und ein Bruchstück* (Frankfurt a.M.: Suhrkamp, 1979), 55–77. On *gestus* and Brecht's theory of the theatre, see Rainer Nägele, "Augenblicke: Eingriffe. Brechts Ästhetik der Wahrnehmung," *The Brecht Yearbook* 17 (1992): 29–52, here 44–45.

13. Wright, *Postmodern Brecht*, 52.

14. Walter Benjamin, "Was ist das epische Theater? (II)," in *Gesammelte Schriften*, vol. II.2, ed. Rolf Tiedemann and Hermann Schweppenhäuser (Frankfurt a.M.: Suhrkamp, 1980), 536.

15. The "Augsburger Fassung" (Augsburg version) has been edited together with annotations from earlier manuscript versions in Wolfgang M. Schwiedrzik, ed., *Brechts* ›*Trommeln in der Nacht*‹ (Frankfurt a.M.: Suhrkamp, 1990).

For an excellent treatment of the different versions, see David Bathrick, *The Dialectic and the Early Brecht: An Interpretive Study of "Trommeln in der Nacht"* (Stuttgart: Akademischer Verlag Hans-Dieter Heinz, 1975). Bathrick did not know of the "Augsburger Fassung" (Augsburg version), which was part of Elisabeth Hauptmann's estate, but he offers a reading of the later versions in comparison with notes and manuscripts that preceded the "Augsburger Fassung" (Augsburg version).

The printed version is much shorter and more pointed than the Augsburg version, an effect Brecht achieved by greatly reducing the final two acts. Kragler appears in a more positive light in the longer version, in which the Africa narrative constitutes the center of Act IV, and the dispute between Kragler and Glubb in Act V is more elaborate. This makes both characters more complex. For a comparison between the two versions of the play, see Wolfgang M. Schwiedrzik, "Grünes Haus oder Piccadilly-Bar?: Zu den wiederaufgefundenen frühen Fassungen von Bertolt Brecht's 'Trommeln in der Nacht,'" in *Brechts* ›*Trommeln in der Nacht*‹, ed. Wolfgang M. Schwiedrzik (Frankfurt a.M.: Suhrkamp, 1990), 101–15.

16. Kragler's displacement is more obvious in the Augsburg version because it privileges theatricality and corporeality more than the printed version. Brecht's reasons for these changes might have been political, as David Bathrick has shown. Bathrick, *The Dialectic and the Early Brecht*, 101–35.

17. About *Trommeln in der Nacht (Drums in the Night)* and the question of genre, see also Guy Stern, "Brechts *Trommeln in der Nacht* als literarische Satire," in *Brechts ›Trommeln in der Nacht‹*, ed. Wolfgang M. Schwiedrzik (Frankfurt a.M.: Suhrkamp, 1990), 386–409. Jan Knopf suggests that tragedy is reversed into comedy because the bourgeoisie of the twentieth century is no longer a tragic character. Knopf, *Brecht Handbuch*, 23.

18. For a definition of *Glosse* (gloss) see Gero von Wilpert, "Glosse," in *Sachwörterbuch der Literatur* (Stuttgart: Kröner, 1979), 314.

19. Bathrick, *The Dialectic and the Early Brecht*, 21.

20. Walter Benjamin, "Was ist das epische Theater? (II)," 536. English translation from Walter Benjamin, "What is the Epic Theater? (II)," in *Selected Writings*, vol. 4, ed. Howard Eiland and Michael W. Jennings, trans. Harry Zohn (Cambridge, Mass.: The Belknap Press, 2003), 305.

21. By examining the interaction between Kragler, the Balickes, and Murk, one can see the psychological and cultural construction of the uncanny. Kragler, returning from the dead, can represent the comfort of immortality, which also contains what Freud called the uncanny aspect of being the "harbinger of death." As such, the "dead man" becomes the enemy of the survivor. For Freud's concept of the uncanny, see Sigmund Freud, "The 'Uncanny,'" in *The Standard Edition of the Complete Psychological Works of Sigmund Freud*, vol. 17, ed. James Strachey (London: Hogarth Press, 1955; London: Hogarth Press, 1986), 217–52.

22. All parenthetical references to the "Augsburger Fassung" (Augsburg version) of *Trommeln in der Nacht (Drums in the Night)* appear as (AF:page) and refer to Bertolt Brecht, "Trommeln in der Nacht," in *Brechts ›Trommeln in der Nacht‹*, ed. Wolfgang M. Schwiedrzik (Frankfurt a.M.: Suhrkamp, 1990), 9–74.

23. Brecht reinforces the resemblance of the irrational romanticism of the "Picadillybar" (in the first half) to the "Zibebe" (in the second half) by having the same actor play the waiter in both locations. "Manke I und II werden vom gleichen Schauspieler gespielt" (Manke I and II are played by the same actor). With these twinned performances, Brecht demonstrates that the same irrationality can be performed on two different social levels—either in the pathetic version in the fancy "Picadillybar," or in a rougher way in the "Zibebe." For a close examination of the Manke brothers, see Stern, "Brechts *Trommeln in der Nacht* als literarische Satire," 401–403.

24. The term *belatedness* comes from Frantz Fanon, who uses it to describe the postcolonial condition in Frantz Fanon, *Black Skin, White Mask*, trans. Charles Lam Markmann (New York: Grove Press, 1967).

25. Bettine Menke, "Das Nach-Leben im Zitat: Benjamins Gedächtnis der Texte," in *Gedächtniskunst: Raum-Bild-Schrift: Studien zur Mnemotechnik*, ed. Anselm Haverkamp and Renate Lachmann (Frankfurt a.M.: Suhrkamp, 1991), 85–86.

26. Fanon, *Black Skin, White Mask*, 112–20. Fanon and Homi K. Bhabha use this terminology to describe the time structure of modernity from a postcolonial perspective. Homi K. Bhabha, *The Location of Culture* (London and New York: Routledge, 1994).

27. The reading of modern history as spectacle comes from Bhabha, *The Location of Culture*, 242.

28. Hans Mayer, "Brecht, Beckett und ein Hund," in *Brechts ›Trommeln in der Nacht‹*, ed. Wolfgang M. Schwiedrzik (Frankfurt a.M.: Suhrkamp, 1990), 409–19.

29. Here I agree with Bathrick, who reads this as politicization in line with official positions of the GDR. See Bathrick, *The Dialectic and the Early Brecht*, 128.

30. In addition to that, David Bathrick rightly stresses the importance of Anna as mediator between the first and the second part of the play, as well as between the different worlds these two parts represent. Bathrick, *The Dialectic and the Early Brecht*, 49.

31. For a close reading on Brecht and nihilism, see Reinhold Grimm, "Brecht und Nietzsche," in *Brecht und Nietzsche oder Geständnisse eines Dichters: Fünf Essays und ein Bruchstück* (Frankfurt a.M.: Suhrkamp 1979), 156–245.

32. For an investigation of disappearance and Nietzsche's notion of "Fernstenliebe," see Grimm, "Brecht und Nietzsche," 229.

33. Michel Foucault, "Nietzsche, Genealogy, History," in *Language, Countermemory, Practice: Selected Essays and Interviews by Michel Foucault*, ed. Donald F. Bouchard, trans. Donald F. Bouchard and Sherry Simon (Ithaca: Cornell University Press, 1977), 139–64.

34. Ibid., 154.

35. Ibid., 142.

36. Wolf-Dietrich Junghans has shown how Brecht's interest in boxing matches is intertwined with his concept of the public sphere in that the fight enables people to gain experience when participation and observation are not separated. Wolf-Dietrich Junghans, "Öffentlichkeiten: Boxen, Theater und Politik," *The Brecht Yearbook* 23 (1998): 56–59.

37. Foucault, "Nietzsche, Genealogy, History," 154.

38. Walter Benjamin, "Lehre vom Ähnlichen," in *Gesammelte Schriften*, vol. II.1, ed. Rolf Tiedemann and Hermann Schweppenhäuser (Frankfurt a.M.: Suhrkamp, 1980), 210. English translation from Walter Benjamin, "Doctrine of the Similar," in *Selected Writings*, vol. 2, ed. Michael W. Jennings, Howard Eiland, and Gary Smith, trans. Michael Jennings (Cambridge, Mass.: The Belknap Press, 1999), 698.

39. Foucault, "Nietzsche, Genealogy, History," 148.

40. Ibid., 148.

CHAPTER 3. MAN BETWEEN
MATERIAL AND SOCIAL ORDER

1. Jürgen Habermas, *Strukturwandel der Öffentlichkeit: Untersuchungen zu einer Kategorie der bürgerlichen Gesellschaft* (Frankfurt a.M.: Suhrkamp, 1990).

2. Oskar Negt and Alexander Kluge share Brecht's observation in their eloquent and still highly relevant book *Öffentlichkeit und Erfahrung: Zur Organisationsanalyse von bürgerlicher und proletarischer Öffentlichkeit* (Frankfurt a.M.: Suhrkamp, 1972), 35–37.

3. Ibid., 84–87.

4. All parenthetical citations of Bertolt Brecht appear as (vol.:page) and refer to Bertolt Brecht, *Werke: Große kommentierte Berliner und Frankfurter Ausgabe*, ed. Werner Hecht, Jan Knopf, Werner Mittenzwei, and Klaus-Detlef Müller, 30 vols. (Frankfurt a.M.: Suhrkamp, 1989–2000).

5. Negt and Kluge, 84–87.

6. Most recently, Fredric Jameson applied the master-slave discourse to Brecht's work in his reading of *Galilei*. Jameson has argued that in order to survive, the slave has to be a true materialist. Fredric Jameson, *Brecht and Method* (London: Verso, 1998), 124.

7. In fact, Brecht started thinking about the changeability of the subject while still under the impression of World War I. The topic is first mentioned in the poem "Das war der Bürger Galgei" (That Was Citizen Galgei). The major rewrite, in which Galy Gay gets transformed into a fascist war machine, appeared in 1938. Brecht wrote a final version of the play in 1954 and noted, "Die Parabel »Mann ist Mann« kann ohne große Mühe konkretisiert werden. Die Verwandlung des Kleinbürgers Galy Gay in eine »menschliche Kampfmaschine« kann statt in Indien in Deutschland spielen. Die Sammlung der Armee zu Kilkoa kann in den Parteitag der NSDAP zu Nürnberg verwandelt werden. Die Stelle des Elefanten Billy Humph kann ein gestohlenes, nunmehr der SA gehörendes Privatauto einnehmen. Der Einbruch kann statt in den Tempel des Herrn Wang in den Laden eines jüdischen Trödlers erfolgen. Jip würde dann als arischer Geschäftsteilhaber von dem Krämer angestellt. Das Verbot sichtbarer Beschädigungen jüdischer Geschäfte wäre mit der Anwesenheit englischer Journalisten zu begründen" (24:51) (The parable "Man Equals Man" can be made concrete without great effort. The metamorphosis of the petit-bourgeois Galy Gay into a "human fighting machine" can play in Germany instead of India. The gathering of the army at Kilkoa can be transformed into the party congress of the NSDAP at Nuremberg. A stolen private car now belonging to the SA can take the place of the elephant Billy Humph. The break-in can take place in the shop of a Jewish second-hand dealer instead of in the temple of Mr. Wang. Jip would then be hired as the Aryan business partner by the shopkeeper. The ban on visible damages to Jewish shops would be explained by the presence of English journalists).

8. Negt and Kluge, *Öffentlichkeit und Erfahrung*, 84. English translation from Oskar Negt and Alexander Kluge, *Public Sphere and Experience*, trans. Peter Labanyi, Jamie Owen Daniel, and Assenka Oksiloff (Minneapolis: University of Minnesota Press, 1993), 43.

9. Walter Benjamin, "Was ist das epische Theater? (I)," in *Gesammelte Schriften*, vol. II.2, ed. Rolf Tiedemann and Hermann Schweppenhäuser (Frankfurt a.M.: Suhrkamp, 1980), 526. English translation from Walter Benjamin, "What is Epic Theatre? (First Version)," in *Understanding Brecht*, trans. Anna Bostock (London: NLB, 1973), 8–9.

10. Jan Knopf, *Brecht Handbuch: Lyrik, Prosa, Schriften* (Stuttgart: J. B. Metzler, 1980), 508.

11. Negt and Kluge, *Öffentlichkeit und Erfahrung*, 84. English translation from Negt and Kluge, *Public Sphere and Experience*, 43–44.

12. Knopf, *Brecht Handbuch*, 506. English translation by Chris Long.

13. See the chapter "Kulturindustrie" (Culture Industry) in: Max Horkheimer and Theodor W. Adorno, "Dialektik der Aufklärung," in Max Horkheimer, ›*Dialektik der Aufklärung*‹ *und Schriften 1940–1950*, ed. Gunzelin Schmid Noerr, vol. 5 of *Gesammelte Schriften* (Frankfurt a.M.: Fischer, 1987), 144–96.

14. Michael Taussig, *Mimesis and Alterity: A Particular History of the Senses* (New York and London: Routledge, 1993), 20.

15. Walter Benjamin, "Das Kunstwerk im Zeitalter seiner technischen Reproduzierbarkeit: Zweite Fassung," in *Gesammelte Schriften*, vol. I.2, ed. Rolf Tiedemann and Hermann Schweppenhäuser (Frankfurt a.M.: Suhrkamp, 1980), 479. English translation from "The Work of Art in the Age of Its Technological Reproducibility," in *Selected Writings*, vol. 4, ed. Howard Eiland and Michael W. Jennings, trans. Harry Zohn and Edmund Jephcott (Cambridge, Mass.: The Belknap Press, 2003), 255.

16. Negt and Kluge, *Öffentlichkeit und Erfahrung*, 85. English translation from Negt and Kluge, *Public Sphere and Experience*, 44.

17. Walter Benjamin, "Das Land, in dem das Proletariat nicht genannt werden darf," in *Gesammelte Schriften*, vol. II.2, ed. Rolf Tiedemann and Hermann Schweppenhäuser (Frankfurt a.M.: Suhrkamp, 1980), 517–18. English translation from Walter Benjamin, "The Land Where the Proletariat May Not Be Mentioned," in *Selected Writings*, vol. 3, ed. Howard Eiland and Michael W. Jennings, trans. Edmund Jephcott (Cambridge, Mass.: The Belknap Press, 2002), 332.

18. Brecht revisits these issues when he attempts to create a new public sphere in the teaching plays. The young comrade in *Die Maßnahme (The Measures Taken)* forgets this lesson because, for him, the revolution is a moral commitment instead of a historical one. His commitment to the cause rather than to a collective construction of reality leads to his death and erasure from history. In a more elaborate teaching play, *Die heilige Johanna der Schlachthöfe (Saint Joan of the Stockyards)*, Brecht presents a workers' strike in the middle of a collapsing meat market. One worker gives the collective the only advice that offers a chance: "Bleibt hier! . . . Geht nicht auseinander! / Nur wenn ihr zusammenbleibt / Könnt ihr euch helfen!" (3:199) (Stay here! . . . Do not disperse! / Only when you stay together / Can you help yourselves!). Johanna, like the young comrade in *Die Maßnahme (The Measures Taken)*, is incapable of accepting this disciplinary imperative. Neither she nor the young comrade recognizes the crucial importance of creating a public sphere through social interaction and contention, and without that public sphere, neither can achieve the unity between ideas (and desires) and the lives they live. Without achieving that unity, they cannot play their properly progressive roles in society and history.

CHAPTER 4. REVOLUTION

1. Walter Benjamin, "Erfahrung und Armut," in *Gesammelte Schriften*, vol. II.1, ed. Rolf Tiedemann and Hermann Schweppenhäuser (Frankfurt a.M.: Suhrkamp, 1980), 213–19.

2. Benjamin, "Erfahrung und Armut," 214. English translation from Walter Benjamin, "Experience and Poverty," in *Selected Writings*, vol. 2, ed. Michael W. Jennings,

Howard Eiland, and Gary Smith, trans. Rodney Livingstone (Cambridge, Mass.: The Belknap Press, 1999), 731.

3. Benjamin, "Erfahrung und Armut," 215. English translation from Benjamin, "Experience and Poverty," 732.

4. Ibid.

5. Benjamin, "Erfahrung und Armut," 216. English translation from Benjamin, "Experience and Poverty," 733.

6. For a discussion of which of Brecht's plays fit the definition of "teaching play," see Burckhardt Lindner, "Das Messer und die Schrift: Für eine Revision der 'Lehrstück-periode,'" *The Brecht Yearbook* 18 (1993): 43–57.

7. Reiner Steinweg, *Das Lehrstück: Brechts Theorie einer politisch-ästhetischen Erziehung* (Stuttgart: Metzler, 1972), 87. English translation by Chris Long.

8. Ibid., 205–11.

9. Burckhardt Lindner coined the useful term *intertextuelle Spielmodelle* (intertextual models of play). Lindner, "Das Messer und die Schrift," 43–44.

10. All parenthetical citations of Bertolt Brecht appear as (vol.:page) and refer to Bertolt Brecht, *Werke: Große kommentierte Berliner und Frankfurter Ausgabe*, ed. Werner Hecht, Jan Knopf, Werner Mittenzwei, and Klaus-Detlef Müller, 30 vols. (Frankfurt a.M.: Suhrkamp, 1989–2000).

11. Walter Benjamin, "Aus dem Brecht-Kommentar," in *Gesammelte Schriften*, vol. II.2, ed. Rolf Tiedemann and Hermann Schweppenhäuser (Frankfurt a.M.: Suhrkamp, 1980), 507. English translation from Walter Benjamin "From the Brecht Commentary," in *Selected Writings*, vol. 2, ed. Michael W. Jennings, Howard Eiland, and Gary Smith, trans. Anna Bostock (Cambridge, Mass.: The Belknap Press, 1999), 375.

12. Lindner, "Das Messer und die Schrift," 53.

13. David Bathrick and Andreas Huyssen consider history the result of the interaction of the players on the stage. David Bathrick and Andreas Huyssen, "Producing Revolution: Heiner Müller's *Mauser* as Learning Play," in Andreas Huyssen, *After the Great Divide: Modernism, Mass Culture, Postmodernism* (Bloomington: Indiana University Press, 1986), 82–93.

14. Benjamin, "Erfahrung und Armut," 218. English translation from Benjamin, "Experience and Poverty," 732.

15. Richard Schechner, "Restoration of Behaviour," in Eugenio Barba and Nicola Savarese, *A Dictionary of Theatre Anthropology: The Secret Art of the Performer*, trans. Richard Fowler (London and New York: Routledge, 1991), 205–10.

16. Ibid., 205.

17. Patrice Pavis, *Dictionary of the Theatre: Terms, Concepts, and Analysis*, trans. Christine Shantz (Toronto: University of Toronto Press, 1998), 202.

18. Ibid.

19. About the different versions of *Der Jasager. Der Neinsager (He Said Yes. He Said No)* see Bertolt Brecht, *Der Jasager und Der Neinsager: Vorlagen, Fassungen und Materialien*, ed. Peter Szondi (Frankfurt a.M.: Suhrkamp, 1966).

20. For a thorough investigation of the shifting of *Einverständnis* (consent), see Peter Szondi, "Brechts Jasager und Neinsager," in *Lektüren und Lektionen: Versuche über Literatur, Literaturtheorie und Literatursoziologie* (Frankfurt a.m.: Suhrkamp, 1973), 125–33.

21. Hans-Thies Lehmann and Helmut Lethen, "Ein Vorschlag zur Gute: Zur doppelten Polarität des Lehrstücks," in *Auf Anregung Bertolt Brechts: Lehrstücke mit Schülern, Arbeitern, Theaterleuten* (Frankfurt a.m.: Suhrkamp, 1978), 302.

22. About the lyrics in *Die Maßnahme (The Measures Taken)*, see Roman Jakobson, "Der grammatische Bau des Gedichts von B. Brecht: *Wir sind sie*," in *Hölderlin-Klee-Brecht: Zur Wortkunst dreier Gedichte* (Frankfurt a.m.: Suhrkamp, 1976), 107–28.

23. About Althusser's concept of despotic time, see Homi Bhabha, *The Location of Culture* (London and New York: Routledge, 1994), 246.

24. Michael Taussig, *Defacement: Public Secrecy, and the Labor of the Negative* (Stanford: Stanford University Press, 1999), 224.

25. On Levinas's concept of the face, see Taussig, *Defacement*, 223–25.

26. Ibid., 224–25.

27. Ibid., 224.

28. Ibid., 253.

29. Eugenio Barba and Nicola Savarese, "The Provisional Face," in *A Dictionary of Theatre Anthropology: The Secret Art of the Performer*, trans. Richard Fowler, (London and New York: Routledge, 1991), 118.

30. Taussig, *Defacement*, 224.

31. Benjamin, "Der Erzähler," in *Gesammelte Schriften*, vol. II.2, ed. Rolf Tiedemann and Hermann Schweppenhäuser (Frankfurt a.m.: Suhrkamp, 1980), 450. English translation from Walter Benjamin, "The Storyteller," in *Selected Writings*, vol. 3, ed. Howard Eiland and Michael W. Jennings, trans. Harry Zohn (Cambridge, Mass.: The Belknap Press, 2002), 151.

CHAPTER 5. BRECHT'S ARCHAEOLOGY OF KNOWLEDGE

1. Fredrik T. Hiebert, an archaeologist, commenting on a civilization that thrived in Central Asia more than four thousand years ago and has just been uncovered due to the access granted to archaeologists following the fall of the USSR. John Noble Wilford, "In Ruin, Symbols on a Stone Hint at a Lost Asian Culture," *New York Times*, 13 May 2001, A1.

2. Walter Benjamin, "Über den Begriff der Geschichte," in *Gesammelte Schriften*, vol. I.2, ed. Rolf Tiedemann and Hermann Schweppenhäuser (Frankfurt a.m.: Suhrkamp, 1980), 701.

3. Victor H. Mair, a specialist in ancient Asian languages and cultures, on a civilization that thrived in Central Asia more than four thousand years ago. Wilford, "In Ruin," A8.

4. All parenthetical citations of Bertolt Brecht appear as (vol.:page) and refer to Bertolt Brecht, *Werke: Große kommentierte Berliner und Frankfurter Ausgabe*, ed. Werner Hecht, Jan Knopf, Werner Mittenzwei, and Klaus-Detlef Müller, 30 vols. (Frankfurt a.M.: Suhrkamp, 1989–2000).

5. Heiner Müller, ed., *Der Untergang des Egoisten Johann Fatzer*, by Bertolt Brecht (Frankfurt a.M.: Suhrkamp, 1994), 7. English translation by Chris Long.

6. Oskar Negt and Alexander Kluge, *Geschichte und Eigensinn* (Frankfurt a.M.: Zweitausendeins, 1981), 1018. English translation by Chris Long.

7. About Fatzer as a document, see Judith Wilke, "The Making of a Document: An Approach to Brecht's *Fatzer* Fragment," *The Drama Review* 43.4 (1999): 122–28.

8. In the context of *Die Maßnahme (The Measures Taken)*, Brecht refers to a poem that he wrote in the *Lesebuch für Städtebewohner (A Reader for Those Who Live in Cities)*—"Wenn ich mit dir rede . . ." (11:165) (When I talk with you . . .)—which describes reality's indifference to the individual.

9. Benjamin, "Über den Begriff der Geschichte," 697. English translation from Walter Benjamin, "On the Concept of History," in *Selected Writings*, vol. 4, ed. Howard Eiland and Michael W. Jennings, trans. Harry Zohn (Cambridge, Mass.: The Belknap Press, 2003), 392.

10. Hans-Thies Lehmann and Helmut Lethen, "Ein Vorschlag zur Güte: Zur doppelten Polarität des Lehrstücks," in *Auf Anregung Bertolt Brechts: Lehrstücke mit Schülern, Arbeitern, Theaterleuten*, ed. Reiner Steinweg (Frankfurt a.M.: Suhrkamp, 1978), 302–17.

11. Friedrich Nietzsche, "Zur Genealolgie der Moral," in *Kritische Studienausgabe*, vol. 5, ed. Giorgio Colli and Mazzino Monitari (München: dtv/de Gruyter, 1988), 352. English translation from Friedrich Nietzsche, *On the Genealogy of Morality*, ed. Keith Ansell-Pearson, trans. Carol Diethe (Cambridge: Cambridge University Press, 1994), 82.

12. Nietzsche, "Zur Genealolgie der Moral," 366. English translation from Nietzsche, *On the Genealogy of Morality*, 93.

13. Sigmund Freud, "Beiträge zur Psychologie des Liebeslebens II—Über die allgemeine Erniedrigung des Liebeslebens," in *Studienausgabe*, vol. 5, ed. Alexander Mitscherlich, Angela Richard, and James Strachey (Frankfurt a.M.: Fischer, 1982), 197–212.

14. Freud, "Beiträge zur Psychologie des Liebeslebens," 209. English translation from Sigmund Freud, "On the Universal Tendency to Debasement in the Sphere of Love (Contributions to the Psychology of Love II)," in *The Standard Edition of the Complete Works of Sigmund Freud*, vol. 11, ed. James Strachey (London: The Hogarth Press, 1957), 190.

15. Nietzsche, "Zur Genealolgie der Moral," 366. English translation from Nietzsche, *On the Genealogy of Morality*, 93.

16. Nietzsche, "Zur Genealolgie der Moral," 295. English translation from Nietzsche, *On the Genealogy of Morality*, 41.

17. Bettine Menke, "Das Nach-Leben im Zitat. Benjamins Gedächtnis der Texte," in *Gedächtniskunst: Raum-Bild-Schrift: Studien zur Mnemotechnik*, ed. Anselm Haverkamp and Renate Lachmann (Frankfurt a.M.: Suhrkamp, 1991), 84. English translation by Chris Long.

18. Sigmund Freud, "Konstruktionen in der Analyse," in *Studienausgabe: Ergänzungsband*, ed. Alexander Mitscherlich, Angela Richard, and James Strachey (Frankfurt a.M.: Fischer, 1982), 318–21.

19. Nietzsche, "Zur Genealolgie der Moral," 254. English translation from Nietzsche, *On the Genealogy of Morality*, 8–9.

20. Nietzsche, "Zur Genealolgie der Moral," 254. English translation from Nietzsche, *On the Genealogy of Morality*, 8.

21. Michel Foucault, "Nietzsche, Genealogy, History," in Donald F. Bouchard, ed., *Language, Countermemory, Practice: Selected Essays and Interviews by Michel Foucault* (Ithaca: Cornell University Press, 1977), 140–44.

22. Reinhart Koselleck, "Historische Kriterien des neuzeitlichen Revolutionsbegriffs," in *Vergangene Zukunft: Zur Semantik geschichtlicher Zeiten* (Frankfurt a.M.: Suhrkamp, 1979), 67–86.

23. Anselm Haverkamp, "Hermeneutischer Prospekt," in *Memoria: Vergessen und Erinnern*, ed. Anselm Haverkamp and Renate Lachmann (München: Fink, 1993), IX–XVI.

24. For example, Brecht alternates between "Mühlheim" and "Mühlhausen" (10.2:1142).

25. Walter Benjamin, "Erfahrung und Armut," in *Gesammelte Schriften*, vol. II.1, ed. Rolf Tiedemann and Hermann Schweppenhäuser (Frankfurt a.M.: Suhrkamp, 1980), 213–19.

26. In his edition of the fragment, Heiner Müller suggests *Fatzer* as a commentary on West German terrorism. Müller, *Der Untergang*, 7–12.

27. Ibid., 7. English translation by Chris Long.

28. Foucault, "Nietzsche, Genealogy, History," 148.

29. Benjamin, "Über den Begriff der Geschichte," 696–98.

30. Ibid., 704.

31. Thomas Weber, "Erfahrung," in *Benjamins Begriffe*, ed. Michael Opitz and Erdmut Wizisla, vol. 1 (Frankfurt a.M.: Suhrkamp, 2000), 246–47.

32. Sigmund Freud, "Jenseits des Lustprinzips," in *Studienausgabe*, vol. 3, ed. Alexander Mitscherlich, Angela Richard, and James Strachey (Frankfurt a.M.: Fischer, 1982), 239–42.

33. Fredric Jameson, *Brecht and Method* (London: Verso, 1991), 92.

34. When, for example, one petit-bourgeois character in *Trommeln in der Nacht (Drums in the Night)* declares revolution and freedom while lounging at a bar table reading the newspaper, the failure of the revolution is already manifest. See Bertolt Brecht, "Trommeln in der Nacht," in *Brechts ›Trommeln in der Nacht‹*, ed. Wolfgang M. Schwiedrzik (Frankfurt a.M.: Suhrkamp, 1990), 46.

35. Benjamin, "Über den Begriff der Geschichte," 691–704.

36. Ibid., 703.

37. Ibid., 695. English translation from Benjamin, "On the Concept of History," 391.

38. Walter Benjamin, "Über das Grauen," (unpublished manuscript) cited here from Rolf Tiedemann, *Dialektik im Stillstand: Versuche zum Spätwerk Walter Benjamins* (Frankfurt a.M.: Suhrkamp, 1983), 101.

39. Benjamin, "Über den Begriff der Geschichte," 703. English translation from Benjamin, "On the Concept of History," 396.

40. Walter Benjamin, "Was ist das epische Theater? (II)," in *Gesammelte Schriften*, vol. II.2, ed. Rolf Tiedemann and Hermann Schweppenhäuser (Frankfurt a.M.: Suhrkamp, 1980), 533.

41. Müller, *Der Untergang*, 7.

42. See, for example, Christof Šubik, "Dialektik im Dickicht der Städte," in *Philosophieren als Theater: Zur Philosophie Bertold Brechts* (Wien: Passagen Verlag, 2000), 157–63.

Index